Contemporary Utilitarianism

MICHAEL BAYLES received his
Ph.D. from Indiana University
in 1967. He has taught at the
University of Missouri and the
University of Idaho, and is now
an Assistant Professor of Philosophy at Brooklyn College.
His papers on moral philosophy have appeared in a number of academic journals.

Contemporary Utilitarianism

EDITED WITH AN INTRODUCTION BY
Michael D. Bayles

Anchor Books
DOUBLEDAY & COMPANY, INC.
GARDEN CITY, NEW YORK

The Anchor Books edition is the first
publication of *Contemporary Utilitarianism*

Anchor Books edition: 1968

Library of Congress Catalog Card Number 68–27107

Copyright © 1968 by Michael D. Bayles

CONTENTS

NOTE TO THE READER

All papers in this collection except Professor Donagan's have appeared elsewhere. Each is reprinted in full as originally published except for Professor Smart's in which he has made a significant change in one argument (for details see the note at the beginning of his paper). Page numbers of the original publications have been inserted in the text in brackets. The text of the original page follows the bracketed number. All references to other papers included in this volume give both the pages of the original publication and those of this volume.

*Contemporary
Utilitarianism*

INTRODUCTION
Michael D. Bayles

This anthology collects in one place a series of ten papers in which the ethical theory, rule-utilitarianism, was developed. The development of this theory was a dialectical process of formulation, criticism, reply and reformulation; the record of this process well illustrates the co-operative development of a philosophical theory.

Rule-utilitarianism is a refinement of utilitarianism, an ethical theory with a long history. Early formulations of utilitarianism may be found in writings of ancient Greeks and Romans. However, it was not until during the latter part of the eighteenth and the nineteenth centuries that it gained a large popularity among philosophers through the writings of the classical utilitarians—Hume, Bentham, Austin, J. S. Mill and Sidgwick.

Utilitarianism is a normative theory of ethics which, in the most general terms, claims one ought to do those actions which produce good or avoid evil for everyone. This theory is compatible with most meta-ethical views. Normative ethics and meta-ethics are the two branches into which ethical theory is usually divided. Meta-ethics may be viewed as a second order study of ethical language and normative theory, while normative ethics is a first order study of the aims and principles of conduct and choice. Two major questions are posed in meta-ethics—"What is the meaning (use) of ethical terms?" and "Can normative theories be classified as correct or incorrect, and if so, upon what basis?" Various answers have been suggested to the former question, but all of them are compatible with utilitarianism. Whether in making ethical judgments one either asserts that actions, people or objects possess natural or non-natural properties, or prescribes behavior, or issues imperatives or expresses emotions is irrelevant to utilitarianism. Different utilitarians have held each of these views. The main meta-ethical doctrine incompatible with utilitarianism is ethical relativism or the belief that it is improper to judge one normative theory to be more correct than another because no method exists by which one can rationally choose between them. As relativism is inconsistent with the claim of any normative theory to be correct, it is no more contrary to utilitarianism than it is to any other theory.

There are two basic problems in normative ethics: One is "What is intrinsically good?" The other is "What ought one to do?" Theories concerned with the first problem may be called theories of value while those concerned with the second may be called theories of obligation. Three kinds of theory of value have been proposed. Some philosophers believe only pleasure is intrinsically good; theories of this sort are called "hedonistic." "Eudaemonistic" theories are held by those philosophers who suggest happiness is the only intrinsic good. Usually happiness is considered to be different from pleasure, but J. S. Mill equated the two. This causes some difference in terminology among contributors to this anthology for some use "hedonism" to refer to theories based on happiness as well as those based on pleasure. The third type of theory is a catch-all for those which do not fit the first two categories. Theories of this sort have been variously called "agathistic," "ideal" or "pluralistic." Any view that something besides pleasure or happiness has intrinsic value is fitted into this category.

Theories of obligation which propose answers to the second problem of normative ethics, what ought one to do, fall into two main groups—deontological and teleological. Teleological theories claim that what one ought to do, or what one's obligations are, depends in some way or other upon producing good and/or avoiding evil. An act must in some way be related to producing good or avoiding evil to be right or obligatory. Deontological or formalistic theories, on the other hand, claim that it is at least sometimes possible for one to have obligations to perform actions which do not produce good or avoid evil in any manner suggested by teleologists. Hence, deontologists have been the main critics of utilitarianism, since it presents the most plausible form of teleological theory.

A rather close connection exists between deontological theories and the meta-ethical theory of intuitionism. As a matter of fact most recent deontologists have been intuitionists. Intuitionists claim that either reason or some special faculty of intuition has direct knowledge of the obligatoriness or disobligatoriness of actions, or the value of persons and objects. If one claims, as deontologists do, that what one ought to do does not depend upon what is good, then one must offer an alternative method for determining what ought to be done. The more likely alternatives seem to be that one is informed or told what is right, usually by revelations from God, or that one has direct knowledge of what is right. Since the seventeenth century most major philosophers have rejected God and revelation as a source of moral knowledge. Hence, some form of intuitionism has presented itself as the most plausible meta-ethical position for deontologists. However, not all intuitionists are deontologists. Both Henry Sidgwick and G. E.

Moore held utilitarian theories of obligation and intuitionist meta-ethical theories.

Teleological theories may be divided into two main
groups depending upon whose good is to be promoted. These groups are egoism and utilitarianism.
Egoistic theories claim that the good to be sought is
that of the actor. The central thesis of egoism may
be stated as "Each person ought to do that which
will most benefit himself." It would seem that on
this view obligations would often result in severe
competition between people, since each person would
be out to get the most good for himself, and this
might involve his depriving others. However, serious
defenders of egoism, e.g., Hobbes and Spinoza, have
generally held that upon a rational examination of
the human situation it appears one best promotes his
own interest by co-operating with others.

Utilitarianism, on the other hand, claims one ought
to do what promotes good or avoids evil for everyone, not just oneself. The net balance of good over
evil which an act produces is called its utility, hence,
the name utilitarianism. The central doctrine of
utilitarianism may thus be stated as "One ought to
do what has utility for everyone." Two aspects of
utilitarianism present themselves for further clarification. The first concerns the end of actions, the good
for which actions should be useful. The second aspect
concerns how one determines the utility of an action.
Both of these aspects must be considered in more
detail.

The central contention of utilitarians concerning
the first aspect, the end or goal for which actions
should be useful, is that they should bring about
what is intrinsically good. Although utilitarianism
is compatible with any theory of value, most utilitarians have held either hedonistic or eudaemonistic
theories; nonetheless, some philosophers such as

Moore have adopted agathistic theories of value along with utilitarianism. Noting the theory of value which a philosopher adopts helps clarify his view of utilitarianism. Combining theories of value with utilitarianism yields three possible varieties—hedonistic, eudaemonistic and agathistic or ideal utilitarianism. Sometimes "utilitarianism" is taken to refer to only the hedonistic and eudaemonistic varieties. However, concern with the theory of value connected with utilitarianism has declined considerably in recent years. One reason for this decline probably lies in the fact that no matter what general claim utilitarians have made concerning the intrinsically good, they have all tended to agree in practice. They have all agreed that food, clothing, health, leisure, happiness, etc., are good. Differences of opinion pertain to the sense in which these things are good, whether they are intrinsically or extrinsically good.

Many utilitarians have taken the end to be not merely producing good, but producing as much good as possible. However, not all utilitarian theories take the end to be the greatest good, some are content with producing good and others with merely avoiding evil. This latter sort is sometimes referred to as "negative utilitarianism." Of course these differences produce other variations in the theories, but these are too complex to be considered here. For present purposes discussion will be restricted to those versions which take the end to be the greatest good.

Although utilitarians believe one ought to do what brings about the greatest good for everyone and have generally agreed as to what is good, a problem still remains concerning the end which actions should promote. One should do what has greatest utility for everyone, but "everyone" is ambiguous since it may be used either collectively or distributively. If "everyone" is used collectively, then one should do what is useful for "everyone taken all together." If "everyone" is used distributively, then one should do what is useful for "each and every one." The practical difference in these two senses may perhaps best be brought out by an example in terms of eudaemonistic utilitarianism. Suppose one could perform only one of two acts, A or B, which would affect the happiness of ten people. If one performs A, then seven people will be very happy and three very unhappy. If one performs B, then none of the people will be very happy or very unhappy. That is, act A will result in the greatest total happiness but act B will result in happiness for each and every person. Thus, if in the utilitarian formula "everyone" has its collective sense one should perform act A, but if "everyone" has its distributive sense one should perform act B. Critics of utilitarianism maintain that if it prescribes act A (classical utilitarians are usually interpreted to have intended the collective sense—the greatest good for the *greatest number*—and, hence, prescribe act A), then it prescribes an act which is clearly contrary to our common sense notions of justice. Further, they contend, since utilitarianism conflicts with justice it cannot be an adequate theory of obligation and is not acceptable. This problem has been a very live issue in recent discussions of utilitarianism and has inclined philosophers such as John Rawls and Richard Brandt, who are sympathetic to utilitarianism, finally to reject it as an adequate theory of obligation without at least some modification.

This problem lies behind the various attitudes taken towards utilitarianism by contemporary philosophers. Some philosophers, such as T. L. S. Sprigge and J. J. C. Smart, find it an adequate theory of obligations. Others, like Brandt, believe it must be supplemented in one or more places. Some, like Rawls, believe it can be accepted only within a framework of justice. Finally, philosophers such as Alan Donagan and H. J. McCloskey believe it to be a totally unacceptable theory. So there are many views as to the acceptability of utilitarianism as a part of normative ethics or what is usually called morals.

The main "bone of contention" in recent discussion of utilitarianism has concerned the second aspect mentioned above, how one determines the utility of an action. The problem is how what one ought to do relates to achieving intrinsic good for everyone. Two main methods have been suggested for determining what one ought to do in terms of utility. (A) This method applies considerations of utility to each specific situation when it arises without reference to other cases. One determines the utility of each different individual act which might be performed. Then one compares the utility of each act with the others. One ought to perform that act which in this specific situation has the greatest utility compared with that of the other individual acts one could perform. A theory of this sort is called "extreme" or "act-utilitarianism." The main feature of act-utilitarianism consists in applying considerations of utility to *this* act in *this* situation. (B) Alternatively, it has been suggested that instead of applying utility to this act in this situation, one should apply it to *kinds* of acts in *types* of situations. A theory of this sort is called "restricted" or "rule-utilitarianism." According to rule-utilitarianism one first determines the utility of performing one kind (class) of acts in a type of situation, or of following a rule which prescribes that one always perform acts of that kind in those types of situation. Then one compares the utility of following this rule with that of following other possible rules. One adopts that rule the following of which has the greatest utility compared with that of other possible rules. Particular acts are then judged by their conformity to this rule. This point constitutes the main difference between act- and rule-utilitarianism; according to rule-utilitarianism particular acts are

judged by their conformity to rules which have been
evaluated by their utility, while according to act-
utilitarianism the individual acts are evaluated by
their utility.

Classical utilitarians either did not distinguish between act- and rule-utilitarianism or were not concerned with this distinction and so did not develop
the differences between them. Consequently, in the
writings of most classical utilitarians one finds elements of both types of theory. However, at the
beginning of the twentieth century G. E. Moore
explicitly interpreted utilitarianism as act-utilitarianism. Moore's discussions were very influential; the result was that for almost half a century philosophers
discussed only act-utilitarianism. Usually, in fact, philosophers equated utilitarianism with hedonistic act-
utilitarianism which is probably the least defensible
variety. About mid-century several philosophers formulated explicit versions of rule-utilitarianism. Since
this development the distinction between act- and
rule-utilitarianism has become more widely recognized and the topic of much debate.

One of the more influential of these explicit formulations of rule-utilitarianism is found in "The Interpretation of the Moral Philosophy of J. S. Mill" by
J. O. Urmson, which appears first in this collection.
Urmson not only formulates an explicit version of
rule-utilitarianism but he also claims that John Stuart
Mill put forth such a view in *Utilitarianism*. Others
have challenged Urmson's claim that Mill consistently
held a rule-utilitarian theory [notably J. D. Mabbott
in "Interpretations of Mill's 'Utilitarianism'," *Philosophical Quarterly*, VI (1956), 115–129], but their
replies, being primarily of historical interest, have
been omitted from this collection.

As has been noted, one reason some philosophers
reject utilitarianism as an adequate theory of obligation is the belief that it does not provide reasons for

acting in a manner most people would deem just. In short, it is claimed utilitarianism does not account for our duty to be just. In the second selection, "Utilitarianism, Universalisation, and Our Duty to Be Just," Jonathan Harrison tries to formulate a rule-utilitarian theory which can account for our duty to be just. In so doing he distinguishes actions the general performance of which is good but which do not individually produce good consequences, and actions the general performance of which is good because they do individually produce good consequences. On the basis of this distinction he then tries to show why one needs to adopt rule-utilitarianism and that it does provide reasons for performing just actions.

In his now famous "Two Concepts of Rules" John Rawls distinguishes between the summary and practice conceptions of rules. Each conception has been applied by philosophers to "moral" rules and is appropriate to certain types of ethical theories. Some of the discussions and debates in ethics may be seen as differences concerning which conception best fits moral rules. The summary conception is appropriate to act-utilitarian theories but is open to strong criticisms concerning promising and punishment. Rawls explicates the practice conception appropriate to some forms of rule-utilitarianism. Rule-utilitarian theories based on the practice conception, Rawls contends, are more defensible than act-utilitarian theories because they avoid the criticisms concerning promising and punishment. This paper presents one of the most important arguments for rule-utilitarianism.

In the following selections, "Extreme and Restricted Utilitarianism" by J. J. C. Smart and "An Examination of Restricted Utilitarianism" by H. J. McCloskey, the authors criticize restricted or rule-utilitarianism. Both of them use the terms "extreme" and "restricted utilitarianism" but have since adopted that of "act-"

and "rule-utilitarianism" in order to bring their terminology into line with the more descriptive language of others. Smart argues from an act-utilitarian position, charging rule-utilitarians with failure to seek the greatest possible good because of superstitious rule-worship. McCloskey, on the other hand, arguing from an intuitionist and deontologist point of view, criticizes several aspects of rule-utilitarianism including conflicts of rules, justice and the general concept of rules.

Richard Brandt's "Toward a Credible Form of Utilitarianism" provides the most comprehensive formulation and defense of rule-utilitarianism to date. This paper may be taken as an indirect reply to the criticisms of Smart and McCloskey. Brandt criticizes act-utilitarianism and shows that rule-utilitarianism avoids some of the criticisms to which the former is open. He also attempts to show that some forms of rule-utilitarianism have the same results as act-utilitarianism and to indicate how one may formulate rule-utilitarian theories which avoid this consequence. Significantly, he also distinguishes between rule-utilitarian theories based upon generally accepted rules of society and those based upon rules which would be best if adopted. An interesting account of methods for handling conflicts between rules is also presented.

Alan Donagan in "Is There a Credible Form of Utilitarianism?" and B. J. Diggs in "Rules and Utilitarianism" offer criticisms of rule-utilitarianism. Donagan claims rule-utilitarianism will often prescribe that it is one's duty to perform an act when one clearly has no obligation to do so although the act's performance may be commendable. He then sketches a non-utilitarian theory. Diggs offers a detailed analysis of types of rules and claims rule-utilitarians mistake the purpose and function of many rules.

In the last two articles H. J. McCloskey and T. L. S. Sprigge debate the utilitarian theory of punishment.

In "A Non-Utilitarian Approach to Punishment" Mc-
Closkey restates and expands on an argument presented in his previous paper in this collection and
elsewhere; he claims utilitarianism simply does not
account for calling certain acts just which most or
all people would say were just. Sprigge, in "A Utilitarian Reply to Dr. McCloskey," analyzes McCloskey's arguments in detail and presents a strong reply
from an act-utilitarian point of view. He agrees with
McCloskey that rule-utilitarianism does not offer an
acceptable alternative to act-utilitarianism and briefly
argues that it either produces the same practical results
as act-utilitarianism or gives up its concern with
general happiness.

Thus Brandt and Sprigge both argue that at least
some forms of rule-utilitarianism have the same practical results as act-utilitarianism, that is, it would never
be the case that rule-utilitarianism of this sort would
imply that one ought to perform one act in a given
situation and act-utilitarianism imply one ought to
do something different. Brandt believes other kinds
of rule-utilitarianism are more credible, but Sprigge
and McCloskey claim they really give up the concern
for the good of everyone. At the time of writing
none of these authors was aware of the important
and well reasoned tenets of a book published late
in 1965 by David Lyons, *Forms and Limits of Utilitarianism* (Oxford: The Clarendon Press). Lyons
carefully distinguishes between rule-utilitarian theories
which imply the same results as act-utilitarianism and
those which do not. One important type of rule-
utilitarianism which does not have the same results
as act-utilitarianism justifies rules in terms of their
"acceptance-utility," that is, the utility of the effects
of generally accepting them as valid, rather than their
"conformity-utility" or the utility of the effects of
actually conforming to them. The main difference
between these two types of utility lies in the fact

that people do not always succeed in conforming to rules they accept as valid so that acceptance-utility allows for a certain amount of weakness of will or failure to live up to one's standards. Brandt and Urmson both use acceptance-utility in their papers.

Granting Lyons' distinction one can see certain implications for the positions adopted by McCloskey and Sprigge concerning a rule-utilitarian view of punishment. For those forms of rule-utilitarianism which give the same results as act-utilitarianism, any defense of an act-utilitarian view of punishment would *ipso facto* be a defense of them. In the case of those forms of rule-utilitarianism which are not practically equivalent to act-utilitarianism the situation is less clear. It would seem that rule-utilitarianisms based upon acceptance-utility permit all the utilitarian defenses Sprigge offers based upon criticisms of the common moral consciousness and the use of fanciful examples. The task of deciding which of Sprigge's defenses may or may not support such rule-utilitarianisms is left to the reader.

THE INTERPRETATION
OF THE MORAL PHILOSOPHY
OF J. S. MILL

J. O. Urmson

It is a matter which should be of great interest to
those who study the psychology of philosophers that
the theories of some great philosophers of the past
are studied with the most patient and accurate scholar-
ship, while those of others are so burlesqued and
travestied by critics and commentators that it is hard
to believe that their works are ever seriously read
with a sympathetic interest, or even that they are
read at all. Amongst those who suffer most in this
way John Stuart Mill is an outstanding example. With
the exception of a short book by Reginald Jackson,[1]
there is no remotely accurate account of his views
on deductive logic, so that, for example, the absurd
view that the syllogism involves *petitio principii* is
almost invariably fathered on him; and, as Von Wright
says, 'A good systematic and critical monograph on
Mill's Logic of Induction still remains to be written'.[2]

FROM *The Philosophical Quarterly*, Vol. III (1953), 33–39.
Reprinted by permission of the author and *The Philosophical
Quarterly*.

[1] *An Examination of the Deductive Logic of J. S. Mill*
(1941).

[2] *A Treatise on Induction and Probability* (1951), p. 164.

But even more perplexing is the almost universal misconstruction placed upon Mill's ethical doctrines; for his *Utilitarianism* is a work which every undergraduate is set to read and which one would therefore expect Mill's critics to have read at least once. But this, apparently, is not so; and instead of Mill's own doctrines a travesty is discussed, so that the most common criticisms of him are simply irrelevant. It will not be the thesis of this paper that Mill's views are immune to criticism, or that they are of impeccable clarity and verbal consistency; it will be maintained that, if interpreted with, say, half the sympathy automatically accorded to Plato, Leibniz, and Kant, an essentially consistent thesis can be discovered which is very superior to that usually attributed to Mill and immune to the common run of criticisms.

One further note must be made on the scope of this paper. Mill, in his *Utilitarianism* attempts to do two things; first, he attempts to state the place of the conception of a *summum bonum* in ethics, secondly, he attempts to give an account of the nature of this ultimate end. We shall be concerned only with the first of these two parts of Mill's ethical theory; we shall not ask what Mill thought the ultimate end was, and how he thought that his view on this point could be substantiated, but only what part Mill considered that the notion of an ultimate end, whatever it be, must play in a sound ethical theory. This part of Mill's doctrine is logically independent of his account of happiness.

Two Mistaken Interpretations of Mill

Some of Mill's expositors and critics have thought that Mill was attempting to analyse or define the notion of right in terms of the *summum bonum*.

[34] Thus Mill is commonly adduced as an example of an ethical naturalist by those who interpret his account of happiness naturalistically, as being one who defined rightness in terms of the natural consequences of actions. Moore, for example, while criticising Mill's account of the ultimate end says: 'In thus insisting that what is right must mean what produces the best possible results Utilitarianism is fully justified'.[3] Others have been less favourable in their estimation of this alleged view of Mill's. But right or wrong, it seems clear to me that Mill did not hold it. Mill's only reference to this analytic problem is on page 27 (of the Everyman edition, to which all references will be made), where he refers to a person 'who sees in moral obligation a transcendent fact, an objective reality belonging to the province of "Things in themselves"', and goes on to speak of this view as an irrelevant opinion 'on this point of Ontology', as though the analysis of ethical terms was not part of ethical philosophy at all as he conceived it, but part of ontology. It seems clear that when Mill speaks of his quest being for the 'criterion of right and wrong' (p. 1), 'concerning the foundation of morality' (p. 1) for a 'test of right and wrong' (p. 2), he is looking for a 'means of ascertaining what is right or wrong' (p. 2), not for a definition of these terms. We shall not, therefore, deal further with this interpretation of Mill; if a further refutation of it is required it should be sought in the agreement of the text with the alternative exposition shortly to be given.

The other mistaken view avoids the error of this first view, and indeed is incompatible with it. It is, probably, the received view. On this interpretation Mill is looking for a test of right or wrong as the ultimate test by which one can justify the ascription

---

[3] *Principia Ethica*, reprinted 1948, p. 106.

of rightness or wrongness to courses of action, rightness and wrongness being taken to be words which we understand. This test is taken to be whether the course of action does or does not tend to promote the ultimate end (which Mill no doubt says is the general happiness). So far there is no cause to quarrel with the received view, for it is surely correct. But in detail the view is wrong. For it is further suggested that for Mill this ultimate test is also the immediate test; the rightness or wrongness of any particular action is to be decided by considering whether it promotes the ultimate end. We may, it might be admitted, on Mill's view sometimes act, by rule of thumb or in a hurry, without actually raising this question; but the actual justification, if there is one, must be directly in terms of consequences, including the consequences of the example that we have set. On this view, then, Mill holds that an action, a particular action, is right if it promotes the ultimate end better than any alternative, and otherwise it is wrong. However we in fact make up our minds in moral situations, so far as justification goes no other factor enters into the matter. It is clear that on this interpretation Mill is immediately open to two shattering objections; first, it is obviously and correctly urged, if one has, for example, promised to do something it is one's duty to do it at least partly because one has promised to do it and not merely because of consequences, [35] even if these consequences are taken to include one's example in promise-breaking. Secondly, it is correctly pointed out that on this view a man who, *ceteris paribus*, chooses the inferior of two musical comedies for an evening's entertainment has done a moral wrong, and this is preposterous.[4] If

---

[4] For one example of this interpretation of Mill and the first and more important objection, see Carritt, *The Theory of Morals*, Ch. IV.

this were in fact the view of Mill, he would indeed be fit for little more than the halting eristic of philosophical infants.

A Revised Interpretation of Mill

I shall now set out in a set of propositions what I take to be in fact Mill's view and substantiate them afterwards from the text. This will obscure the subtleties but will make clearer the main lines of interpretation.

A. A particular action is justified as being right by showing that it is in accord with some moral rule. It is shown to be wrong by showing that it trangresses some moral rule.

B. A moral rule is shown to be correct by showing that the recognition of that rule promotes the ultimate end.

C. Moral rules can be justified only in regard to matters in which the general welfare is more than negligibly affected.

D. Where no moral rule is applicable the question of the rightness or wrongness of particular acts does not arise, though the worth of the actions can be estimated in other ways.

As a terminological point it should be mentioned that where the phrase 'moral rule' occurs above Mill uses the phrase 'secondary principle' more generally, though he sometimes says 'moral law'. By these terms, whichever is preferred, Mill is referring to such precepts as 'Keep promises', 'Do no murder', or 'Tell no lies'. A list of which Mill approves is to be found in *On Liberty* (p. 135).

There is, no doubt, need of further explanation of these propositions; but that, and some caveats, can best be given in the process of establishing that these are in fact Mill's views. First, then, to establish from

the text that in Mill's view particular actions are
shown to be right or wrong by showing that they
are or are not in accord with some moral rule. (i) He
says with evident approbation on p. 2: 'The intuitive,
no less than what may be termed the inductive, school
of ethics, insists on the necessity of general laws.
They both agree that the morality of an individual
action is not a question of direct perception, but
of the application of a law to an individual case.
They recognise also, to a great extent, the same moral
laws'. Mill reproaches these schools only with being
unable to give a unifying rationale of these laws
(as he will do in proposition B). (ii) He says on
page 22: 'But to consider the rules of morality as
improvable is one thing; to pass over the intermediate
generalisations entirely, and endeavour to test each
individual action directly by the first principle, is another. It is a strange notion that the acknowledgement
of a first principle is inconsistent with the admission
of secondary ones'. He adds, with feeling: 'Men really
[36] ought to leave off talking a kind of nonsense on
this subject which they would neither talk nor listen
to on other matters of practical concernment'. (iii)
Having admitted on p. 23 that 'rules of conduct
cannot be so framed as to require no exceptions', he
adds (p. 24) 'We must remember that only in these
cases of conflict between secondary principles is it
requisite that first principles should be appealed to.
There is no case of moral obligation in which some
secondary principle is not involved; and if only one,
there can seldom be any real doubt which one it is, in
the mind of any person by whom the principle itself is
recognised'. This quotation supports both propositions
A and D. It shows that for Mill moral rules are
not merely rules of thumb which aid the unreflective
man in making up his mind, but an essential part
of moral reasoning. The relevance of a moral rule is
the criterion of whether we are dealing with a case

of right or wrong or some other moral or prudential situation. (iv) The last passage which we shall select to establish this interpretation of Mill (it would be easy to find more) is also a joint confirmation of propositions A and D, showing that our last was not an *obiter dictum* on which we have placed too much weight. In the chapter entitled 'On the connection between justice and utility', Mill has maintained that it is a distinguishing mark of a just act that it is one required by a specific rule or law, positive or moral, carrying also liability to penal sanctions. He then writes this important paragraph (p. 45), which in view of its importance and the neglect that it has suffered must be quoted at length: 'The above is, I think, a true account, as far as it goes, of the origin and progressive growth of the idea of justice. But we must observe, that it contains, as yet, nothing to distinguish that obligation from moral obligation in general. For the truth is, that the idea of penal sanction, which is the essence of law, enters not only into the conception of injustice, but into that of any kind of wrong. We do not call anything wrong, unless we mean to imply that a person ought to be punished in some way or other for doing it; if not by law, by the opinion of his fellow-creatures; if not by opinion, by the reproaches of his own conscience. This seems to be the real turning point of the distinction between morality and simple expediency. It is a part of the notion of Duty in every one of its forms, that a person may rightfully be compelled to fulfil it. Duty is a thing which may be exacted from a person, as one exacts a debt. Unless we think that it may be exacted from him, we do not call it his duty. . . . There are other things, on the contrary, which we wish that people should do, which we like or admire them for doing, perhaps dislike or despise them for not doing, but yet admit that they are not bound to do; it is not a case of moral obligation; we do not blame them, that is, we do not think that they are proper objects of punishment. . . . I think there is no doubt that this distinction lies at the bottom of the notions of right and wrong; that we call any conduct wrong, or employ, instead, some other term of dislike or disparagement, according as we think that the person ought, or ought not, to be punished for it; and we say, it would be right to do so and so, or merely that it would be desirable or laudable, according as we would wish to see the person [37] whom it concerns, compelled, or only persuaded and exhorted, to act in that manner'. How supporters of the received view have squared it with this passage I do not know; they do not mention it. If they have noticed it at all it is, presumably, regarded as an example of Mill's inconsistent eclecticism. Mill here makes it quite clear that in his view right and wrong are derived from moral rules; in other cases where the ultimate end is no doubt affected appraisal of conduct must be made in other ways. For example, if one's own participation in the ultimate end is impaired without breach of moral law, it is (*Liberty*, p. 135) imprudence or lack of self-respect, it is not wrong-doing. So much for the establishment of this interpretation of Mill, in a positive way, as regards points A and D. We must now ask whether there is anything in Mill which is inconsistent with it and in favour of the received view.

It is impossible to show positively that there is nothing in Mill which favours the received view against the interpretation here given, for it would require a complete review of everything that Mill says. We shall have to be content with examining two points which might be thought to tell in favour of the received view.

(*a*) On p. 6 Mill says: 'The creed which accepts as the foundation of morals, Utility, or the Greatest Happiness Principle, holds that actions are right in proportion as they tend to promote happiness, wrong as they tend to promote the reverse of Happiness'. This seems to be the well-known sentence which is at the bottom of the received interpretation. Of course, it could be taken as a loose and inaccurate statement of the received view, if the general argument required it. But note that strictly one can say that a certain action tends to produce a certain result only if one is speaking of type- rather than token-actions. Drinking alcohol may tend to promote exhilaration, but my drinking this particular glass either does or does not produce it. It seems, then, that Mill can well be interpreted here as regarding moral rules as forbidding or enjoining types of action, in fact as making the point that the right moral rules are the ones which promote the ultimate end (my proposition B), not as saying something contrary to proposition A. And this, or something like it, is the interpretation which consistency requires. Mill's reference to 'tendencies of actions' at the top of p. 22 supports the stress here laid on the word 'tend', and that context should be examined by those who require further conviction.

(*b*) Mill sometimes refers to moral rules as 'intermediate generalisations' (e.g., p. 22) from the supreme principle, or as 'corollaries' of it (also p. 22). These are probably the sort of phrases which lead people to think that they play a purely heuristic role in ethical thinking for Mill. As for the expression 'intermediate generalisation', Mill undoubtedly thinks that we should, and to some extent do, arrive at and improve our moral rules by such methods as observing that a certain type of action has had bad results of a social kind in such an overwhelming majority of cases that it ought to be banned. (But this is an over-simplification; see the note on p. 58 on how we ought to arrive at moral rules, and the pessimistic account of how we in fact arrive [38] at them in

Liberty, p. 69–70). But this account of the genesis of moral rules does not require us to interpret them as being anything but rules when once made. It really seems unnecessary to say much of the expression 'corollary'; Mill obviously cannot wish it to be taken literally; in fact it is hard to state the relation of moral rules to a justifying principle with exactitude and Mill, in a popular article in *Fraser*, did not try very hard to do so.

Moral Rules and the Ultimate End

We have already been led in our examination of possible objections to proposition A to say something in defence of the view that Mill thought that a moral rule is shown to be correct by showing that the recognition of that rule promotes the ultimate end (proposition B). A little more may be added on this point, though it seems fairly obvious that if we are right in saying that the supreme principle is not to be evoked, in Mill's view, in the direct justification of particular right acts, it must thus come in in an indirect way in view of the importance that Mill attached to it. And it is hard to think what the indirect way is if not this. (i) On p. 3 Mill reproaches other moral philosophers with not giving a satisfactory account of moral rules in terms of a fundamental principle, though they have correctly placed moral rules as governing particular actions. It would be indeed the mark of an inconsistent philosopher if he did not try to repair the one serious omission which he ascribes to others. (ii) Mill ascribes to Kant (p. 4) the use of utilitarian arguments because, Mill alleges, he in fact supports the rules of morality by showing the evil consequences of not adopting them or adopting alternatives. Thus Mill is here regarding as distinctively utilitarian the justification or rejection of moral rules on the ground of consequences. He could hardly have wished to suggest that Kant would directly justify, even inadvertently, particular actions on such grounds. But it is perhaps not to the point to argue this matter more elaborately. If anyone has been convinced by what has gone before, he will not need much argument on this point; with others it is superfluous to make the attempt.

In What Fields Are Moral Rules of Right and Wrong Applicable?

The applicability of moral rules is, says Mill, 'the characteristic difference which marks off, not justice, but morality in general, from the remaining provinces of Expediency and Worthiness' (p. 46). Mill says little or nothing in *Utilitarianism* about the boundary between morality and worthiness (surely it would be better to have said the boundary between right and wrong on the one hand and other forms of both moral and non-moral appraisal on the other?). It seems reasonable to suppose that he would have recognised that the use of moral rules must be confined to matters in which the kind of consequence is sufficiently invariable for there not to be too many exceptions. But this is a pragmatic limitation; Mill does have something to say about a limitation in principle in *Liberty* which I have crudely summarised in my proposition C—moral rules can be justifiably maintained in regard only to matters in which the general welfare is more than negligibly affected. [39]

It is important to note that Mill in *Liberty* is concerned with freedom from moral sanctions as well as the sanctions of positive law. The distinction between self-regarding and other actions is regarded by him as relevant to moral as well as to political philosophy. The most noteworthy passage which bears on the

scope of moral rules is on page 135. Here he mentions such things as encroachment on the rights of
others as being 'fit objects of moral reprobation, and,
in grave cases, of moral retribution and punishment'.
But self-regarding faults (low tastes and the like) are
'not properly immoralities and to whatever pitch they
are carried, do not constitute wickedness . . . . . The
term duty to oneself, when it means anything more
than prudence, means self-respect or self-develop-
ment'. Self-regarding faults render the culprit 'necessarily and properly a subject of distaste, or, in extreme cases, even of contempt', but this is in the
sphere of worthiness not of right and wrong.

So much then for Mill's account of the logic of
moral reasoning. It must be emphasised that no more
has been attempted than a skeleton plan of Mill's
answer, and that Mill puts the matter more richly
and more subtly in his book. Even on the question
of general interpretation more store must be laid on
the effect of a continuous reading in the light of the
skeleton plan than on the effect of the few leading
quotations introduced in this paper. It is emphatically
not the contention of this paper that Mill has given a
finally correct account of these matters which is immune to all criticism; an attempt has been made only
to give a sympathetic account without any criticism
favourable or unfavourable. But I certainly do maintain that the current interpretations of Mill's *Utilitarianism* are so unsympathetic and so incorrect that
the majority of criticisms which have in fact been
based on them are irrelevant and worthless.

◈

UTILITARIANISM,
UNIVERSALISATION,
AND OUR DUTY TO BE JUST
Jonathan Harrison

"In considering what common interest requires,
we are, besides the immediate effects of actions, to
consider what their general tendencies are, what
they open the way to, and what would actually be
the consequences if all were to act alike. If under
the pretence of greater indigence, superfluity to the
owner, or intention to give to a worthier person, I
may take away a man's property, or adjudge it
from him in a court of justice; another or all, in
the same circumstances may do so; and thus the
boundaries of property would be overthrown, and
general anarchy, distrust and savageness be introduced."—Richard Price.[1]

According to Utilitarianism, it is often said, an action is right if it produces at least as much good as
any other action which the agent could have done in

FROM the *Proceedings of the Aristotelian Society*, Vol. LIII
(1952–53), 105–34. Reprinted by permission of the Editor of
the Aristotelian Society. Copyright 1953 The Aristotelian
Society.

[1] Richard Price: *A Review of the Principal Questions in
Morals*, edited by D. Daiches Raphael, p. 164.

the circumstances in which he was placed. Besides
being right, it is also a duty, if it produces more
good than any other action that the agent could have
done. When we are faced with a situation in which
we have to choose between a number of actions,
each of which would produce as much good or more
than anything else we could do, but of none of which
is it true that they would produce more good than
anything else we could do, then we have not a duty
to perform any particular one of these actions to the
exclusion of the others. What is our duty is to do
one or other of these actions; but it is a matter of
indifference which of them we do, and we have
done our duty, whichever one of them we perform.[2] [106]

There are, therefore, some right actions which are
not duties, and so the words "right" and "a duty"
cannot mean the same thing. This fact has been regarded as unimportant,[3] because it has been supposed
that the circumstances in which we are faced with a
choice between a number of right actions, none of
which are duties, occur but seldom.

However, it seems to me that such situations, so far
from being rare, are arising all the time. At any moment of the day, when I am not engaged in doing anything in particular, there are at least half a dozen
actions I can think of which I could do, which it
would be perfectly right for me to do, but none of
which could, by any stretch of the imagination, be
said to be duties. It is often supposed that, in such circumstances, I have no duties, but this is a mistake.
Among the actions which I could do at this moment
are some wrong ones; I might, for example, throw my

---

[2] See G. E. Moore: *Ethics*, pp. 32–35. The definition of
utilitarianism used here would not have satisfied Professor
Moore, but it will do for our purposes.

[3] See W. D. Ross: *The Right and the Good*, pp. 3–4.

muffin in my friend's face, or wantonly break the window of the cafe in which I am drinking tea with him. Since it is within my power to perform, at this very moment, some wrong actions, I must, at this very moment, have some duty incumbent upon me, namely, the duty of refraining from performing any of these wrong actions. And furthermore, a man of more ascetic temperament and sterner moral character than myself might well argue that, at this very moment, I was not doing my duty; that my money might be better employed in succouring the needy; my time in furthering the development of a noble cause; my mind in contemplating the benevolence of my Maker or the enormities of my sins.

For these reasons, it seems to me that, so far from right actions almost always being duties, right actions are hardly ever duties. What is my duty is to perform one of the number of alternative right actions which I could perform; in doing any one of them I do my duty, though I could equally well have done it in doing any other. The occasion [107] when we can say of one particular action that it, and it alone, is a duty, occurs comparatively seldom.

Utilitarianism might, then, be defined as the theory which holds that an action is right if there is no action within the power of the agent which would produce more good than it, and that it is my duty to perform some right action or other. The circumstances in which there is only one right action within the power of the agent will fall under this principle as a special case, and, when this special case arises, that right action will also be a duty.

I will not bore my readers by citing any of the well-known objections to utilitarianism, but there is one particular difficulty in this theory which, for the purpose of this article, is of special interest. There are some actions which we think we have a duty to do, although they themselves produce no good conse-

quences, because such actions would produce good
consequences if they were generally practised. There
are some actions which we think we have a duty to
refrain from doing, even though they themselves produce no harmful consequences, because such actions
would produce harmful consequences if the performance of them became the general rule. I think I have
a duty to vote for that person whose party I think
would govern the nation best, although I do not think
that the addition of my vote to the total number of
votes which are cast for him is going to make any
difference to the result of the election, simply because
I realise that, if all his other supporters were to do as
I do, and fail to go to the polls, the man would not
be elected. I refrain from walking on the grass of a
well-kept park lawn, not because I think that my walking on the grass is going to damage the lawn to such
an extent as to detract from anybody's pleasure in
contemplating it, but because I realise that, if everybody else who walked in the park were to do likewise,
the grass in the park would be spoilt. These two duties
cannot be derived from the duty of setting a good
example, or of refraining from setting a bad example,
for I should still feel them incumbent upon me, even
if no-one were to [108] know that I had defaced my
ballot paper, and even if the park was empty of everyone but me.

   Such facts, if they are facts, have not been entirely
neglected by Utilitarians. Hume, for example, may
have had them in mind when he distinguished between justice and benevolence. Of the social virtues
of benevolence and humanity he says: "And as the
good, resulting from their benign influence is in itself
complete and entire, it also excites the moral sentiment
of approbation, without any reflection on farther consequences, and without any more enlarged views of
the concurrence or imitation of the other members

of society."[4] Whereas of justice he says: "The case is not the same with the social virtues of justice and fidelity. They are highly useful, or indeed absolutely necessary to the well-being of mankind; but the benefit resulting from them is not the consequence of every individual single act; but arises from the whole scheme or system concurred in by the whole, or the greater part of the society."[5] Comparing the virtues of justice and benevolence, he says: "The happiness and prosperity of mankind, arising from the social virtue of benevolence and its subdivisions, may be compared to a wall, built by many hands, which still rises by each stone that is heaped upon it, and receives increase proportional to the diligence and care of each workman. The same happiness, raised by the social virtue of justice and its subdivisions, may be compared to the building of a vault, where each individual stone would, of itself, fall to the ground; nor is the whole fabric supported but by the mutual assistance and combination of its corresponding parts."[6]

Benevolent actions, if I have interpreted Hume rightly, themselves produce good consequences, and would produce good consequences whether anybody else performed benevolent actions or not. A just action, however, would not [109] produce good consequences if it was the only instance of its kind. Just actions only produce good consequences so long as the performance of just actions is the rule rather than the exception. This is why one may often be bound to perform a just action which has consequences which are harmful. I must perform it, even when it itself has harmful consequences, because it is an action of a kind the general performance of which is necessary

---

[4] L. A. Selby-Bigge: *Hume's Enquiries*, second edition, 1902, p. 304.

[5] *Loc. cit.*

[6] *Op. cit.*, p. 305.

to society. This is why justice is "conventional" in
a way in which benevolence is not. Justice is conventional in that the benefit to be derived from it depends upon its customary observance. No benefit will
be obtained from my practice of justice unless my
fellows practise it too, and the same is true of them.
This is not to say that I make an explicit agreement
with them that we shall all behave justly in order to
gain the benefits of justice. Indeed, our obligation to
be just could not be derived from any such agreement, because the obligation to keep agreements is itself a subdivision of justice. Both I and my neighbours are not just because we agree to be just, but
because we each realise that the common practice of
justice is in the interest of all of us.

However, it is not certain that Hume did hold the
view which I have just attributed to him. This view
may easily be confused with, and Hume himself, I
am afraid, failed to distinguish it from, another rather
similar view. There are some actions which, besides
being of a sort which would produce good consequences if generally performed, are themselves necessary to the production of these good consequences. If
two men are rowing a boat, the boat will progress
only so long as they both row, and will fail to progress
if either of them stop rowing. In this case, the actions
of either oarsman are necessary if the good which
consists in the progress of the boat is to be secured.
Such actions, since they are necessary conditions of
the production of a certain good, do themselves produce good consequences, and so they must clearly be
distinguished from those actions which, though they
are of a sort the general performance of which would
produce good consequences, do not produce [110]
good consequences themselves. Moreover, the good
which consists in the movement of the boat cannot be
split into parts, and part attributed to the actions of
one oarsman, and part to the actions of the other; the

whole of this good must be produced, or none of it. Hence the good in question must be considered as being equally the consequence of the actions of either man, and it is the whole of this good which each man must take into account when he is considering whether or not he has a duty to row. Now it may have been Hume's view that justice is a duty, not because just actions are of a sort which would produce good consequences if generally practised, but because just actions are severally necessary if any good is to be produced by the general practice of justice.

There are arguments which might be used to try to show that Hume held the latter of the two views which I have just distinguished; which tend to show that Hume thought that we had a duty to be just because, if we were not just, the whole of the good consequent upon the general performance of justice would be lost; rather than that he thought that we should perform just actions because they were of a sort the general performance of which would produce good consequences, even when they themselves did not. In the first place, he sometimes speaks as if the performance of every just action is necessary if any just action is to produce good consequences. I must be just, even when it seems that the consequences of my being just are bad, because, if I am not just, the good which the general practice of justice brings about will be lost. In the second place, he thinks that, in a state of nature, it will be nobody's duty to be just, because if, in such a state, only one of us behaves justly, no good will result. Whereas what he should have said—and, perhaps, what he would have said—if he had held that a just action is made right by the fact that it is of a sort the general performance of which would produce good consequences, is, that it is our duty to be just, even in a state of nature. For it is still true, even in a state of nature, that the general performance of just actions would produce good consequences, even [111] though individual just actions, performed in that state, do not produce good consequences; hence, it seems, we would have a duty to be just in a state of nature, even if, by being just, we produce consequences which are indifferent, or even bad.

The fact that Hume thought that we would not have a duty to be just in a state of nature, and the fact that he sometimes speaks as if the performance of every just action is necessary if any just action is to have good consequences, seems to indicate that Hume thought that we had a duty to perform just actions because they, together with other just actions, were severally necessary to the production of the good resultant upon the practice of justice. But there are some arguments which tend to show, either that he thought that we had a duty to practise just actions because they were of a sort the general performance of which would have good consequences, or that, if he did not actually hold this, his theory is as a result a worse one than I have supposed it to be.

Firstly, the view that we must be just in this particular case, so that the good consequent upon the practice of justice as a whole should be brought about, is unrealistic. It is simply false that the performance of every just action is necessary if the good produced by the practice of justice is to be secured. If this were true, the human race would have perished miserably many years ago. An occasional act of injustice here and there does not undermine the whole beneficial effect of the practice of justice, and, if such actions are performed in secret, they may sometimes not even produce any harmful effects at all.

Secondly, the view that we must be just, because just actions are severally necessary to the production of the good of justice, would make our duty to be just more rigid than we in fact believe it to be. Our normal view on the practice of justice in hard cases is this. We think that we should not turn aside from justice whenever it seems that an unjust action would produce some good, but, on the other hand, we do think that there are occasions on which unjust actions should be performed, because the good to be [112] gained is considerable. But, if the whole of the good consequent upon the practice of justice were dependent upon the performance of just actions in every particular case, it is difficult to believe that the consequences of any individual unjust action, considered in itself, could ever be good enough to justify me in performing it. I must, therefore, apply rules of justice in all circumstances, however trivial, and however great the immediate good to be gained by neglecting them.

Thirdly, if Hume did hold the view that we must perform just actions because just actions are necessary if the general practice of justice is to have any value, then his theory is incapable of accounting for the difficulties with which utilitarianism is faced, and for which it was, in part, intended to account. This theory was, in part, intended to explain how we could have a duty to perform some actions the consequences of which were indifferent or positively bad, and it is one of the great merits of the view that we have a duty to perform actions because they are of a sort which would produce good consequences if generally practised, that it does enable us to explain how it is that we have a duty to perform some actions which, in themselves, have bad or indifferent consequences. But the theory that it is our duty to perform just actions because their performance is necessary for the good of justice to be realised does not, in fact, do this. It does not, as does the other theory, admit and account for the fact that we have a duty to perform some actions which do not themselves produce good consequences, for it does not recognise that there are such duties. All that can be said, if we adopt it, is that there are some actions, which seem to produce no good consequences, or even to produce bad consequences, when we take a narrow and restricted view. When we take a more enlarged view, and consider these actions along with other actions of the same sort, it will be seen that, in actual fact, they really do produce good consequences; they produce good consequences because they are one of a set of actions the several performance of which is necessary if a certain good is to be produced. [113] This view, therefore, does not find a place in the utilitarian scheme of duties for our duty to perform actions which do not themselves have good consequences. It merely denies that we have any such duties, and tries to explain how the illusion that we have arises.

Utilitarians—as well as moral philosophers who have not been utilitarians—have not always failed to notice the fact that we think actions are right if they are of a sort which would produce good consequences if generally practised, or are wrong if they are of a sort which would produce bad consequences if other people did the same. Mill, for example, remarked: "In the case of abstinences—indeed of things which people forbear to do from moral considerations, though the consequences in the particular case might be beneficial—it would be unworthy of an intelligent agent not to be consciously aware that the action is of a class which, if practised generally, would be generally injurious, and that this is the ground of the obligation to abstain from it."[7] But utilitarians have not always realised that, in admitting that the performance of such actions is a duty, they are departing from, or, at least, modifying, utilitarianism as it is stated above. And that they are departing from, or modifying, utili-

---

[7] John Stuart Mill: *Utilitarianism*, Everyman edition, pp. 17–18.

tarianism, as it is usually thought of, is clear. For actions which are permissible, according to utilitarianism as I have defined it above, might well not be permissible, according to utilitarianism in this modified form. For it may very well be true of an action, both that there is no other action within the power of the agent that would produce better consequences than it, and that it is an instance of a class of actions which would produce harmful consequences if they were to be generally performed. In this case, I should, according to utilitarianism as it is normally thought of, be acting rightly if I performed it; whereas, according to this modified form of utilitarianism, I should be acting wrongly. [114]

But the principle that I should perform actions, if they are of a sort which would produce good consequences if generally performed, and should refrain from performing actions which would produce bad consequences, if generally performed, is not free from difficulty.

In the first place, the principle is, as it stands, insufficiently precise. An action, it says, is right if it is of a sort which would produce good consequences, if generally practised, and wrong if it is of a sort which would produce harmful consequences, if generally practised. But no action is an instance of just one sort or class of actions; every action is an instance of many such sorts. It may well be that among the many classes of action of which a given action is an instance, there may be some classes which would have good consequences, if generally performed, some classes which would have bad consequences, if generally performed, and yet other classes, the general performance of which would be indifferent. When we say that the consequences, for good or for ill, of the class of actions of which a given action is a member should be taken into account when we are considering whether or not that action ought to be performed, about which of the many classes, of which the action in question is an instance, are we talking? Which of these classes should be considered, when we are wondering whether such an action is a right and proper one for us to do?

Some of the classes, of which it is a member, should not be considered by us because the consequences which they would have, if generally performed, are different from the consequences their sub-classes would have, if they were generally performed. Suppose, for example, that a red-headed man with one eye, a wart on his right cheek, and a mermaid tattooed on his left forearm, were to tell a lie on a Tuesday. It might be argued that it was quite permissible for him to have told this lie, because his action in telling the lie belongs to the class of actions performed on a Tuesday, and the consequences of the general performance of actions on a Tuesday is indifferent. But the class of actions performed on a Tuesday is not the sort of class [115] which it is important to consider, when meditating upon the consequences of the general performance of certain classes of actions. For the class of actions performed on a Tuesday contains within itself a number of sub-classes: deceitful actions on a Tuesday, self-sacrificing actions on a Tuesday, revengeful actions on a Tuesday, and so on. The consequences of the general performance of actions in these sub-classes will differ both from one another and from the consequences of the general performance of that wider class which is the genus. Since this is the case, it would be unreasonable for us to consider the consequences of the general performance of actions on a Tuesday. For the consequences of the general practice of lying on a Tuesday are different from those of the general practice of actions of any sort on a Tuesday, and it is the consequences of the general performance of the more specific class of actions which it is important for us to consider.

It can be important for us to consider the consequences of the general performance of a certain class of actions only if that class contains within itself no sub-classes, the consequences of the general practice of which is either better or worse than the consequences of the general practice of actions belonging to it. It would be inaccurate to say that this class is of the wrong sort because it is too generic. For the class of actions performed between 3.0 p.m. and 3.01 p.m. on Tuesday is a good deal more specific than it is, and yet is of the wrong sort for precisely the same reason.

If, on the other hand—to revert to our original example—we were to consider, not the consequences of the general practice of lying, but the consequences of the general practice of lying by one-eyed, red-headed men, with warts on their right cheeks and mermaids tattooed on their left forearms, then the class of actions we were considering would be a wrong one, but for a different reason. The class of actions performed on Tuesday afternoon was a wrong one to consider, because it could be "relevantly specified"; that is to say, by the addition of characteristics such as "being the telling of a lie" I could obtain a more [116] specific class of actions, the consequences of the general performance of which would be different from the consequences of the general performance of actions belonging to it. The class of actions, "lies told by one-eyed, red-headed men, with warts on their right cheeks, and mermaids tattooed on their left forearms", is a wrong one because it can be "irrelevantly generalised"; that is to say, by subtracting characteristics such as "being an action performed by a one-eyed man" I can obtain more general classes of actions, the consequences of the general performance of which do not differ from the consequences of the general performance of actions belonging to it.

In the second place, the principle seems to rule

out as being wrong a number of actions which everybody normally thinks to be permissible, and would
make obligatory as duties many actions which people
do not normally consider to be such. The principle
that I should perform actions, the general practice of
which would be beneficial, is often used as an argument for pacifism, and with some plausibility. If everybody were to refrain from participating in wars,
there would be no wars; hence it is my duty to refrain
from participating in wars, whether anybody else co-
operates with me or not. But the same principle can
be used to justify actions which even a pacifist would
condemn. If nobody were to lay violent hands upon
the persons of his neighbours, or upon their property,
everyone would live in peace with his fellow men—
and what a desirable state of affairs this would be! But
must the policeman for this reason refrain from forci-
bly apprehending the criminal, the judge from send-
ing him to prison, and the gaoler from keeping him
there? Similarly, the principle that I should refrain
from performing actions which would be harmful if
generally performed would make it obligatory for me
to refrain from performing many actions which I
have, no doubt, a duty not to do. But it would also
make it obligatory for me to refrain from performing many actions which we would all regard as being
permissible, if not positively as duties. It would make
it [117] my duty, for example, not to become a professional philosopher, because, in a world in which
everybody became professional philosophers, it would
be impossible to survive. The same principle would
prohibit entry into almost any trade or profession,
with the possible exception of that of agricultural
labourer.

But in answering the first difficulty, the means of
answering this second difficulty have already been
provided. It is true, for example, that if we consider
violent actions generally, then, if everybody refrained

from violent actions, good consequences would result. But the class of violent actions is not the class which it is important to consider, when we are wondering whether an action is of a sort which would have good or bad consequences if generally performed. The class of violent actions is not the right class for us to consider because it can relevantly be made more specific. It contains within itself, as sub-classes, such species of violent actions as the violence of a parent towards a child, the violence of a policeman towards a criminal, the violence of a criminal towards a householder, the violence of one soldier to another, the violence of one small boy to another small boy. Since the consequences of the general practice of these sub-classes of violent action may be, and very probably are, different from the consequences of the universal practice of violent actions in general, then it is the consequences of the general practice of the species which we should consider, not of the genus. So, too, participation in wars is a class of actions which can be made relevantly more specific, if it is limited by the addition of suitable characteristics. It contains sub-classes, such as participation in wars on behalf of an aggressor, participation in wars on behalf of a country which is resisting aggression, participation in wars as a mercenary on behalf of a country of which one is not a citizen, participation in religious wars, participation in disciplinary wars on behalf of some international authority. Since the consequences of the general performance of these species will differ from the consequences of the general performance of the genus, then it is the species which should be considered, not the genus. [118] To take the third example, if everyone were to become university lecturers, the consequences would, no doubt, be deplorable. But the entering into the profession of university lecturer is a class of actions which contains species such as that of becoming a university lecturer by men who have no

aptitude for medicine, no liking for the civil service,
and who have a capacity for acquiring and disseminat-
ing information which would be unsuitable for school-
children, but of not much use or interest to ordinary
adults. Becoming a university lecturer is a class of
actions which can be relevantly specified, and, since
this is so, it is the consequences of the general practice
of the species which we should consider, not the
consequences of the general practice of the genus.

Actions are right if they are of a sort which would
produce good consequences, if generally practised.
Now being right is a property of the individual action. Being generally practised (or seldom, or always,
or never practised, as the case may be) is a property
of the sort of action this action is, or of the class of
actions of which it is a member. But of what is producing good consequences a property? When actions
of this sort are not generally practised, producing
good consequences will, of course, be a property of
nothing. But when actions of this sort are generally
practised, of what will producing good consequences
be a property? Not of the sort, because sorts or classes
cannot produce good consequences, or fail to produce
them, though instances of the sort or members of the
class can. Producing good consequences must, then,
be a property of the individual actions. But if we say
that every individual action of the sort produces good
consequences, then our principle does not meet the
difficulty which it was introduced to meet, namely,
the difficulty that there are actions which are right,
although they do not produce good consequences.
Whereas if we say that only some of the individual
actions of the sort produce good consequences, we are
faced with this perplexing situation: the rightness of
some instances of the sort is derived from the good
consequences produced by other instances of the sort.
We are faced, too, with this [119] further difficulty. A
utilitarian, if he is to deserve the name at all, must try

to derive the rightness of actions in some way from the good ends which they serve. So it may be objected that, if the general practice of a sort of action produces good consequences, even when some actions of the sort produce no good consequences, or even bad consequences, would not even better consequences be produced if people were to refrain from performing those actions of the sort which did not produce good consequences, and performed only those that did?[8] But if this is the case, then it cannot be argued that the rightness of those actions which do not produce good consequences is dependent on the fact that in some way they serve a good end, for this, so far from being a fact, is, as the preceding argument has shown, simply not true.

The argument I have just stated does not, I think, show that the man who holds that our duty to perform a certain action may be founded upon the good consequences of the general performance of similar actions cannot properly be called a utilitarian, but it does serve to elicit an important property which such classes of action must have. Consider, for example, the class of actions "drinking cocoa for breakfast". It may well be that actions of this class would have good consequences, if generally performed, and it may even be that this class of actions cannot relevantly be made more specific, in the way in which I have explained. But even so, the fact, if it is a fact, that actions of this sort would produce good consequences, if they were to be generally performed, could not possibly be an adequate reason for thinking that either I, or anybody else, has a duty to drink cocoa for breakfast. If I have a duty to drink cocoa for breakfast at all, this duty is derived from the effects of drinking cocoa on my health and temper,

---

[8] *See* D. G. C. Macnabb: David Hume: *His Theory of Knowledge and Morality*, p. 182.

i.e., on the effects of the particular action to be performed, [120] not upon the effects of the general performance of similar actions.

If this is so, then the mere fact that actions of a certain class would have good consequences if they were generally performed cannot be sufficient to make performance of such actions a duty, even when the class in question cannot relevantly be made more specific. Something more is necessary. Actions of the class in question must be so related to one another that, if they are not performed in the majority of cases, then they will not produce good consequences —or, at any rate, not such good consequences—in any. They must be related to one another in such a way that the good consequences produced by those of them which do produce good consequences are dependent upon a sufficient number of those of them which do not have good consequences being performed. Mr. R. F. Harrod, in an excellent article on the subject,[9] has characterised such classes (in the way in which one would expect of an economist) thus: *"There are certain acts which when performed on n similar occasions have consequences more than n times as great as those resulting from one performance. And it is in this class of cases that obligations arise."*[10] By obligation, apparently, Mr. Harrod does not mean just any sort of obligation. He means our obligation to perform certain actions, although we could produce better consequences by not performing them.

The difference between the view just outlined and the other theory which Hume might have held is this. According to the other theory, the performance of any action was necessary if the others were to produce good consequences. Hence the good conse-

[9] R. F. Harrod: "Utilitarianism Revised", *Mind*, 1936.
[10] *Op. cit.*, p. 148.

quences produced by the general performance of the class of actions was equally dependent upon the performance of every member of the class. According to the view just outlined, not every member of the class of actions in question must be performed if the [121] others are to continue to have any value. I may omit to perform any one (or any two, or any three) of those actions which themselves produce no good consequences, without detracting from the value of those which do. But if we were to neglect to perform all the actions in the class which themselves had no good consequences, then the good consequences produced by the others would be seriously affected. Hence our objection is answered. Not to perform any one of the actions which themselves produce no good consequences would not detract from the good produced by the general performance of actions of the class, provided that the others continued to be performed. But not to perform any at all would seriously diminish it, if not take it away altogether.

Hence we must perform certain actions, which produce no good consequences, or even harmful consequences themselves, because, if everybody took the liberty of infringing the rule demanding their performance in the same circumstances, its utility would be lost. But we do not think that such rules should be applied in all circumstances. We do not, it is true, think that we should fail to apply a rule, simply because one particular failure to apply it would produce no bad consequences, or even if application of the rule produced harmful consequences, provided that these consequences are not harmful beyond a certain point. But we do not think that such rules should be applied, however disastrous the consequences of applying them are. We think that, if the consequences of a certain application of a rule are disastrous, or even bad beyond a certain point, then the rule should be set aside in this particular case. In other words, when benevolence conflicts with justice, we do not, as Hume seemed to imply, think that justice should always override benevolence. In what circumstances, then, should justice prevail, and in what circumstances benevolence?

We should, I think, only apply a rule to a hard case if the gain which would result from failing to apply the rule in all cases as hard or harder exceeds the loss which would result from failure to apply the rule to those cases. [122] To suppose that the utility of a rule must be destroyed, or even greatly diminished, by failure to apply it in certain restricted instances is a mistake. If we were only to fail to apply it to the hardest of hard cases, the rule might be neglected so rarely that its utility might be undiminished. It is only when we cease to apply the rule to cases less hard that the utility of the rule is impaired, and, even so, the gain from relieving the hard cases may be sufficient to counterbalance the loss of some of the benefit derived from the general application of the rule. If the gain from relieving the hard cases is only just sufficient to balance the loss of utility to the rule, then it is a matter of indifference whether we apply the rule or not. If the gain is insufficient to do this, then the rule should be applied. Mr. Harrod, in the article I have just mentioned, sums up the matter thus: "A lie is justified when the balance of pain or loss of pleasure is such that, if a lie was told in all circumstances when there was no less a balance of pain or loss of pleasure, the harm due to the total loss of confidence did not exceed the sum of harm due to truthfulness in every case."[11] It should be remembered that, though the gain due to failing to apply a rule to a case which is not very hard is, in respect of every individual failure to apply the rule, smaller than the gain resulting from failure to apply a rule

---

[11] *Op. cit.*, p. 149.

to a case which is very hard, not very hard cases occur much more frequently than very hard cases, and, in this respect, the not very hard cases have the advantage. On the other hand, the fact that not very hard cases are frequent means that the loss of utility to the rule by failure to apply it to them will be correspondingly greater than the loss of utility caused by failure to apply it to the very hard cases.

Readers will have noticed that this modified form of utilitarianism agrees with intuitionism in the form in which it is held by Sir David Ross in that, according to both him and it, we should not break certain rules simply because [123] the consequences of breaking them are better than the consequences of keeping them. But it is, in one important respect, superior to Sir David Ross's theory. He thinks that we should pay our debts, keep our promises, honour our agreements, and tell the truth even in circumstances when we could produce more good by failing to do so. On the other hand, he quite properly does not hold the extreme view, that these rules should be observed, however great are the advantages of breaking them. In his own language, he thinks that we have a *prima facie* duty to bring about as much good as we can, as well as *prima facie* duties to keep our promises and tell the truth, and so on. When our *prima facie* duty to produce as much good as we can conflicts with our other duties, he thinks that sometimes it is a duty to perform the former *prima facie* duty, sometimes a duty to perform one of the others. But he is quite unable to provide us with any principle which will tell us when we should tell the truth, or keep the promise, and when we should tell the lie, or break the promise, in order to produce good consequences. He is quite sure that the principle by which we decide between these two conflicting rules is not what utilitarianism, as he understands it, says it is. According to the unmodified form of utilitarianism, we should tell the truth only so long as the consequences of truth-telling are better than the consequences of lying. If the consequences of truth-telling are just as good, or just as bad, as the consequences of lying, then it does not matter whether we tell the truth or not. If the consequences of lying are better than the consequences of telling the truth, then we should lie. Sir David Ross, on the other hand, thinks that we should not lie if the consequences of lying are only slightly better than the consequences of telling the truth, but that we should lie, if the consequences of lying are greatly better. But just how much better the consequences of lying must be than the consequences of telling the truth he is unable to tell us. But this modified form of utilitarianism can tell us, and it is, in this respect, if in no other, superior to Sir David Ross's view. [124]

Utilitarianism, in its modified form, may also provide us with the solution to another of Sir David Ross's problems. What happens when, for example, my *prima facie* duty to tell the truth conflicts with my *prima facie* duty to keep my promises? Sir David Ross tells us that, when this happens, it is sometimes my duty to tell the truth, and sometimes my duty to keep my promise. But again, he is unable to provide us with any principle whereby we can decide between such conflicting *prima facie* duties. This, indeed, accords with his general view that, though rules can be given concerning what actions are *prima facie* duties, no rules can be given concerning what actions are duties.

Sir David Ross, though he thinks no principles can be given about duties, thinks that we do at least know enough about them to be able to reject the traditional utilitarian's way of solving the problem. We should not, he thinks, tell the lie and keep the promise, or tell the truth and break the promise, according to which of these two alternatives produce the most good. On this point he is probably right. But, it should be noticed, this is not the principle which the modified form of utilitarianism which we are discussing would recommend. We should not consider just the consequences of telling this lie and keeping this promise, or telling this truth and breaking this promise. We should consider what would be the consequences if everybody were to tell such lies in order to keep such promises or, what comes to the same thing, to break such promises in order to enunciate such truths. It may well be that, after reflection upon the general practice of such actions, we conclude that we should keep the promise and tell the lie, even though the consequences of breaking the promise and telling the truth would be better. It should be remembered, too, that the consequences of the general practice of keeping this sort of promise, or of telling this sort of truth, may differ from the consequences of the general practice of promise-keeping or truth-telling as genera. [125]

So far, so good. But it may well be objected that we have no duty to perform an action simply because it is of a sort which would produce good consequences, if performed by everybody, or to refrain from performing it, because the general performance of it would be bad. Surely, it might be argued, we must be realistic about matters of duty. We should not base our conduct upon what would happen, if certain conditions, which may be unfulfilled, were realised. We should base our conduct upon what, after the fullest consideration possible in the time at our disposal, it seems most likely will happen. If, therefore, I can relieve a hard case by failing to apply a rule of justice, I should do so, even if the consequences of everybody doing the same would be bad, so long as I have reason to suppose that everybody will not do the same. Even if good consequences would be brought about by the general performance of a certain type of action, I have no duty to perform it, so long as I have good reason to believe that actions of that type will not, in fact, be generally performed. This, it might seem, is what Hobbes thought, and Hume—some of the time —because they both thought that we had not a duty to be just in a state of nature, *i.e.* in a state in which nobody else is just. Hume, though he thought that we had no duty to be just in a state of nature, thought that our duty to be benevolent was still incumbent upon us, for our duty to be benevolent, unlike our duty to be just, is in no way dependent upon the performance of benevolent actions by other people. Hence, in a state of nature, I have a duty to be benevolent to my fellows and to women[12] and domestic animals, though I have no duty to be just to them. [126]

Mr. Harrod has an answer to this problem, which does not seem to me to be satisfactory. He says: "I believe that, where the practice is not general, a second refining process is required. Will the gain due to its application by all conscientious, *i.e.* moral, people *only* be sufficient to offset the loss which the crude utilitarian principle registers? It may be objected that there are no moral people. To meet this, for the word moral in the second refining principle, say people sufficiently moral to act disinterestedly in this kind of case."[13]

This answer, however, cannot be accepted. It is be-

---

[12] "In many nations the female sex are reduced to like slavery, and are rendered incapable of all property, in opposition to their lordly masters. But though the males, when united, have in all countries bodily force sufficient to maintain this severe tyranny, yet such are the insinuation, address and charms of their fair companions, that women are commonly able to break the confederacy, and share with the other sex in all the rights and privileges of society." L. A. Selby-Bigge: *Hume's Enquiries*, p. 191.

[13] *Op. cit.*, p. 151.

ing objected that we do not have a duty to apply the principle where nobody else applies it, and Mr. Harrod replies that we have a duty to apply it if there are enough moral people to do likewise. But wherein lies their morality? In applying the principle? But then, they cannot be moral if the principle is not moral, and it is the morality of the principle which is being called in question—and actually, by Mr. Harrod himself, set aside, in favour of the principle as doubly refined. And how many people are there moral enough to apply the principle in a state of nature? Surely, none at all, for a state of nature is defined as one in which there is nobody moral enough to apply the principle.

I think that Mr. Harrod, under the guise of defending the principle that the good or bad consequences of the general performance of a certain type of action should be considered, is really siding with its opponents. For I think that he really believes that it is important to know how many people there are sufficiently moral to apply the principle which I apply, because he thinks that it is important for me to know how likely it is that other people will apply the principle, before I can make up my mind whether I myself have a duty to apply it. But this is just what opponents of the principle think. They think that I have not a duty to be just rather than to relieve a hard case, even if the consequences which would result if everybody [127] were to be unjust in similar cases would be bad, so long as I have reason to believe that other people will not be unjust in similar cases. They think that I have not a duty to be just in a state of nature, even though good consequences would result if everybody were to be just, because I have reason to believe that I shall be alone in my practice of justice.

To the man who objects that one may be unjust to relieve a hard case, even if such an action would have

bad consequences if everybody else were to do the
same, provided that I have reason to believe that nobody else will do the same, one is inclined to make
the following answer. I am not in a better position to
estimate what other people will do than they are to
estimate what I will do and, if everybody were to
relieve hard cases because they thought that it was
unlikely that other people would do the same, bad
consequences would result. We are inclined to say, if
nobody were just in a state of nature, because they
thought it unlikely that justice would also be practised by others, then we would never get out of a
state of nature. If it be objected that we were never in
a state of nature, it may be replied that we are all in
a state of nature with regard to some things. Men may
not be in a state of nature with regard to debt-paying,
nor Englishmen with regard to queueing, but nations
are in a state of nature with regard to international
agreements, and housewives are, very likely, in a state
of nature with regard to saving scrap, when they are
told that, if everybody handed in their old dustbin
lids, enough metal would be saved to build a battle-
ship.

But, of course, in making these answers, we are not
justifying the principle—though we are making it
more plausible—for we are falling back on the very
principle we are trying to justify. Nor is it possible
to justify the principle. If it is true, then it must be
accepted as true without reason, though this does
not mean that it is irrational to accept it. In this respect it is like any fundamental moral principle, so the
fact that it cannot be justified must not be held against
it. [128]

But the probability or otherwise of other people
doing what I do does have a bearing on my duty to
do an action (or to refrain from doing it) if it would
have good (or bad) consequences if everybody else
did the same. It is true that, if I only have good

reason for thinking that other people will not do what I do, then my duty to be just in a hard case still applies. For other people's reasons for thinking that theirs will not be the general practice are as good as mine and, if everybody failed to apply a rule in a hard case merely because they had good reasons for thinking that others would not do the same, bad consequences would result. But if I had conclusive reasons for thinking that other people would not do the same, then it would be my duty to relieve the hard case. For only one person can have conclusive reasons for thinking that others will not relieve the hard cases he relieves, and, from one person's relieving hard cases, no disastrous consequences follow. Similarly, in a state of nature, if I only have good reasons for thinking that others will not apply the rules I apply, my duty to apply these rules remains. But if I have conclusive reasons for thinking that others will not apply the rules I apply, my duty to apply them ceases. For if everybody were to fail to apply these rules only in circumstances in which they knew that nobody else would do the same, no bad consequences would follow. If these two examples seem artificial, this is only because I have considered extreme cases. It is unlikely that I should know that nobody but I will fail to apply a rule of justice in a hard case, and it is unlikely that I should know that no-one but I will be just in a state bordering upon a state of nature. But I may sometimes know that the majority of people will not apply a rule to cases as hard as the case to which I fail to apply it, or know that the majority of people are too short sighted and unrestrained to apply a rule of justice in cases where others do not. In such cases, supposing imitation by a minority of people only is not sufficient to produce any good (or bad) effects, my duty to apply the rule ceases. [129]

This, however, is not an exception to the principles

already expounded, but a consequence of them. What
I am saying, in other words, is that my knowledge of
the behaviour of other people is a characteristic which
relevantly specifies the class of actions the consequences of the general practice of which it is my
duty to consider. I have a duty to perform a certain
action, although believing that other people will not
perform it, because, if everybody who believed that
other people would not perform it were to do similar
actions, good consequences would result. I have not a
duty to perform an action, when knowing that other
people will not do likewise because, if people performed similar actions only when they knew no-one
else would do the same, no good consequences would
follow.

My duty to perform actions of a sort which would
have good consequences if they were generally practised will thus depend, in some measure, upon my
ignorance of the behaviour of other people. I must
not, for example, turn aside from applying a principle
of justice in a hard case when I do not know that
other people will not do the same, because I have
every reason to believe that they will have much the
same reasons for failing to apply a rule of justice to
similar hard cases as I have for failing to apply it to
this one, and because, if everybody were to do what
I propose doing, disastrous consequences would follow. But, if I were omniscient about the behaviour
of other people, then it would be my duty to do that
action, which itself has good consequences. But this
is not because the principle that we ought always to
perform those actions which would have good consequences, if generally performed, and to refrain from
performing those actions which would have bad consequences, if generally performed, is not applicable
to people who have complete knowledge of the behaviour of others. It is because, to people who have
complete knowledge of the behaviour of others, the

two principles, that we should perform those actions which themselves have good consequences, and that we should perform those actions which are of a sort which would have good consequences, [130] if practised generally, enjoin the same actions. If everybody having complete knowledge of the behaviour of other people were to perform those actions which themselves had good consequences, good consequences would result; whereas, if all people not having complete knowledge of the behaviour of other people were to perform those actions which themselves had good consequences, bad consequences would result. In the case of people having complete knowledge of the behaviour of others, the unmodified utilitarian principle falls under the modified principle as a special case, and an omniscient being would be justified in acting upon it, though beings like ourselves would not.[14] This does not mean, of course, that the two principles are identical. They would not be identical, even if they always enjoined identical actions, whereas they only do this in very special circumstances. Even when they enjoin identical actions, it is the modified utilitarian principle which is obligatory. The unmodified principle derives its obligatoriness from its accordance with the modified principle, and it is not obligatory in its own right.

It will not have escaped the reader, and it certainly

---

[14] Cf. Butler: *Works, Gladstone's Edition*, vol. II, p. 190 n. "For instance: As we are not competent judges, what is upon the whole for the good of the world, there may be other immediate ends appointed us to pursue, besides that one of doing good, or producing happiness. Though the good of the creation be the only end of the Author of it, yet he may have laid us under particular obligations, which we may discern and feel ourselves under, quite distinct from a perception, that the observance or violation of them is for the happiness or misery of our fellow-creatures." Also C. D. Broad: *Five Types of Ethical Theory*, pp. 81–2.

did not escape Mr. Harrod, that there is some connection between the modified utilitarian principle and
the Kantian categorical imperative. Now I do not
think that the modified utilitarian principle can be
deduced, as Kant thought moral principles could be
deduced from the idea of law in general. The claim
that moral principles can be deduced from the idea
of law in general depends, I think, upon the claim
that there is only one set of principles upon [131]
which, taken singly or together, it is possible for
everybody to act, coupled with a definition of "law"
according to which no principle upon which everybody cannot act can properly be said to be a law. It
does not seem to me that the claim that there is only
one set of principles upon which everyone can act
is justified. A universe in which everybody acted
morally is perfectly conceivable, but so is a universe
in which everybody acted morally, with the exception
that everybody committed suicide at the age of fifty.
The fact that it is possible for everybody to commit
suicide at the age of fifty (and, at the same time, to
be moral in other respects) does not seem to me to
show that it is obligatory, or even permissible, to do
this.

Nor do I think that imperfect duties can be derived
from the impossibility of one's being able to will that
everybody should fail to perform an imperfect duty.
First of all it is not clear to me that this is impossible.
If a man were sufficiently callous to murder his own
wife, might he not be sufficiently callous, supposing
he had the power, to will that other men should
murder theirs? Besides, why cannot one will that everybody should fail to perform an (imperfect) duty?
Not because of the moral repugnance such general
negligence would cause us; Kant is supposed to be
giving our inability to will that an action should be
generally performed as a reason for thinking that it is
wrong, and not *vice versa*. Are we unable to will

general neglect of a duty, because such neglect would be contrary to our interest? Kant speaks as if I cannot will that people should not help others in distress, because, in that case, no one would help me when I am in distress. But, if the fact that an action has consequences which are detrimental to my interest is a bad reason for thinking that it is wrong, surely the fact that I cannot, from self-interest, will its universal performance, is a worse one.

But the modified utilitarian principle, though it is not impossible for everybody to fail to act upon it, and though it is not impossible, though it may be immoral, for one to will that everybody should transgress it, does conform to [132] some suggestions which may be found in the works of Kant. First of all, the unmodified utilitarian principle is self-defeating, whereas the modified principle is not. If everybody were to act upon the unmodified utilitarian principle, everybody would fail to apply rules of justice to certain hard cases, and bad consequences would result. But the purpose of the people who applied the unmodified utilitarian principle would be to produce good consequences, and so the general application of the rule they were practising would defeat the ends which determined them to adopt it.

Secondly, suppose that I apply the unmodified utilitarian principle to a certain case, knowing that, if other people apply the modified principle, I can produce good consequences by doing so. In this case, my conduct, though beneficial is, in a certain sense, inconsistent. It is not inconsistent in the sense that it is impossible for me to do what I do, nor in the sense that it is impossible for everybody to do what I do, nor in the sense that it is impossible for me to do what I do, while others do what they do. My principle is inconsistent with theirs in the sense that both of them could not be acted upon by everybody or, for that matter, by anybody. Since my own prin-

ciple would be self-defeating if universally adopted, I
do not regard it as fit for application by everybody,
but take the liberty of allowing myself to make an
exception to the ones that I do regard as suitable.
Should it be argued, on behalf of a more nearly Kantian position, that my principle is really "Apply the
unmodified utilitarian formula, so long as everybody
else applies the modified formula," and that this principle cannot be acted upon by everybody. I reply that
this argument rests upon a confusion. A judge is applying the principle "Condemn all murderers" just as
much when he frees an innocent man as when he
sentences a murderer. Similarly, the rest of the world,
which is applying the modified utilitarian formula,
may just as much be acting on the principle "Apply
the unmodified utilitarian formula, so long as everybody else applies the modified formula" as am I, who
apply the unmodified [133] formula. What is impossible, is not that everybody should apply this principle,
but that it should ever enjoin more than one person to
apply the unmodified utilitarian formula.

The result is some reconciliation between the doctrine of Kant and the teleological ethical principles
which he despised. An end, we must say, stands in
much the same relation to the morality of principles
as do the "facts" in relation to the truth of propositions, and we can no more decide what principles are
and are not moral, by means of consistency alone,
without reference to ends, than we can settle what
propositions are true, by means of consistency alone,
without reference to "facts." But though the fitness
of any principle to be a moral principle cannot be
decided without some reference to an end, the principle must be such that this end is harmoniously and
coherently realised by its universal application and,
if it can be successfully applied only by a given individual who relies upon the methods of others being

more orthodox than his own, the principle is not one which deserves to be called "moral."

In other words, the unmodified utilitarian principle is not eligible to be part of a system of universal legislation, whereas the modified principle is, though it is not the only principle which is. In this respect the modified principle does, while the unmodified principle does not, conform to one of the conditions which any principle must fulfil if it is to be regarded as a principle on which we ought to act, and this condition it is one of Kant's great merits to have emphasised. No principle is fit to be a moral principle unless it is fit that it should be universally adopted and universally applied, though a principle may be unfit for universal adoption, even where universal adoption is logically possible. Our attitude to a principle cannot be a distinctively moral one unless we are prepared to accept, and sometimes to recommend, its universal application. The unmodified utilitarian principle conforms to neither of these two conditions. It is not fit for universal adoption, because the very grounds, namely, that it serves a good [134] end, which recommend its application by one person, prohibit its application by everybody. And our attitude to it cannot be a moral one. For we can be prepared to apply it ourselves only so long as others do not, and hence we cannot possibly be prepared to recommend that it be adopted by others besides ourselves.

TWO CONCEPTS
OF RULES*
John Rawls

In this paper I want to show the importance of the distinction between justifying a practice[1] and justifying a particular action falling under it, and I want to explain the logical basis of this distinction and how it is possible to miss its significance. While the distinction has frequently been made,[2] and is now

* This is a revision of a paper given at the Harvard Philosophy Club on April 30, 1954.

FROM *The Philosophical Review*, Vol. LXIV (1955), 3–32. Reprinted by permission of the author and *The Philosophical Review*.

[1] I use the word "practice" throughout as a sort of technical term meaning any form of activity specified by a system of rules which defines offices, roles, moves, penalties, defenses, and so on, and which gives the activity its structure. As examples one may think of games and rituals, trials and parliaments.

[2] The distinction is central to Hume's discussion of justice in *A Treatise of Human Nature*, bk. III, pt. 11, esp. secs. 2–4. It is clearly stated by John Austin in the second lecture of *Lectures on Jurisprudence* (4th ed.; London, 1873), I, 116ff. (1st ed., 1832). Also it may be argued that J. S. Mill took it for granted in *Utilitarianism;* on this point cf. J. O. Urmson, "The Interpretation of the Moral Philosophy of J. S. Mill," *Philosophical Quarterly*, Vol. III (1953) [reprinted in this volume, pp. 13–24]. In addition to the arguments given by

becoming commonplace, there remains the task of
explaining the tendency either to overlook it altogether, or to fail to appreciate its importance.

To show the importance of the distinction I am
going to defend utilitarianism against those objections
which have traditionally been made against it in connection with punishment and the obligation to keep
promises. I hope to show that if one uses the distinction in question then one can state utilitarianism [4] in
a way which makes it a much better explication of
our considered moral judgments than these traditional
objections would seem to admit.[3] Thus the importance of the distinction is shown by the way it
strengthens the utilitarian view regardless of whether
that view is completely defensible or not.

To explain how the significance of the distinction
may be overlooked, I am going to discuss two conceptions of rules. One of these conceptions conceals
the importance of distinguishing between the justification of a rule or practice and the justification of a

---

Urmson there are several clear statements of the distinction in
A System of Logic (8th ed.; London, 1872), bk. VI, ch. xii
pars. 2, 3, 7. The distinction is fundamental to J. D. Mabbott's
important paper, "Punishment," *Mind*, n.s., vol. XLVIII (April,
1939). More recently the distinction has been stated with
particular emphasis by S. E. Toulmin in *The Place of Reason
in Ethics* (Cambridge, 1950), see esp. ch. xi, where it plays a
major part in his account of moral reasoning. Toulmin doesn't
explain the basis of the distinction, nor how one might overlook its importance, as I try to in this paper, and in my review of his book (*Philosophical Review*, Vol. LX [October,
1951]), as some of my criticisms show, I failed to understand
the force of it. See also H. D. Aiken, "The Levels of Moral
Discourse," *Ethics*, vol. LXII (1952), A. M. Quinton, "Punishment," *Analysis*, vol. XIV (June, 1954), and P. H. Nowell-
Smith, *Ethics* (London, 1954), pp. 236-239, 271-273.

[3] On the concept of explication see the author's paper
Philosophical Review, Vol. LX (April, 1951).

particular action falling under it. The other conception makes it clear why this distinction must be made and what is its logical basis.

I

The subject of punishment, in the sense of attaching legal penalties to the violation of legal rules, has always been a troubling moral question.[4] The trouble about it has not been that people disagree as to whether or not punishment is justifiable. Most people have held that, freed from certain abuses, it is an acceptable institution. Only a few have rejected punishment entirely, which is rather surprising when one considers all that can be said against it. The difficulty is with the justification of punishment: various arguments for it have been given by moral philosophers, but so far none of them has won any sort of general acceptance; no justification is without those who detest it. I hope to show that the use of the aforementioned distinction enables one to state the utilitarian view in a way which allows for the sound points of its critics.

For our purposes we may say that there are two justifications of punishment. What we may call the retributive view is that punishment is justified on the grounds that wrongdoing merits punishment. It is morally fitting that a person who does wrong [5] should suffer in proportion to his wrongdoing. That a criminal should be punished follows from his guilt,

---

[4] While this paper was being revised, Quinton's appeared; footnote 2 supra. There are several respects in which my remarks are similar to his. Yet as I consider some further questions and rely on somewhat different arguments, I have retained the discussion of punishment and promises together as two test cases for utilitarianism.

and the severity of the appropriate punishment depends on the depravity of his act. The state of affairs where a wrongdoer suffers punishment is morally better than the state of affairs where he does not; and it is better irrespective of any of the consequences of punishing him.

What we may call the utilitarian view holds that on the principle that bygones are bygones and that only future consequences are material to present decisions, punishment is justifiable only by reference to the probable consequences of maintaining it as one of the devices of the social order. Wrongs committed in the past are, as such, not relevant considerations for deciding what to do. If punishment can be shown to promote effectively the interest of society it is justifiable, otherwise it is not.

I have stated these two competing views very roughly to make one feel the conflict between them: one feels the force of *both* arguments and one wonders how they can be reconciled. From my introductory remarks it is obvious that the resolution which I am going to propose is that in this case one must distinguish between justifying a practice as a system of rules to be applied and enforced, and justifying a particular action which falls under these rules; utilitarian arguments are appropriate with regard to questions about practices, while retributive arguments fit the application of particular rules to particular cases.

We might try to get clear about this distinction by imagining how a father might answer the question of his son. Suppose the son asks, "Why was *J* put in jail yesterday?" The father answers, "Because he robbed the bank at *B*. He was duly tried and found guilty. That's why he was put in jail yesterday." But suppose the son had asked a different question, namely, "Why do people put other people in jail?" Then the father might answer, "To protect good people from bad people" or "To stop people from doing things that would make it uneasy for all of us; for otherwise we wouldn't be able to go to bed at night and sleep in peace." There are two very different questions here. One question emphasizes the proper name: it asks why *J* was punished rather than someone else, or it asks what he was punished for. The other question asks why we have the institution of punishment: [6] why do people punish one another rather than, say, always forgiving one another?

Thus the father says in effect that a particular man is punished, rather than some other man, because he is guilty, and he is guilty because he broke the law (past tense). In his case the law looks back, the judge looks back, the jury looks back, and a penalty is visited upon him for something he did. That a man is to be punished, and what his punishment is to be, is settled by its being shown that he broke the law and that the law assigns that penalty for the violation of it.

On the other hand we have the institution of punishment itself, and recommend and accept various changes in it, because it is thought by the (ideal) legislator and by those to whom the law applies that, as a part of a system of law impartially applied from case to case arising under it, it will have the consequence, in the long run, of furthering the interests of society.

One can say, then, that the judge and the legislator stand in different positions and look in different directions: one to the past, the other to the future. The justification of what the judge does, *qua* judge, sounds like the retributive view; the justification of what the (ideal) legislator does, *qua* legislator, sounds like the utilitarian view. Thus both views have a point (this is as it should be since intelligent and sensitive persons have been on both sides of the argument); and one's initial confusion disappears once one sees that these views apply to persons holding different offices with different duties, and situated differently with respect to the system of rules that make up the criminal law.[5]

One might say, however, that the utilitarian view is more fundamental since it applies to a more fundamental office, for the judge carries out the legislator's will so far as he can determine it. Once the legislator decides to have laws and to assign penalties for their violation (as things are there must be both the law and the penalty) an institution is set up which involves a retributive conception of particular cases. It is part of the concept of the criminal law as a system of rules that the application [7] and enforcement of these rules in particular cases should be justifiable by arguments of a retributive character. The decision whether or not to use law rather than some other mechanism of social control, and the decision as to what laws to have and what penalties to assign, may be settled by utilitarian arguments; but if one decides to have laws then one has decided on something whose working in particular cases is retributive in form.[6]

The answer, then, to the confusion engendered by the two views of punishment is quite simple: one distinguishes two offices, that of the judge and that of the legislator, and one distinguishes their different stations with respect to the system of rules which make up the law; and then one notes that the different sorts of considerations which would usually be offered as reasons for what is done under the cover of these offices can be paired off with the competing justifications of punishment. One recon-

---

[5] Note the fact that different sorts of arguments are suited to different offices. One way of taking the differences between ethical theories is to regard them as accounts of the reasons expected in different offices.

[6] In this connection see Mabbott, *op. cit.*, pp. 163–164.

ciles the two views by the time-honored device of making them apply to different situations.

But can it really be this simple? Well, this answer allows for the apparent intent of each side. Does a person who advocates the retributive view necessarily advocate, as an *institution*, legal machinery whose essential purpose is to set up and preserve a correspondence between moral turpitude and suffering? Surely not.[7] What retributionists have rightly insisted upon is that no man can be punished unless he is guilty, that is, unless he has broken the law. Their fundamental criticism of the utilitarian account is that, as they interpret it, it sanctions an innocent person's being punished (if one may call it that) for the benefit of society.

On the other hand, utilitarians agree that punishment is to be inflicted only for the violation of law. They regard this much as understood from the concept of punishment itself.[8] The point of [8] the utilitarian account concerns the institution as a system of rules: utilitarianism seeks to limit its use by declaring it justifiable only if it can be shown to foster effectively the good of society. Historically it is a

---

[7] On this point see Sir David Ross, *The Right and the Good* (Oxford, 1930), pp. 57–60.

[8] See Hobbes's definition of punishment in *Leviathan*, ch. xxviii; and Bentham's definition in *The Principle of Morals and Legislation*, ch. xii, par. 36, ch. xv, par. 28, and in *The Rationale of Punishment*, (London, 1830), bk. I, ch. i. They could agree with Bradley that: "Punishment is punishment only when it is deserved. We pay the penalty, because we owe it, and for no other reason; and if punishment is inflicted for any other reason whatever than because it is [8] merited by wrong, it is a gross immorality, a crying injustice, an abominable crime, and not what it pretends to be." *Ethical Studies* (2nd ed.; Oxford, 1927), pp. 26–27. Certainly by definition it isn't what it pretends to be. The innocent can only be punished by mistake; deliberate "punishment" of the innocent necessarily involves fraud.

protest against the indiscriminate and ineffective use of the criminal law.[9] It seeks to dissuade us from assigning to penal institutions the improper, if not sacrilegious, task of matching suffering with moral turpitude. Like others, utilitarians want penal institutions designed so that, as far as humanly possible, only those who break the law run afoul of it. They hold that no official should have discretionary power to inflict penalties whenever he thinks it for the benefit of society; for on utilitarian grounds an institution granting such power could not be justified.[10]

The suggested way of reconciling the retributive and the utilitarian justifications of punishment seems to account for what both sides have wanted to say. There are, however, two further questions which arise, and I shall devote the remainder of this section to them.

First, will not a difference of opinion as to the proper criterion of just law make the proposed reconciliation unacceptable to retributionists? Will they not question whether, if the utilitarian principle is

[9] Cf. Leon Radzinowicz, *A History of English Criminal Law: The Movement for Reform 1750–1833* (London, 1948), esp. ch. xi on Bentham.

[10] Bentham discusses how corresponding to a punitory provision of a criminal law there is another provision which stands to it as an antagonist and which needs a name as much as the punitory. He calls it, as one might expect, the *anaetiosostic*, and of it he says: "The punishment of guilt is the object of the former one: the preservation of innocence that of the latter." In the same connection he asserts that it is never thought fit to give the judge the option of deciding whether a thief (that is, a person whom he believes to be a thief, for the judge's belief is what the question must always turn upon) should hang or not, and so the law writes the provision: "The judge shall not cause a thief to be hanged unless he have been duly convicted and sentenced in course of law" (*The Limits of Jurisprudence Defined*, ed. C. W. Everett [New York, 1945], pp. 238–239).

used as the criterion, it follows that those who have broken the law are guilty in a way which satisfies their demand [9] that those punished deserve to be punished? To answer this difficulty, suppose that the rules of the criminal law are justified on utilitarian grounds (it is only for laws that meet his criterion that the utilitarian can be held responsible). Then it follows that the actions which the criminal law specifies as offenses are such that, if they were tolerated, terror and alarm would spread in society. Consequently, retributionists can only deny that those who are punished deserve to be punished if they deny that such actions are wrong. This they will not want to do.

The second question is whether utilitarianism doesn't justify too much. One pictures it as an engine of justification which, if consistently adopted, could be used to justify cruel and arbitrary institutions. Retributionists may be supposed to concede that utilitarians *intend* to reform the law and to make it more humane; that utilitarians do not *wish* to justify any such thing as punishment of the innocent; and that utilitarians may appeal to the fact that punishment presupposes guilt in the sense that by punishment one understands an institution attaching penalties to the infraction of legal rules, and therefore that it is logically absurd to suppose that utilitarians in justifying *punishment* might also have justified punishment (if we may call it that) of the innocent. The real question, however, is whether the utilitarian, in justifying punishment, hasn't used arguments which commit him to accepting the infliction of suffering on innocent persons if it is for the good of society (whether or not one calls this punishment). More generally, isn't the utilitarian committed in principle to accepting many practices which he, as a morally sensitive person, wouldn't want to accept? Retributionists are inclined to hold that there is no way to

stop the utilitarian principle from justifying too much
except by adding to it a principle which distributes
certain rights to individuals. Then the amended criterion is not the greatest benefit of society *simpliciter*,
but the greatest benefit of society subject to the
constraint that no one's rights may be violated. Now
while I think that the classical utilitarians proposed
a criterion of this more complicated sort, I do not
want to argue that point here.[11] What I want to
show is that [10] there is *another* way of preventing
the utilitarian principle from justifying too much, or
at least of making it much less likely to do so: namely,
by stating utilitarianism in a way which accounts
for the distinction between the justification of an
institution and the justification of a particular action
falling under it.

I begin by defining the institution of punishment
as follows: a person is said to suffer punishment
whenever he is legally deprived of some of the normal
rights of a citizen on the ground that he has violated
a rule of law, the violation having been established
by trial according to the due process of law, provided
that the deprivation is carried out by the recognized
legal authorities of the state, that the rule of law
clearly specifies both the offense and the attached
penalty, that the courts construe statutes strictly, and
that the statute was on the books prior to the time
of the offense.[12] This definition specifies what I shall
understand by punishment. The question is whether
utilitarian arguments may be found to justify institutions widely different from this and such as one
would find cruel and arbitrary.

This question is best answered, I think, by taking

---

[11] By the classical utilitarians I understand Hobbes, Hume,
Bentham, J. S. Mill, and Sidgwick.

[12] All these features of punishment are mentioned by
Hobbes; cf. *Leviathan*, ch. xxviii.

up a particular accusation. Consider the following from Carritt:

> . . . the utilitarian must hold that we are justified in inflicting pain always and only to prevent worse pain or bring about greater happiness. This, then, is all we need to consider in so-called punishment, which must be purely preventive. But if some kind of very cruel crime becomes common, and none of the criminals can be caught, it might be highly expedient, as an example, to hang an innocent man, if a charge against him could be so framed that he were universally thought guilty; indeed this would only fail to be an ideal instance of utilitarian 'punishment' because the victim himself would not have been so likely as a real felon to commit such a crime in the future; in all other respects it would be perfectly deterrent and therefore felicific.[13]

Carritt is trying to show that there are occasions when a utilitarian argument would justify taking an action which would be generally condemned; and thus that utilitarianism justifies too much. But the failure of Carritt's argument lies in the fact that [11] he makes no distinction between the justification of the general system of rules which constitutes penal institutions and the justification of particular applications of these rules to particular cases by the various officials whose job it is to administer them. This becomes perfectly clear when one asks who the "we" are of whom Carritt speaks. Who is this who has a sort of absolute authority on particular occasions to decide that an innocent man shall be "punished" if everyone can be convinced that he is guilty? Is this person the legislator, or the judge, or the body of private citizens, or what? It is utterly crucial to know

---

[13] *Ethical and Political Thinking* (Oxford, 1947), p. 65.

who is to decide such matters, and by what authority, for all of this must be written into the rules of the institution. Until one knows these things one doesn't know what the institution is whose justification is being challenged; and as the utilitarian principle applies to the institution one doesn't know whether it is justifiable on utilitarian grounds or not.

Once this is understood it is clear what the counter-move to Carritt's argument is. One must describe more carefully what the *institution* is which his example suggests, and then ask oneself whether or not it is likely that having this institution would be for the benefit of society in the long run. One must not content oneself with the vague thought that, when it's a question of *this* case, it would be a good thing if *somebody* did something even if an innocent person were to suffer.

Try to imagine, then, an institution (which we may call "telishment") which is such that the officials set up by it have authority to arrange a trial for the condemnation of an innocent man whenever they are of the opinion that doing so would be in the best interests of society. The discretion of officials is limited, however, by the rule that they may not condemn an innocent man to undergo such an ordeal unless there is, at the time, a wave of offenses similar to that with which they charge him and telish him for. We may imagine that the officials having the discretionary authority are the judges of the higher courts in consultation with the chief of police, the minister of justice, and a committee of the legislature.

Once one realizes that one is involved in setting up an *institution*, [12] one sees that the hazards are very great. For example, what check is there on the officials? How is one to tell whether or not their actions are authorized? How is one to limit the risks involved in allowing such systematic deception? How is one to avoid giving anything short of complete discretion to the authorities to telish anyone they like? In addition to these considerations, it is obvious that people will come to have a very different attitude towards their penal system when telishment is adjoined to it. They will be uncertain as to whether a convicted man has been punished or telished. They will wonder whether or not they should feel sorry for him. They will wonder whether the same fate won't at any time fall on them. If one pictures how such an institution would actually work, and the enormous risks involved in it, it seems clear that it would serve no useful purpose. A utilitarian justification for this institution is most unlikely.

It happens in general that as one drops off the defining features of punishment one ends up with an institution whose utilitarian justification is highly doubtful. One reason for this is that punishment works like a kind of price system: by altering the prices one has to pay for the performance of actions it supplies a motive for avoiding some actions and doing others. The defining features are essential if punishment is to work in this way; so that an institution which lacks these features, e.g., an institution which is set up to "punish" the innocent, is likely to have about as much point as a price system (if one may call it that) where the prices of things change at random from day to day and one learns the price of something after one has agreed to buy it.[14] [13]

---

[14] The analogy with the price system suggests an answer to the question how utilitarian considerations insure that punishment is proportional to the offense. It is interesting to note that Sir David Ross, after making the distinction between justifying a penal law and justifying a particular application of it, and after stating that utilitarian considerations have a large place in determining the former, still holds back from accepting the utilitarian justification of punishment on the

If one is careful to apply the utilitarian principle to the institution which is to authorize particular actions, then there is *less* danger of its justifying too much. Carritt's example gains plausibility by its indefiniteness and by its concentration on the particular case. His argument will only hold if it can be shown that there are utilitarian arguments which justify an institution whose publicly ascertainable offices and powers are such as to permit officials to exercise that kind of discretion in particular cases. But the requirement of having to build the arbitrary features of the particular decision into the institutional practice makes the justification much less likely to go through.

II

I shall now consider the question of promises. The objection to utilitarianism in connection with promises seems to be this: it is believed that on the utilitarian view when a person makes a promise the

---

grounds that justice requires that punishment be proportional to the offense, and that utilitarianism is unable to account for this. Cf. *The Right and the Good*, pp. 61–62. I do not claim that utilitarianism can account for this requirement as Sir David might wish, but it happens, nevertheless, that if utilitarian considerations are followed penalties will be proportional to offenses in this sense: the order of offenses according to seriousness can be paired off [13] with the order of penalties according to severity. Also the absolute level of penalties will be as low as possible. This follows from the assumption that people are rational (i.e., that they are able to take into account the "prices" the state puts on actions), the utilitarian rule that a penal system should provide a motive for preferring the less serious offense, and the principle that punishment as such is an evil. All this was carefully worked out by Bentham in *The Principles of Morals and Legislation*, chs. xiii–xv.

only ground upon which he should keep it, if he should keep it, is that by keeping it he will realize the most good on the whole. So that if one asks the question "Why should I keep *my* promise?" the utilitarian answer is understood to be that doing so in *this* case will have the best consequences. And this answer is said, quite rightly, to conflict with the way in which the obligation to keep promises is regarded.

Now of course critics of utilitarianism are not unaware that one defense sometimes attributed to utilitarians is the consideration involving the practice of promise-keeping.[15] In this connection [14] they are supposed to argue something like this: it must be admitted that we feel strictly about keeping promises, more strictly than it might seem our view can account for. But when we consider the matter carefully it is always necessary to take into account the effect which our action will have on the practice of making promises. The promisor must weigh, not only the effects of breaking his promise on the particular case, but also the effect which his breaking his promise will have on the practice itself. Since the practice is of great utilitarian value, and since breaking one's promise always seriously damages it, one will seldom be justified in breaking one's promise. If we view our individual promises in the wider context of the practice of promising itself we can account for the strictness of the obligation to keep promises. There is

---

[15] Ross, *The Right and the Good*, pp. 37–39, and *Foundations of Ethics* (Oxford, 1939), pp. 92–94. I know of no utilitarian who has used this argument except W. A. Pickard-Cambridge in "Two Problems about Duty," *Mind*, n.s., XLI (April, 1932), 153–157, although the argument goes with G. E. Moore's version of utilitarianism in *Principia Ethica* (Cambridge, 1903). To my knowledge it does not appear in the classical utilitarians; and if one interprets their view correctly this is no accident.

always one very strong utilitarian consideration in favor of keeping them, and this will insure that when the question arises as to whether or not to keep a promise it will usually turn out that one should, even where the facts of the particular case taken by itself would seem to justify one's breaking it. In this way the strictness with which we view the obligation to keep promises is accounted for.

Ross has criticized this defense as follows:[16] however great the value of the practice of promising, on utilitarian grounds, there must be some value which is greater, and one can imagine it to be obtainable by breaking a promise. Therefore there might be a case where the promisor could argue that breaking his promise was justified as leading to a better state of affairs on the whole. And the promisor could argue in this way no matter how slight the advantage won by breaking the promise. If one were to challenge the promisor his defense would be that what he did was best on the whole in view of all the utilitarian considerations, which in this case *include* the importance of the practice. Ross feels that such a defense would be unacceptable. I think he is right insofar as he is protesting against the appeal to consequences in general and without further explanation. Yet it is extremely difficult to weigh the force of Ross's argument. The kind of case imagined seems unrealistic and one feels that it needs to be described. One is inclined to think that it would [15] either turn out that such a case came under an exception defined by the practice itself, in which case there would not be an appeal to consequences in general on the particular case, or it would happen that the circumstances were so peculiar that the conditions which the practice presupposes no longer obtained. But certainly Ross is right in thinking that it strikes us as

---

[16] Ross, *The Right and the Good*, pp. 38–39.

wrong for a person to defend breaking a promise by a general appeal to consequences. For a general utilitarian defense is not open to the promisor: it is not one of the defenses allowed by the practice of making promises.

Ross gives two further counterarguments:[17] First, he holds that it overestimates the damage done to the practice of promising by a failure to keep a promise. One who breaks a promise harms his own name certainly, but it isn't clear that a broken promise always damages the practice itself sufficiently to account for the strictness of the obligation. Second, and more important, I think, he raises the question of what one is to say of a promise which isn't known to have been made except to the promisor and the promisee, as in the case of a promise a son makes to his dying father concerning the handling of the estate.[18] In this sort of case the consideration relating to the practice doesn't weigh on the promisor at all, and yet one feels that this sort of promise is as binding as other promises. The question of the effect which breaking it has on the practice seems irrelevant. The only consequence seems to be that

---

[17] Ross, *ibid.*, p. 39. The case of the nonpublic promise is discussed again in *Foundations of Ethics*, pp. 95–96, 104–105. It occurs also in Mabbott, "Punishment," *op. cit.*, pp. 155–157, and in A. I. Melden, "Two Comments on Utilitarianism," *Philosophical Review*, Vol. LX (October, 1951), 519–523, which discusses Carritt's example in *Ethical and Political Thinking*, p. 64.

[18] Ross's example is described simply as that of two men dying alone where one makes a promise to the other. Carritt's example (cf. n. 17 supra) is that of two men at the North Pole. The example in the text is more realistic and is similar to Mabbott's. Another example is that of being told something in confidence by one who subsequently dies. Such cases need not be "desert-island arguments" as Nowell-Smith seems to believe (cf. his *Ethics*, pp. 239–244).

one can break the promise without running any risk
of being censured; but the obligation itself seems not
the least weakened. Hence it is doubtful whether
the effect on the practice ever weighs in the particular case; certainly it cannot account for the strictness of the obligation where [16] it fails to obtain. It
seems to follow that a utilitarian account of the obligation to keep promises cannot be successfully carried
out.

From what I have said in connection with punishment, one can foresee what I am going to say about
these arguments and counterarguments. They fail to
make the distinction between the justification of a
practice and the justification of a particular action
falling under it, and therefore they fall into the mistake of taking it for granted that the promisor, like
Carritt's official, is entitled without restriction to bring
utilitarian considerations to bear in deciding whether
to keep *his* promise. But if one considers what the
practice of promising is one will see, I think, that
it is such as not to allow this sort of general discretion
to the promisor. Indeed, the point of the practice
is to abdicate one's title to act in accordance with
utilitarian and prudential considerations in order that
the future may be tied down and plans coordinated
in advance. There are obvious utilitarian advantages
in having a practice which denies to the promisor,
as a defense, any general appeal to the utilitarian
principle in accordance with which the practice itself
may be justified. There is nothing contradictory, or
surprising, in this: utilitarian (or aesthetic) reasons
might properly be given in arguing that the game
of chess, or baseball, is satisfactory just as it is, or
in arguing that it should be changed in various respects, but a player in a game cannot properly appeal
to such considerations as reasons for his making one
move rather than another. It is a mistake to think
that if the practice is justified on utilitarian grounds

then the promisor must have complete liberty to use utilitarian arguments to decide whether or not to keep his promise. The practice forbids this general defense; and it is a purpose of the practice to do this. Therefore what the above arguments presuppose—the idea that if the utilitarian view is accepted then the promisor is bound if, and only if, the application of the utilitarian principle to his own case shows that keeping it is best on the whole—is false. The promisor is bound because he promised: weighing the case on its merits is not open to him.[19] [17]

Is this to say that in particular cases one cannot deliberate whether or not to keep one's promise? Of course not. But to do so is to deliberate whether the various excuses, exceptions and defenses, which are understood by, and which constitute an important part of, the practice, apply to one's own case.[20] Various defenses for not keeping one's promise are allowed, but among them there isn't the one that, on general utilitarian grounds, the promisor (truly) thought his action best on the whole, even though there may be the defense that the consequences of keeping one's promise would have been *extremely* severe. While there are too many complexities here to consider all the necessary details, one can see that the general defense isn't allowed if one asks the following question: what would one say of someone who, when asked why he broke his promise, replied simply that breaking it was best on the whole? Assuming that his reply is sincere, and that his belief was reasonable (i.e., one need not consider the possibility that he was mistaken), I think that one would

---

[19] What I have said in this paragraph seems to me to coincide with Hume's important discussion in the *Treatise of Human Nature*, bk. III, pt. II, sec. 5; and also sec. 6, par. 8.

[20] For a discussion of these, see H. Sidgwick, *The Methods of Ethics* (6th ed.; London, 1901), bk. III, ch. vi.

question whether or not he knows what it means to say "I promise" (in the appropriate circumstances). It would be said of someone who used this excuse without further explanation that he didn't understand what defenses the practice, which defines a promise, allows to him. If a child were to use this excuse one would correct him; for it is part of the way one is taught the concept of a promise to be corrected if one uses this excuse. The point of having the practice would be lost if the practice did allow this excuse.

It is no doubt part of the utilitarian view that every practice should admit the defense that the consequences of abiding by it would have been extremely severe; and utilitarians would be inclined to hold that some reliance on people's good sense and some concession to hard cases is necessary. They would hold that a practice is justified by serving the interests of those who take part in it; and as with any set of rules there is understood a background of circumstances under which it is expected to be applied and which need not—indeed which cannot—be fully stated. Should these circumstances change, then even if [18] there is no rule which provides for the case, it may still be in accordance with the practice that one be released from one's obligation. But this sort of defense allowed by a practice must not be confused with the general option to weigh each particular case on utilitarian grounds which critics of utilitarianism have thought it necessarily to involve.

The concern which utilitarianism raises by its justification of punishment is that it may justify too much. The question in connection with promises is different: it is how utilitarianism can account for the obligation to keep promises at all. One feels that the recognized obligation to keep one's promise and utilitarianism are incompatible. And to be sure, they are incompatible if one interprets the utilitarian view as necessarily holding that each person has complete liberty to weigh every particular action on general utilitarian grounds. But must one interpret utilitarianism in this way? I hope to show that, in the sorts of cases I have discussed, one cannot interpret it in this way.

III

So far I have tried to show the importance of the distinction between the justification of a practice and the justification of a particular action falling under it by indicating how this distinction might be used to defend utilitarianism against two long-standing objections. One might be tempted to close the discussion at this point by saying that utilitarian considerations should be understood as applying to practices in the first instance and not to particular actions falling under them except insofar as the practices admit of it. One might say that in this modified form it is a better account of our considered moral opinions and let it go at that. But to stop here would be to neglect the interesting question as to how one can fail to appreciate the significance of this rather obvious distinction and can take it for granted that utilitarianism has the consequence that particular cases may always be decided on general utilitarian grounds.[21] I want to [19] argue that this mistake

---

[21] So far as I can see it is not until Moore that the doctrine is expressly stated in this way. See, for example, *Principia Ethica*, p. 147, where it is said that the statement "I am morally bound to perform this action" is identical with the statement "*This* action will produce the procedure the greatest possible amount of good in [19] the Universe" (my italics). It is important to remember that those whom I have called the classical utilitarians were largely interested in social institutions. They were among the leading economists and political theo-

may be connected with misconceiving the logical status of the rules of practices; and to show this I am going to examine two conceptions of rules, two ways of placing them within the utilitarian theory.

The conception which conceals from us the significance of the distinction I am going to call the summary view. It regards rules in the following way: one supposes that each person decides what he shall do in particular cases by applying the utilitarian principle; one supposes further that different people will decide the same particular case in the same way and that there will be recurrences of cases similar to those previously decided. Thus it will happen that in cases of certain kinds the same decision will be made either by the same person at different times or by different persons at the same time. If a case occurs frequently enough one supposes that a rule is formulated to cover that sort of case. I have called this conception the summary view because rules are pictured as summaries of past decisions arrived at by the *direct* application of the utilitarian principle to particular cases. Rules are regarded as reports that cases of a certain sort have been found on *other* grounds to be properly decided in a certain way (although, of course, they do not *say* this).

---

rists of their day, and they were not infrequently reformers interested in practical affairs. Utilitarianism historically goes together with a coherent view of society, and is not simply an ethical theory, much less an attempt at philosophical analysis in the modern sense. The utilitarian principle was quite naturally thought of, and used, as a criterion for judging social institutions (practices) and as a basis for urging reforms. It is not clear, therefore, how far it is necessary to amend utilitarianism in its classical form. For a discussion of utilitarianism as an integral part of a theory of society, see L. Robbins, *The Theory of Economic Policy in English Classical Political Economy* (London, 1952).

There are several things to notice about this way of placing rules within the utilitarian theory.[22]

---

[22] This footnote should be read after sec. 3 and presupposes what I have said there. It provides a few references to statements by leading utilitarians of the summary conception. In general it appears that when they discussed the logical features of rules the summary conception prevailed and that it was typical of the way they talked about moral rules. I cite a rather lengthy group of passages from Austin as a full illustration.

John Austin in his *Lectures on Jurisprudence* meets the objection that deciding [20] in accordance with the utilitarian principle case by case is impractical by saying that this is a misinterpretation of utilitarianism. According to the utilitarian view ". . . our conduct would conform to *rules* inferred from the tendencies of actions, but would not be determined by a direct resort to the principle of general utility. Utility would be the test of our conduct, ultimately, but not immediately: the immediate test of the rules to which our conduct would conform, but not the immediate test of specific or individual actions. Our rules would be fashioned on utility; our conduct, on our rules" (vol. I, p. 116). As to how one decides on the tendency of an action he says: "If we would try the tendency of a specific or individual act, we must not contemplate the act as if it were single and insulated, but must look at the class of acts to which it belongs. We must suppose that acts of the class were generally done or omitted, and consider the probable effect upon the general happiness or good. We must guess the consequences which would follow, if the class of acts were general; and also the consequences which would follow, if they were generally omitted. We must then compare the consequences on the positive and negative sides, and determine on which of the two the *balance* of advantage lies. . . . If we truly try the tendency of a specific or individual act, we try the tendency of the class to which that act belongs. The *particular* conclusion which we draw, with regard to the single act, implies a *general* conclusion embracing all similar acts. . . . To the rules thus inferred, and lodged in the memory, our conduct would conform *immediately* if it were truly adjusted to utility" (*ibid.*, p. 117). One might think that Austin

meets the objection by stating the practice conception of rules;
and perhaps he did intend to. But it is not clear that he has
stated this conception. Is the generality he refers to of the
statistical sort? This is suggested by the notion of tendency.
Or does he refer to the utility of setting up a practice? I
don't know; but what suggests the summary view is his subsequent remarks. He says: "To consider the specific consequences of single or individual acts, would *seldom* [my italics]
consist with that ultimate principle" (*ibid.*, p. 117). But
would one ever do this? He continues: ". . . this being admitted, the necessity of pausing and calculating, which the
objection in question supposes, is an imagined necessity. To
preface each act or forbearance by a conjecture and comparison of consequences, were clearly *superfluous* [my italics]
and mischievous. It were clearly superfluous, inasmuch as
the *result of that process* [my italics] would be embodied
in a known *rule*. It were clearly mischievous, inasmuch as
the *true* result would be expressed by that rule, whilst the
process would probably be faulty, if it were done on the
spur of the occasion" (*ibid.*, pp. 117–118). He goes on: "If
our experience and observation of particulars were not *gen-
eralized*, our experience and observation of particulars would
seldom avail us in *practice*. . . . The inferences suggested
to our minds by repeated experience and observation are,
therefore, drawn in *principles*, or compressed into *maxims*.
These we carry about us ready for use, and apply to
individual cases promptly . . . without reverting to the
process by which they were obtained; or without recall-
ing, and arraying before our minds, the numerous and
intricate considerations of which they are *handy abridg-
ments* [my italics]. . . . True theory is a *compendium* of
particular truths. . . . Speaking then, generally, human conduct is inevitably *guided* [my italics] by *rules*, or by
principles or *maxims*" (*ibid.*, pp. 117–118). I need not trouble to show how all these remarks incline to the summary
view. Further, when Austin comes to deal with [21] cases
"of comparatively rare occurrence" he holds that specific considerations may outweigh the general. "Looking at the reasons
from which we had inferred the rule, it were absurd to think
it inflexible. We should therefore dismiss the *rule;* resort di-

rectly to the *principle* upon which our rules were fashioned; and calculate *specific* consequences to the best of our knowledge and ability" (*ibid.*, pp. 120–121). Austin's view is interesting because it shows how one may come close to the practice conception and then slide away from it.

In *A System of Logic,* bk. VI, ch. xii, par. 2, Mill distinguishes clearly between the position of judge and legislator and in doing so suggests the distinction between the two concepts of rules. However, he distinguishes the two positions to illustrate the difference between cases where one is to apply a rule already established and cases where one must formulate a rule to govern subsequent conduct. It's the latter case that interests him and he takes the "maxim of policy" of a legislator as typical of rules. In par. 3 the summary conception is very clearly stated. For example, he says of rules of conduct that they should be taken provisionally, as they are made for the most numerous cases. He says that they "point out" the manner in which it is least perilous to act; they serve as an "admonition" that a certain mode of conduct has been found suited to the most common occurrences. In *Utilitarianism,* ch. ii, par. 24, the summary conception appears in Mill's answer to the same objection Austin considered. Here he speaks of rules as "corollaries" from the principle of utility; these "secondary" rules are compared to "landmarks" and "direction-posts." They are based on long experience and so make it unnecessary to apply the utilitarian principle to each case. In par. 25 Mill refers to the task of the utilitarian principle in adjudicating between competing moral rules. He talks here as if one then applies the utilitarian principle directly to the particular case. On the practice view one would rather use the principle to decide which of the ways that make the practice consistent is the best. It should be noted that while in par. 10 Mill's definition of utilitarianism makes the utilitarian principle apply to morality, i.e., to the rules and precepts of human conduct, the definition in par. 2 uses the phrase "actions are right in *proportion* as they *tend* to promote happiness" [my italics] and this inclines towards the summary view. In the last paragraph of the essay "On the Definition of Political Economy," *Westminster Review* (October, 1836), Mill says that it is only in art, as distinguished

[23]1. The point of having rules derives from the fact that similar cases tend to recur and that one can decide cases more quickly if one records past decisions in the form of rules. If similar cases didn't recur, one would be required to apply the utilitarian principle directly, case by case, and rules reporting past decisions would be of no use.

2. The decisions made on particular cases are logically prior to rules. Since rules gain their point from the need to apply the utilitarian principle to many similar cases, it follows that a particular case (or several cases similar to it) may exist whether or not there is a rule covering that case. We are pictured

---

from science, that one can properly speak of exceptions. In a question of practice, if something is fit to be done "in the majority of cases" then it is made the rule. "We may . . . in talking of art *unobjectionably* speak of the *rule* and the *exception*, meaning by the rule the cases in which there exists a preponderance . . . of inducements for acting in a particular way; and by the exception, the cases in which the preponderance is on the contrary side." These remarks, too, suggest the summary view.

In Moore's *Principia Ethica*, ch. v, there is a complicated and difficult discussion of moral rules. I will not examine it here except to express my suspicion that the summary conception prevails. To be sure, Moore speaks frequently of the utility of rules as generally followed, and of actions as generally practiced, but it is possible that these passages fit the statistical notion of generality which the summary conception allows. This conception is suggested by Moore's taking the utilitarian principle as applying directly to particular actions (pp. 147–148) and by his notion of a rule as something indicating which [22] of the few alternatives likely to occur to anyone will generally produce a greater total good in the immediate future (p. 154). He talks of an "ethical law" as a prediction, and as a generalization (pp. 146, 155). The summary conception is also suggested by his discussion of exceptions (pp. 162–163) and of the force of examples of breaching a rule (pp. 163–164).

as recognizing particular cases prior to there being a rule which covers them, for it is only if we meet with a number of cases of a certain sort that we formulate a rule. Thus we are able to describe a particular case as a particular case of the requisite sort whether there is a rule regarding *that* sort of case or not. Put another way: what the *A*'s and the *B*'s refer to in rules of the form 'Whenever *A* do *B*' may be described as *A*'s and *B*'s whether or not there is the rule 'Whenever *A* do *B*', or whether or not there is any body of rules which make up a practice of which that rule is a part.

To illustrate this consider a rule, or maxim, which could arise in this way: suppose that a person is trying to decide whether to tell someone who is fatally ill what his illness is when he has been asked to do so. Suppose the person to reflect and then decide, on utilitarian grounds, that he should not answer truthfully; and suppose that on the basis of this and other like occasions he formulates a rule to the effect that when asked by someone fatally ill what his illness is, one should not tell him. The point to notice is that someone's being fatally ill and asking what his illness is, and someone's telling him, are things that can be described as such whether or not there is this rule. The performance of the action to which the rule refers doesn't require the stage-setting of a practice of which this rule is a part. This is [23] what is meant by saying that on the summary view particular cases are logically prior to rules.

3. Each person is in principle always entitled to reconsider the correctness of a rule and to question whether or not it is proper to follow it in a particular case. As rules are guides and aids, one may ask whether in past decisions there might not have been a mistake in applying the utilitarian principle to get the rule in question, and wonder whether or not it

is best in this case. The reason for rules is that
people are not able to apply the utilitarian principle
effortlessly and flawlessly; there is need to save time
and to post a guide. On this view a society of
rational utilitarians would be a society without rules
in which each person applied the utilitarian principle
directly and smoothly, and without error, case by
case. On the other hand, ours is a society in which
rules are formulated to serve as aids in reaching these
ideally rational decisions on particular cases, guides
which have been built up and tested by the experience of generations. If one applies this view to
rules, one is interpreting them as maxims, as "rules
of thumb"; and it is doubtful that anything to which
the summary conception did apply would be called
a *rule*. Arguing as if one regarded rules in this way
is a mistake one makes while doing philosophy.

4. The concept of a *general* rule takes the following form. One is pictured as estimating on what
percentage of the cases likely to arise a given rule
may be relied upon to express the correct decision,
that is, the decision that would be arrived at if one
were to correctly apply the utilitarian principle case
by case. If one estimates that by and large the
rule will give the correct decision, or if one estimates
that the likelihood of making a mistake by applying
the utilitarian principle directly on one's own is
greater than the likelihood of making a mistake by
following the rule, and if these considerations held
of persons generally, then one would be justified in
urging its adoption as a general rule. In this way
general rules might be accounted for on the summary
view. It will still make sense, however, to speak of
applying the utilitarian principle case by case, for
it was by trying to foresee the results of doing this
that one got the initial estimates upon which acceptance of the rule depends. That one is [24] taking a
rule in accordance with the summary conception

will show itself in the naturalness with which one speaks of the rule as a guide, or as a maxim, or as a generalization from experience, and as something to be laid aside in extraordinary cases where there is no assurance that the generalization will hold and the case must therefore be treated on its merits. Thus there goes with this conception the notion of a particular exception which renders a rule suspect on a particular occasion.

The other conception of rules I will call the practice conception. On this view rules are pictured as defining a practice. Practices are set up for various reasons, but one of them is that in many areas of conduct each person's deciding what to do on utilitarian grounds case by case leads to confusion, and that the attempt to coordinate behavior by trying to foresee how others will act is bound to fail. As an alternative one realizes that what is required is the establishment of a practice, the specification of a new form of activity; and from this one sees that a practice necessarily involves the abdication of full liberty to act on utilitarian and prudential grounds. It is the mark of a practice that being taught how to engage in it involves being instructed in the rules which define it, and that appeal is made to those rules to correct the behavior of those engaged in it. Those engaged in a practice recognize the rules as defining it. The rules cannot be taken as simply describing how those engaged in the practice in fact behave: it is not simply that they act as if they were obeying the rules. Thus it is essential to the notion of a practice that the rules are publicly known and understood as definitive; and it is essential also that the rules of a practice can be taught and can be acted upon to yield a coherent practice. On this conception, then, rules are not generalizations from the decisions of individuals applying the utilitarian principle directly and independently to recurrent particular cases. On the con-

trary, rules define a practice and are themselves the
subject of the utilitarian principle.

To show the important differences between this
way of fitting rules into the utilitarian theory and the
previous way, I shall consider the differences between
the two conceptions on the points previously discussed. [25]

1. In contrast with the summary view, the rules of
practices are logically prior to particular cases. This
is so because there cannot be a particular case of an
action falling under a rule of a practice unless there
is the practice. This can be made clearer as follows:
in a practice there are rules setting up offices, specifying certain forms of action appropriate to various
offices, establishing penalties for the breach of rules,
and so on. We may think of the rules of a practice
as defining offices, moves, and offenses. Now what is
meant by saying that the practice is logically prior to
particular cases is this: given any rule which specifies
a form of action (a move), a particular action which
would be taken as falling under this rule given that
there is the practice would not be *described as* that
sort of action unless there was the practice. In the
case of actions specified by practices it is logically
impossible to perform them outside the stage-setting
provided by those practices, for unless there is the
practice, and unless the requisite proprieties are fulfilled, whatever one does, whatever movements one
makes, will fail to count as a form of action which
the practice specifies. What one does will be described
in some *other* way.

One may illustrate this point from the game of baseball. Many of the actions one performs in a game of
baseball one can do by oneself or with others whether
there is the game or not. For example, one can throw
a ball, run, or swing a peculiarly shaped piece of
wood. But one cannot steal base, or strike out, or
draw a walk, or make an error, or balk; although one

can do certain things which appear to resemble these
actions such as sliding into a bag, missing a grounder
and so on. Striking out, stealing a base, balking, etc.,
are all actions which can only happen in a game. No
matter what a person did, what he did would not be
described as stealing a base or striking out or drawing
a walk unless he could also be described as playing
baseball, and for him to be doing this presupposes the
rule-like practice which constitutes the game. The
practice is logically prior to particular cases: unless
there is the practice the terms referring to actions
specified by it lack a sense.[23] [26]

2. The practice view leads to an entirely different
conception of the authority which each person has to
decide on the propriety of following a rule in particular cases. To engage in a practice, to perform those
actions specified by a practice, means to follow the
appropriate rules. If one wants to do an action which
a certain practice specifies then there is no way to do
it except to follow the rules which define it. Therefore, it doesn't make sense for a person to raise the
question whether or not a rule of a practice correctly
applies to *his* case where the action he contemplates
is a form of action defined by a practice. If someone

---

[23] One might feel that it is a mistake to say that a practice
is logically prior to the forms of action it specifies on the
grounds that if there were never any [26] instances of actions
falling under a practice then we should be strongly inclined
to say that there wasn't the practice either. Blue-prints for a
practice do not make a practice. That there is a practice entails that there are instances of people having been engaged
and now being engaged in it (with suitable qualifications).
This is correct, but it doesn't hurt the claim that any given
particular instance of a form of action specified by a practice
presupposes the practice. This isn't so on the summary picture,
as each instance must be "there" prior to the rules, so to speak,
as something from which one gets the rule by applying the
utilitarian principle to it directly.

were to raise such a question, he would simply show
that he didn't understand the situation in which he
was acting. If one wants to perform an action specified by a practice, the only legitimate question concerns the nature of the practice itself ("How do I go
about making a will?").

This point is illustrated by the behavior expected
of a player in games. If one wants to play a game,
one doesn't treat the rules of the game as guides as to
what is best in particular cases. In a game of baseball
if a batter were to ask "Can I have four strikes?" it
would be assumed that he was asking what the rule
was; and if, when told what the rule was, he were to
say that he meant that on this occasion he thought it
would be best on the whole for him to have four
strikes rather than three, this would be most kindly
taken as a joke. One might contend that baseball
would be a better game if four strikes were allowed
instead of three; but one cannot picture the rules as
guides to what is best on the whole in particular
cases, and question their applicability to particular
cases as particular cases.

3 and 4. To complete the four points of comparison with the summary conception, it is clear from
what has been said that [27] rules of practices are not
guides to help one decide particular cases correctly as
judged by some higher ethical principle. And neither
the quasi-statistical notion of generality, nor the notion of a particular exception, can apply to the rules of
practices. A more or less general rule of a practice
must be a rule which according to the structure of the
practice applies to more or fewer of the kinds of
cases arising under it; or it must be a rule which is
more or less basic to the understanding of the practice. Again, a particular case cannot be an exception
to a rule of a practice. An exception is rather a qualification or a further specification of the rule.

It follows from what we have said about the practice conception of rules that if a person is engaged in a practice, and if he is asked why *he* does what *he* does, or if he is asked to defend what he does, then his explanation, or defense, lies in referring the questioner to the practice. He cannot say of *his* action, if it is an action specified by a practice, that he does it rather than some other because he thinks it is best on the whole.[24] When a man engaged in a practice is queried about his action he must assume that the questioner either doesn't know that he is engaged in it ("Why are you in a hurry to pay him?" "I promised to pay him today") or doesn't know what the practice is. One doesn't so much justify one's particular action as explain, or show, that it is in accordance with the practice. The reason for this is that it is only against the stage-setting of the practice that one's particular action is described as it is. Only by reference to the practice can one *say* what one is doing. To explain or to defend one's own action, as a particular action, one fits it into the practice which defines it. If this is not accepted it's a sign that a different question is being raised as to whether one is justified in accepting the practice, or in tolerating it. When the challenge is to the practice, citing the rules (saying what the practice is) is naturally to no avail. But when the challenge is to the particular action defined by the practice, there is nothing one can do but refer to the rules. Concerning particular actions [28] there is only a question for one who isn't clear as to what the practice is, or who doesn't know that it is being engaged in. This is to be contrasted with the case of a maxim which may be taken as pointing to the correct decision on the case as de-

---

[24] A philosophical joke (in the mouth of Jeremy Bentham): "When I run to the other wicket after my partner has struck a good ball I do so because it is best on the whole."

cided on *other* grounds, and so giving a challenge on
the case a sense by having it question whether these
other grounds really support the decision on this case.

If one compares the two conceptions of rules I
have discussed, one can see how the summary conception misses the significance of the distinction between justifying a practice and justifying actions
falling under it. On this view rules are regarded as
guides whose purpose it is to indicate the ideally
rational decision on the given particular case which
the flawless application of the utilitarian principle
would yield. One has, in principle, full option to use
the guides or to discard them as the situation war-
rants without one's moral office being altered in any
way: whether one discards the rules or not, one always holds the office of a rational person seeking case
by case to realize the best on the whole. But on the
practice conception, if one holds an office defined by
a practice then questions regarding one's actions in
this office are settled by reference to the rules which
define the practice. If one seeks to question these
rules, then one's office undergoes a fundamental
change: one then assumes the office of one empowered to change and criticize the rules, or the office
of a reformer, and so on. The summary conception
does away with the distinction of offices and the
various forms of argument appropriate to each. On
that conception there is one office and so no offices
at all. It therefore obscures the fact that the utilitarian
principle must, in the case of actions and offices defined by a practice, apply to the practice, so that
general utilitarian arguments are not available to those
who act in offices so defined.[25] [29]

---

[25] How do these remarks apply to the case of the promise
known only to father and son? Well, at first sight the son certainly holds the office of promisor, and so he isn't allowed by
the practice to weigh the particular case on general utilitarian

Some qualifications are necessary in what I have said. First, I may have talked of the summary and the practice conceptions of rules as if only one of them could be true of rules, and if true of any rules, then necessarily true of *all* rules. I do not, of course, mean this. (It is the critics of utilitarianism who make this mistake insofar as their arguments against utilitarianism presuppose a summary conception of the rules of practices.) Some rules will fit one conception, some rules the other; and so there are rules of practices (rules in the strict sense), and maxims and "rules of thumb."

Secondly, there are further distinctions that can be made in classifying rules, distinctions which should be made if one were considering other questions. The distinctions which I have drawn are those most relevant for the rather special matter I have discussed, and are not intended to be exhaustive.

Finally, there will be many border-line cases about which it will be difficult, if not impossible, to decide which conception of rules is applicable. One expects border-line cases with any concept, and they are especially likely in connection with such involved concepts as those of a practice, institution, game, rule, and so on. Wittgenstein has shown how fluid these

---

grounds. Suppose instead that he wishes to consider himself in the office of one empowered to criticize and change the practice, leaving aside the question as to his right to move from his previously assumed office to another. Then he may consider utilitarian arguments as applied to the practice; but [29] once he does this he will see that there are such arguments for not allowing a general utilitarian defense in the practice for this sort of case. For to do so would make it impossible to ask for and to give a kind of promise which one often wants to be able to ask for and to give. Therefore he will not want to change the practice, and so as a promisor he has no option but to keep his promise.

notions are.[26] What I have done is to emphasize and sharpen two conceptions for the limited purpose of this paper.

IV

What I have tried to show by distinguishing between two conceptions of rules is that there is a way of regarding rules which allows the option to consider particular cases on general utilitarian grounds; whereas there is another conception which does not admit of such discretion except insofar as the rules themselves authorize it. I want to suggest that the tendency while doing philosophy to picture rules in accordance with the summary [30] conception is what may have blinded moral philosophers to the significance of the distinction between justifying a practice and justifying a particular action falling under it; and it does so by misrepresenting the logical force of the reference to the rules in the case of a challenge to a particular action falling under a practice, and by obscuring the fact that where there is a practice, it is the practice itself that must be the subject of the utilitarian principle.

It is surely no accident that two of the traditional test cases of utilitarianism, punishment and promises, are clear cases of practices. Under the influence of the summary conception it is natural to suppose that the officials of a penal system, and one who has made a promise, may decide what to do in particular cases on utilitarian grounds. One fails to see that a general discretion to decide particular cases on utilitarian grounds is incompatible with the concept of a practice; and that what discretion one does have is itself

---

[26] *Philosophical Investigations* (Oxford, 1953), I, pars. 65–71, for example.

defined by the practice (e.g., a judge may have discretion to determine the penalty within certain limits). The traditional objections to utilitarianism which I have discussed presuppose the attribution to judges, and to those who have made promises, of a plenitude of moral authority to decide particular cases on utilitarian grounds. But once one fits utilitarianism together with the notion of a practice, and notes that punishment and promising are practices, then one sees that this attribution is logically precluded.

That punishment and promising are practices is beyond question. In the case of promising this is shown by the fact that the form of words "I promise" is a performative utterance which presupposes the stage-setting of the practice and the proprieties defined by it. Saying the words "I promise" will only be promising given the existence of the practice. It would be absurd to interpret the rules about promising in accordance with the summary conception. It is absurd to say, for example, that the rule that promises should be kept could have arisen from its being found in past cases to be best on the whole to keep one's promise; for unless there were already the understanding that one keeps one's promises as part of the practice itself there couldn't have been any cases of promising.

It must, of course, be granted that the rules defining promising [31] are not codified, and that one's conception of what they are necessarily depends on one's moral training. Therefore it is likely that there is considerable variation in the way people understand the practice, and room for argument as to how it is best set up. For example, differences as to how strictly various defenses are to be taken, or just what defenses are available, are likely to arise amongst persons with different backgrounds. But irrespective of these variations it belongs to the concept of the practice of promising that the general utilitarian defense is not

available to the promisor. That this is so accounts for
the force of the traditional objection which I have
discussed. And the point I wish to make is that when
one fits the utilitarian view together with the practice
conception of rules, as one must in the appropriate
cases, then there is nothing in that view which entails that there must be such a defense, either in the
practice of promising, or in any other practice.

Punishment is also a clear case. There are many actions in the sequence of events which constitute someone's being punished which presuppose a practice.
One can see this by considering the definition of punishment which I gave when discussing Carritt's criticism of utilitarianism. The definition there stated refers to such things as the normal rights of a citizen,
rules of law, due process of law, trials and courts of
law, statutes, etc., none of which can exist outside
the elaborate stage-setting of a legal system. It is also
the case that many of the actions for which people
are punished presuppose practices. For example, one is
punished for stealing, for trespassing, and the like,
which presuppose the institution of property. It is impossible to say what punishment is, or to describe a
particular instance of it, without referring to offices,
actions, and offenses specified by practices. Punishment is a move in an elaborate legal game and presupposes the complex of practices which make up
the legal order. The same thing is true of the less
formal sorts of punishment: a parent or guardian or
someone in proper authority may punish a child, but
no one else can.

There is one mistaken interpretation of what I have
been saying which it is worthwhile to warn against.
One might think that the use I am making of the
distinction between justifying a practice and justifying the particular actions falling under it involves
[32] one in a definite social and political attitude in
that it leads to a kind of conservatism. It might seem

that I am saying that for each person the social practices of his society provide the standard of justification for his actions; therefore let each person abide by them and his conduct will be justified.

This interpretation is entirely wrong. The point I have been making is rather a logical point. To be sure, it has consequences in matters of ethical theory; but in itself it leads to no particular social or political attitude. It is simply that where a form of action is specified by a practice there is no justification possible of the particular action of a particular person save by reference to the practice. In such cases the action is what it is in virtue of the practice and to explain it is to refer to the practice. There is no inference whatsoever to be drawn with respect to whether or not one should accept the practices of one's society. One can be as radical as one likes but in the case of actions specified by practices the objects of one's radicalism must be the social practices and people's acceptance of them.

I have tried to show that when we fit the utilitarian view together with the practice conception of rules, where this conception is appropriate,[27] we can formulate it in a way which saves it from several traditional objections. I have further tried to show how the logical force of the distinction between justifying a prac-

---

[27] As I have already stated, it is not always easy to say where the conception is appropriate. Nor do I care to discuss at this point the general sorts of cases to which it does apply except to say that one should not take it for granted that it applies to many so-called "moral rules." It is my feeling that relatively few actions of the moral life are defined by practices and that the practice conception is more relevant to understanding legal and legal-like arguments than it is to the more complex sort of moral arguments. Utilitarianism must be fitted to different conceptions of rules depending on the case, and no doubt the failure to do this has been one source of difficulty in interpreting it correctly.

tice and justifying an action falling under it is connected with the practice conception of rules and cannot be understood as long as one regards the rules of practices in accordance with the summary view. Why, when doing philosophy, one may be inclined to so regard them, I have not discussed. The reasons for this are evidently very deep and would require another paper.

EXTREME AND RESTRICTED UTILITARIANISM[1]
J. J. C. Smart

I

Utilitarianism is the doctrine that the rightness of actions is to be judged by their consequences. What do we mean by 'actions' here? Do we mean particular actions or do we mean classes of actions? According to which way we interpret the word 'actions' we get two different theories, both of which merit the appellation 'utilitarian'.

(1) If by 'actions' we mean particular individual actions we get the sort of doctrine held by Bentham, Sidgwick, and Moore. According to this doctrine we test individual actions by their consequences, and general rules, like 'keep promises', are mere rules of thumb

FROM *The Philosophical Quarterly*, Vol. VI (1956), 344–354, with revisions. Reprinted by permission of the author and *The Philosophical Quarterly*. The major revision which Professor Smart has made occurs on pp. 351–2 of the original publication (pp. 111–113 in this volume) concerning a game theoretical solution of the act-utilitarian's problem. Since publication of this article Professor Smart has preferred to follow Brandt's terminology of "act-" and "rule-utilitarianism" instead of "extreme" and "restricted utilitarianism."

[1] Based on a paper read to the Victorian Branch of the Australasian Association of Psychology and Philosophy, October, 1955.

which we use only to avoid the necessity of estimating the probable consequences of our actions at every step. The rightness or wrongness of keeping a promise on a particular occasion depends only on the goodness or badness of the consequences of keeping or of breaking the promise on that particular occasion. Of course part of the consequences of breaking the promise, and a part to which we will normally ascribe decisive importance, will be the weakening of faith in the institution of promising. However, if the goodness of the consequences of breaking the rule is *in toto* greater than the goodness of the consequences of keeping it, then we must break the rule, irrespective of whether the goodness of the consequences of *everybody's* obeying the rule is or is not greater than the consequences of *everybody's* breaking it. To put it shortly, rules do not matter, save *per accidens* as rules of thumb and as *de facto* social institutions with which the utilitarian has to reckon when estimating consequences. I shall call this doctrine 'extreme utilitarianism'.

(2) A more modest form of utilitarianism has recently become fashionable. The doctrine is to be found in Toulmin's book *The Place of Reason in Ethics*, in Nowell-Smith's *Ethics* (though I think Nowell-Smith has qualms), in John Austin's *Lectures on Jurisprudence* (Lecture II), and even in J. S. Mill, if Urmson's interpretation of him is correct (*Philosophical Quarterly*, Vol. III, pp. 33–39, 1953 [reprinted in this volume, pp. 13–24]). Part of its charm is that it appears to resolve the dispute in moral philosophy between intuitionists and utilitarians in a way which is very neat. The above philosophers hold, or seem to hold, that moral rules are more than rules of thumb. In general the rightness of an action is *not* to be tested by evaluating its consequences but only by considering whether or not it falls under a certain rule. Whether the rule is to be considered an accepta-

ble moral rule, is, however, to be [345] decided by considering the consequences of adopting the rule. Broadly, then, actions are to be tested by rules and rules by consequences. The only cases in which we must test an individual action directly by its consequences are (*a*) when the action comes under two different rules, one of which enjoins it and one of which forbids it, and (*b*) when there is no rule whatever that governs the given case. I shall call this doctrine 'restricted utilitarianism'.

It should be noticed that the distinction I am making cuts across, and is quite different from, the distinction commonly made between hedonistic and ideal utilitarianism. Bentham was an extreme hedonistic utilitarian and Moore an extreme ideal utilitarian, and Toulmin (perhaps) could be classified as a restricted ideal utilitarian. A hedonistic utilitarian holds that the goodness of the consequences of an action is a function only of their pleasurableness and an ideal utilitarian, like Moore, holds that pleasurableness is not even a necessary condition of goodness. Mill seems, if we are to take his remarks about higher and lower pleasures seriously, to be neither a pure hedonistic nor a pure ideal utilitarian. He seems to hold that pleasurableness is a necessary condition for goodness, but that goodness is a function of other qualities of mind as well. Perhaps we can call him a quasi-ideal utilitarian. When we say that a state of mind is good I take it that we are expressing some sort of *rational preference*. When we say that it is pleasurable I take it that we are saying that it is enjoyable, and when we say that something is a higher pleasure I take it that we are saying that it is more truly, or more deeply, enjoyable. I am doubtful whether 'more deeply enjoyable' does not just mean 'more enjoyable, even though not more enjoyable on a first look', and so I am doubtful whether quasi-ideal utilitarianism, and possibly ideal utilitarianism too, would not collapse into hedonistic utilitarianism on a closer scrutiny of the logic of words like 'preference', 'pleasure', 'enjoy', 'deeply enjoy', and so on. However, it is beside the point of the present paper to go into these questions. I am here concerned only with the issue between extreme and restricted utilitarianism and am ready to concede that both forms of utilitarianism can be either hedonistic or non-hedonistic.

The issue between extreme and restricted utilitarianism can be illustrated by considering the remark 'But suppose everyone did the same'. (Cf. A. K. Stout's article in *The Australasian Journal of Philosophy*, Vol. 32, pp. 1–29.) Stout distinguishes two forms of the universalisation principle, the causal form and the hypothetical form. To say that you ought not to do an action A because it would have bad results if everyone (or many people) did action A may be merely to point out that while the action A would otherwise be the optimific one, nevertheless when you take into account that doing A will probably cause other people to do A too, you can see that A is not, on a broad view, really optimific. If this causal influence could be avoided (as may happen in the case of a secret desert island promise) then we would disregard the universalisation principle. This is the causal [346] form of the principle. A person who accepted the universalisation principle in its hypothetical form would be one who was concerned only with what would happen *if* everyone did the action A: he would be totally unconcerned with the question of whether in fact everyone would do the action A. That is, he might say that it would be wrong not to vote because it would have bad results of everyone took this attitude, and he would be totally unmoved by arguments purporting to show that my refusing to vote has no effect whatever on other people's propensity to vote. Making use of Stout's distinction, we can

say that an extreme utilitarian would apply the universalisation principle in the causal form, while a restricted utilitarian would apply it in the hypothetical
form.

How are we to decide the issue between extreme
and restricted utilitarianism? I wish to repudiate at
the outset that milk and water approach which describes itself sometimes as 'investigating what is implicit in the common moral consciousness' and sometimes as 'investigating how people ordinarily talk about
morality'. We have only to read the newspaper correspondence about capital punishment or about what
should be done with Formosa to realise that the common moral consciousness is in part made up of superstitious elements, of morally bad elements, and of
logically confused elements. I address myself to good
hearted and benevolent people and so I hope that if
we rid ourselves of the logical confusion the superstitious and morally bad elements will largely fall
away. For even among good hearted and benevolent
people it is possible to find superstitious and morally
bad reasons for moral beliefs. These superstitious and
morally bad reasons hide behind the protective screen
of logical confusion. With people who are not logically confused but who are openly superstitious or
morally bad I can of course do nothing. That is, our
ultimate pro-attitudes may be different. Nevertheless
I propose to rely on *my own* moral consciousness
and to appeal to *your* moral consciousness and to
forget about what people ordinarily say. 'The obligation to obey a rule', says Nowell-Smith (*Ethics*, p.
239), 'does not, *in the opinion of ordinary men*', (my
italics), 'rest on the beneficial consequences of obeying it in a particular case'. What does this prove?
Surely it is more than likely that ordinary men are
confused here. Philosophers should be able to examine
the question more rationally.

II

For an extreme utilitarian moral rules are rules of thumb. In practice the extreme utilitarian will mostly guide his conduct by appealing to the rules ('do not lie', 'do not break promises', etc.) of common sense morality. This is not because there is anything sacrosanct in the rules themselves but because he can argue that probably he will most often act in an extreme utilitarian way if he does not think as a utilitarian. For one thing, actions have frequently to be done in a hurry. Imagine a man seeing a person drowning. He jumps in and rescues him. There is no time to reason the [347] matter out, but usually this will be the course of action which an extreme utilitarian would recommend if he did reason the matter out. If, however, the man drowning had been drowning in a river near Berchtesgaden in 1938, and if he had had the well known black forelock and moustache of Adolf Hitler, an extreme utilitarian would, if he had time, work out the probability of the man's being the villainous dictator, and if the probability were high enough he would, on extreme utilitarian grounds, leave him to drown. The rescuer, however, has not time. He trusts to his instincts and dives in and rescues the man. And this trusting to instincts and to moral rules can be justified on extreme utilitarian grounds. Furthermore, an extreme utilitarian who knew that the drowning man was Hitler would nevertheless praise the rescuer, not condemn him. For by praising the man he is strengthening a courageous and benevolent disposition of mind, and in general this disposition has great positive utility. (Next time, perhaps, it will be Winston Churchill that the man saves!) We must never forget that an extreme utilitarian may praise actions which he knows to be wrong. Saving Hitler was wrong, but it was a member of a class of actions which are generally right, and the motive to do actions of this class is in general an optimific one. In considering questions of praise and blame it is not the expediency of the praised or blamed action that is at issue, but the expediency of the praise. It can be expedient to praise an inexpedient action and inexpedient to praise an expedient one.

Lack of time is not the only reason why an extreme utilitarian may, on extreme utilitarian principles, trust to rules of common sense morality. He knows that in particular cases where his own interests are involved his calculations are likely to be biased in his own favour. Suppose that he is unhappily married and is deciding whether to get divorced. He will in all probability greatly exaggerate his own unhappiness (and possibly his wife's) and greatly underestimate the harm done to his children by the break up of the family. He will probably also underestimate the likely harm done by the weakening of the general faith in marriage vows. So probably he will come to the correct extreme utilitarian conclusion if he does not in this instance think as an extreme utilitarian but trusts to common sense morality.

There are many more and subtle points that could be made in connection with the relation between extreme utilitarianism and the morality of common sense. All those that I have just made and many more will be found in Book IV Chapters 3–5 of Sidgwick's *Methods of Ethics*. I think that this book is the best book ever written on ethics, and that these chapters are the best chapters of the book. As they occur so near the end of a very long book they are unduly neglected. I refer the reader, then, to Sidgwick for the classical exposition of the relation between (extreme) utilitarianism and the morality of common sense. One further point raised by Sidgwick in this connection is whether an (extreme) utilitarian ought on (extreme) utilitarian principles to propagate (extreme) utilitarianism among the [348] public. As most people are not very philosophical and not good at empirical calculations, it is probable that they will most often act in an extreme utilitarian way if they do not try to think as extreme utilitarians. We have seen how easy it would be to misapply the extreme utilitarian criterion in the case of divorce. Sidgwick seems to think it quite probable that an extreme utilitarian should not propagate his doctrine too widely. However, the great danger to humanity comes nowadays on the plane of public morality—not private morality. There is a greater danger to humanity from the hydrogen bomb than from an increase of the divorce rate, regrettable though that might be, and there seems no doubt that extreme utilitarianism makes for good sense in international relations. When France walked out of the United Nations because she did not wish Morocco discussed, she said that she was within her rights because Morocco and Algiers are part of her metropolitan territory and nothing to do with U.N. This was clearly a legalistic if not superstitious argument. We should not be concerned with the so-called 'rights' of France or any other country but with whether the cause of humanity would best be served by discussing Morocco in U.N. (I am not saying that the answer to this is 'Yes'. There are good grounds for supposing that more harm than good would come by such a discussion.) I myself have no hesitation in saying that on extreme utilitarian principles we ought to propagate extreme utilitarianism as widely as possible. But Sidgwick had respectable reasons for suspecting the opposite.

The extreme utilitarian, then, regards moral rules as rules of thumb and as sociological facts that have to be taken into account when deciding what to do, just as facts of any other sort have to be taken into account. But in themselves they do not justify any action.

III

The restricted utilitarian regards moral rules as more than rules of thumb for short-circuiting calculations of consequences. Generally, he argues, consequences are not relevant at all when we are deciding what to do in a particular case. In general, they are relevant only to deciding what rules are good reasons for acting in a certain way in particular cases. This doctrine is possibly a good account of how the modern unreflective twentieth century Englishman often thinks about morality, but surely it is monstrous as an account of how it is most rational to think about morality. Suppose that there is a rule R and that in 99% of cases the best possible results are obtained by acting in accordance with R. Then clearly R is a useful rule of thumb; if we have not time or are not impartial enough to assess the consequences of an action it is an extremely good bet that the thing to do is to act in accordance with R. But is it not monstrous to suppose that if we *have* worked out the consequences and if we have perfect faith in the impartiality of our calculations, and if we *know* that in this instance to break R will have better results than to keep it, we should nevertheless obey the rule? Is it not to erect R into a sort of idol if we keep it when [349] breaking it will prevent, say, some avoidable misery? Is not this a form of superstitious rule-worship (easily explicable psychologically) and not the rational thought of a philosopher?

The point may be made more clearly if we consider Mill's comparison of moral rules to the tables in the nautical almanack. (*Utilitarianism*, Everyman edition, pp. 22–23). This comparison of Mill's is adduced by Urmson as evidence that Mill was a restricted utilitarian, but I do not think that it will bear this interpretation at all. (Though I quite agree with Urmson that many other things said by Mill are in harmony with restricted rather than extreme utilitarianism. Probably Mill had never thought very much about the distinction and was arguing for utilitarianism, restricted or extreme, against other and quite non-utilitarian forms of moral argument.) Mill says: 'Nobody argues that the art of navigation is not founded on astronomy, because sailors cannot wait to calculate the Nautical Almanack. Being rational creatures, they go out upon the sea of life with their minds made up on the common questions of right and wrong, as well as on many of the far more difficult questions of wise and foolish. . . . Whatever we adopt as the fundamental principle of morality, we require subordinate principles to apply it by'. Notice that this is, as it stands, only an argument for subordinate principles as rules of thumb. The example of the nautical almanack is misleading because the information given in the almanack is in all cases the same as the information one would get if one made a long and laborious calculation from the original astronomical data on which the almanack is founded. Suppose, however, that astronomy were different. Suppose that the behaviour of the sun, moon and planets was very nearly as it is now, but that on rare occasions there were peculiar irregularities and discontinuities, so that the almanack gave us rules of the form 'in 99% of cases where the observations are such and such you can deduce that your position is so and so'. Furthermore, let us suppose that there were methods which enabled us, by direct and laborious calculation from the original astronomical data, not using the rough and ready tables of the almanack, to get our correct position in 100% of cases. Seafarers might use the almanack because they never had time for the long calculations and they were content with a 99% chance of success in calculating their positions. Would it not be absurd, however, if they *did* make the direct calculation, and finding that it disagreed with the almanack calculation, nevertheless they ignored it and stuck to the almanack conclusion? Of course the case would be altered if there were a high enough probability of making slips in the direct calculation: then we might stick to the almanack result, liable to error though we knew it to be, simply because the direct calculation would be open to error for a different reason, the fallibility of the computer. This would be analogous to the case of the extreme utilitarian who abides by the conventional rule against the dictates of his utilitarian calculations simply because he thinks that his calculations are probably affected by personal bias. But if the navigator were sure of his direct calculations [350] would he not be foolish to abide by his almanack? I conclude, then, that if we change our suppositions about astronomy and the almanack (to which there are no exceptions) to bring the case into line with that of morality (to whose rules there are exceptions), Mill's example loses its appearance of supporting the restricted form of utilitarianism. Let me say once more that I am not here concerned with how ordinary men think about morality but with how they ought to think. We could quite well imagine a race of sailors who acquired a superstitious reverence for their almanack, even though it was only right in 99% of cases, and who indignantly threw overboard any man who mentioned the possibility of a direct calculation. But would this behaviour of the sailors be rational?

Let us consider a much discussed sort of case in which the extreme utilitarian might go against the conventional moral rule. I have promised to a friend, dying on a desert island from which I am subsequently rescued, that I will see that his fortune (over which I have control) is given to a jockey club. However, when I am rescued I decide that it would be better to give the money to a hospital, which can do more good with it. It may be argued that I am wrong to give the money to the hospital. But why? (*a*) The hospital can do more good with the money than the jockey club can. (*b*) The present case is unlike most cases of promising in that no one except me knows about the promise. In breaking the promise I am doing so with complete secrecy and am doing nothing to weaken the general faith in promises. That is, a factor, which would normally keep the extreme utilitarian from promise breaking even in otherwise unoptimific cases, does not at present operate. (*c*) There is no doubt a slight weakening in my own character as an habitual promise keeper, and moreover psychological tensions will be set up in me every time I am asked what the man made me promise him to do. For clearly I shall have to say that he made me promise to give the money to the hospital, and, since I am an habitual truth teller, this will go very much against the grain with me. Indeed I am pretty sure that in practice I myself would keep the promise. But we are not discussing what my moral habits would probably make me do; we are discussing what I ought to do. Moreover, we must not forget that even if it would be most rational of me to give the money to the hospital it would also be most rational of you to punish or condemn me if you did, most improbably, find out the truth (e.g. by finding a note washed ashore in a bottle). Furthermore, I would agree that though it was most rational of me to give the money to the hospital it would be most rational of you to condemn me for it. We revert again to Sidgwick's distinction between the utility of the action and the utility of the praise of it.

Many such issues are discussed by A. K. Stout in the article to which I have already referred. I do not wish to go over the same ground again, especially as I think that Stout's arguments support my own point of view. It will be useful, however, to consider one other example that he gives. Suppose that during hot weather there is an edict that no water must be [351] used for watering gardens. I have a garden and I reason that most people are sure to obey the edict, and that as the amount of water that I use will be by itself negligible no harm will be done if I use the water secretly. So I do use the water, thus producing some lovely flowers which give happiness to various people. Still, you may say, though the action was perhaps optimific, it was unfair and wrong.

There are several matters to consider. Certainly my action should be condemned. We revert once more to Sidgwick's distinction. A right action may be rationally condemned. Furthermore, this sort of offence is normally found out. If I have a wonderful garden when everybody else's is dry and brown there is only one explanation. So if I water my garden I am weakening my respect for law and order, and as this leads to bad results an extreme utilitarian would agree that I was wrong to water the garden. Suppose now that the case is altered and that I can keep the thing secret: there is a secluded part of the garden where I grow flowers which I give away anonymously to a home for old ladies. Are you still so sure that I did the wrong thing by watering my garden? However, this is still a weaker case than that of the hospital and the jockey club. There will be tensions set up within myself: my secret knowledge that I have broken the rule will make it hard for me to exhort others to keep the rule. These psychological ill effects in myself may be not inconsiderable: directly and indirectly they may lead to harm which is at least of the same order as the

happiness that the old ladies get from the flowers.
You can see that on an extreme utilitarian view there
are two sides to the question.

So far I have been considering the duty of an
extreme utilitarian in a predominantly non-utilitarian
society. The case is altered if we consider the extreme
utilitarian who lives in a society every member, or
most members, of which can be expected to reason
as he does. Should he water his flowers now? (Granting, what is doubtful, that in the case already considered he would have been right to water his flowers.)
Clearly not. A simple argument, employing the game-
theoretical concept of a mixed strategy, suggests that
each extreme utilitarian should give himself a very
small probability (say by tossing dice) of watering
his garden. Suppose that there are m potential garden
waterers and that $f(n)$ is the damage done by exactly
n people watering their gardens. Now if each of them
gives himself a probability p of watering his garden
it is easy to calculate, in terms of p, the probabilities
p_1, p_2, . . . p_m of 1, 2, . . . m persons respectively
watering their gardens. Let a be the benefit to each
gardener of watering his garden. Then if V is the
total probable benefit to the community of gardeners
we have

$$V = p_1(a - f(1)) + p_2(2a - f(2)) + \ldots p_m(ma - f(m))$$

Assuming that numerical values can be given to a
and to values of the function $f(n)$ we calculate the
value of p for which $\dfrac{dV}{dp} = 0$. This gives the value of
p which maximises the total probable benefit. In practical cases of course numerical values of $f(n)$ and a
cannot be determined, but a good approximation
can usually be got by taking p as equal to zero.
However the mathematical analysis is of theoretical
interest for the discussion of utilitarianism. Too many

writers mistakenly suppose that the only two relevant alternatives are that no one does something and that everyone does it. [352]

I now pass on to a type of case which may be thought to be the trump card of restricted utilitarianism. Consider the rule of the road. It may be said that since all that matters is that everyone should do the same it is indifferent which rule we have, 'go on the left hand side' or 'go on the right hand side'. Hence the only *reason* for going on the left hand side in British countries is that this is the rule. Here the rule does seem to be a reason, in itself, for acting in a certain way. I wish to argue against this. The rule in itself is not a reason for our actions. We would be perfectly justified in going on the right hand side if (*a*) we knew that the rule was to go on the left hand side, and (*b*) we were in a country peopled by super-anarchists who always on principle did the opposite of what they were told. This shows that the rule does not give us a reason for acting so much as an indication of the probable actions of others, which helps us to find out what would be our own most rational course of action. If we are in a country not peopled by anarchists, but by non-anarchist extreme Utilitarians, we expect, other things being equal, that they will keep rules laid down for them. Knowledge of the rule enables us to predict their behaviour and to [353] harmonise our own actions with theirs. The rule 'keep to the left hand side', then, is not a logical *reason* for action but an anthropological *datum* for planning actions.

I conclude that in every case if there is a rule R the keeping of which is in general optimific, but such that in a special sort of circumstances the optimific behaviour is to break R, then in these circumstances we should break R. Of course we must consider all the less obvious effects of breaking R, such as reducing people's faith in the moral order, before coming to the conclusion that to break R is right: in fact we shall rarely come to such a conclusion. Moral rules, on the extreme utilitarian view, are rules of thumb only, but they are not bad rules of thumb. But if we *do* come to the conclusion that we should break the rule and if we have weighed in the balance our own fallibility and liability to personal bias, what good reason remains for keeping the rule? I can understand 'it is optimific' as a reason for action, but why should 'it is a member of a class of actions which are usually optimific' or 'it is a member of a class of actions which as a class are more optimific than any alternative general class' be a good reason? You might as well say that a person ought to be picked to play for Australia just because all his brothers have been, or that the Australian team should be composed entirely of the Harvey family because this would be better than composing it entirely of any other family. The extreme utilitarian does not appeal to artificial feelings, but only to our feelings of benevolence, and what better feelings can there be to appeal to? Admittedly we can have a pro-attitude to anything, even to rules, but such artificially begotten pro-attitudes smack of superstition. Let us get down to realities, human happiness and misery, and make these the objects of our pro-attitudes and anti-attitudes.

The restricted utilitarian might say he is talking only of *morality*, not of such things as rules of the road. I am not sure how far this objection, if valid, would affect my argument, but in any case I would reply that as a philosopher I conceive of ethics as the study of how it would be *most rational* to act. If my opponent wishes to restrict the word 'morality' to a narrower use he can have the word. The fundamental question is the question of rationality of action *in general*. Similarly if the restricted utilitarian were to appeal to ordinary usage and say 'it might be most rational to leave Hitler to drown but it would surely not be *wrong* to rescue him', I should again let him have the words 'right' and 'wrong' and should stick to 'rational' and 'irrational'. We already saw that it would be rational to praise Hitler's rescuer, even though it would have been most rational not to have rescued Hitler. In ordinary language, no doubt, 'right' and 'wrong' have not only the meaning 'most rational to do' and 'not most rational to do' but also have the meaning 'praiseworthy' and 'not praiseworthy'. Usually to the utility of an action corresponds utility of praise of it, but as we saw, this is not always so. Moral language could thus do with tidying up, for example by reserving 'right' for 'most rational' [354] and 'good' as an epithet of praise for the motive from which the action sprang. It would be more becoming in a philosopher to try to iron out illogicalities in moral language and to make suggestions for its reform than to use it as a court of appeal whereby to perpetuate confusions.

One last defence of restricted utilitarianism might be as follows. 'Act optimifically' might be regarded as itself one of the rules of our system (though it would be odd to say that this rule was justified by its optimificality). According to Toulmin (*The Place of Reason in Ethics*, pp. 146–8) if 'keep promises', say, conflicts with another rule we are allowed to argue the case on its merits, as if we were extreme utilitarians. If 'act optimifically' is itself one of our rules then there will always be a conflict of rules whenever to keep a rule is not itself optimific. If this is so, restricted utilitarianism collapses into extreme utilitarianism. And no one could read Toulmin's book or Urmson's article on Mill without thinking that Toulmin and Urmson are of the opinion that they have thought of a doctrine which does *not* collapse into extreme utilitarianism, but which is, on the contrary, an improvement on it.

AN EXAMINATION
OF RESTRICTED
UTILITARIANISM

H. J. McCloskey

It is my purpose in this paper to show that *restricted utilitarianism* is no more tenable as an ethical theory than is the better known *extreme utilitarianism* which it is intended to supersede.[1] According to restricted utilitarianism we justify particular actions by reference to general rules or practices and the rules by reference to the principle of utility. Hence according to this theory particular actions may be obligatory even though they are not productive to the maximum good possible.

This theory arises out of its exponents' dissatisfaction with extreme utilitarianism, according to

FROM *The Philosophical Review*, Vol. LXVI (1957), 466–485. Reprinted by permission of the author and *The Philosophical Review*. Since publication of this article Dr. McCloskey has preferred to use the terminology of "act-" and "rule-utilitarianism" instead of "extreme" and "restricted utilitarianism."

[1] The terminology is that adopted by J. J. C. Smart in "Extreme and Restricted Utilitarianism," *Philosophical Quarterly*, Vol. VI (1956), 344 [reprinted in this volume, pp. 99–115]. All subsequent references to Smart's views relate to this article.

which "it is always the duty of every agent to do
that one, among all the actions which he can do on
any given occasion, whose total consequence will have
the greatest intrinsic value" (G. E. Moore). This is
evident in the writings of its contemporary exponents
and sympathizers, such as J. O. Urmson and John
Rawls. Urmson, for instance, argues that restricted
utilitarianism is much superior to extreme utilitarianism just because it escapes the standard, fatal objections to that theory.[2] This is why he regards it
as important to show that the traditional interpretation of John Stuart Mill as an extreme utilitarian is
mistaken. Rawls argues along the same lines, illustrat-
ing in some detail the superiority of the restricted
theory by reference to the objections that are urged
against the extreme view in connection with punishment and the obligation to keep promises.[3] Rawls and
Urmson in their respective articles are simply voicing
an almost general feeling among contemporary utilitarians that the simple device of treating the Principle
of Utility not as a justification of particular obligations but of general [467] practices or principles
provides a general solution to the traditional objections to utilitarianism. There are some grounds for
this confidence; and it is significant that J. J. C.
Smart, who seeks to defend extreme against restricted
utilitarianism, does so almost entirely by pointing to
inadequacies in the restricted utilitarian theory. Smart
does not show that extreme utilitarianism can meet
the objections that are commonly urged against it

---

[2] J. O. Urmson, "The Interpretation of the Moral Philosophy of J. S. Mill," *Philosophical Quarterly*, Vol. III (1953),
33 [reprinted in this volume, pp. 13–24].

[3] John Rawls, "Two Concepts of Rules," *Philosophical Review*, Vol. LXIV (1955), 3 [reprinted in this volume, pp. 59–
98]. All subsequent references to Rawls's views relate to this
article.

and with which the restricted theory seeks to deal. Instead, he concentrates on attempting to show that the restricted theory cannot meet any objections encountered by the extreme theory and that in its attempts to do so, it involves itself in absurdities; and only to a much lesser extent does he concern himself with showing that some of the more usual, but less telling, objections to extreme utilitarianism are not real objections. The most acute difficulties encountered by the extreme theory are those involving considerations of justice—for example, punishment; and it is of note that Smart fails to consider such cases and that he gives no indication how the extreme theory might be made to cope with them. On the other hand, in spite of Smart's contention to the contrary, the restricted theory does seem to assist utilitarianism in escaping many of these difficulties; but it is not completely successful in this, and it does encounter new and serious difficulties of its own. These difficulties are as fatal to the claims of the restricted theory as are the difficulties commonly urged against utilitarianism to the claims of the extreme theory. To bring this out, it is necessary to note and examine the main varieties of restricted utilitarianism.

Pure and mixed. (a) According to what might be called the *pure* restricted theory, the principle of utility is the primary principle by reference to which "rules in practice" are justified. It is appealed to only when considering the rules in practice and never when discussing the rightness or wrongness of actions. Urmson explains restricted utilitarianism in this way, but I know of no utilitarian who, in an undeviating way, defends pure restricted utilitarianism. It is nonetheless an important position because many exponents of restricted utilitarianism write as if this is the view they wish to defend and as if they have not succeeded in distinguishing it from the other varieties. Smart concentrates his attention on this variety, probably for these reasons. (b) Secondly, [468] there is the *mixed* variety. According to this variety, the principle of utility is the primary principle which justifies the "rules in practice," but it is also a rule or secondary principle which competes with the other rules. Stephen Toulmin most nearly of all the restricted utilitarians espouses this version, but it seems to be that to which practically all restricted utilitarians are forced by pressure of difficulties.

Conditional and unconditional. (a) *Unconditional* restricted utilitarianism is that which treats the rules as being rules which in themselves prescribe no exceptions or spheres in which they do not hold. (b) *Conditional* restricted utilitarian theories are those according to which the practices or rules are such that they allow, as not being covered by the practice, special types of cases which might at first appear to fall under the practice. An unconditional restricted utilitarian theory might be to the effect that stealing is never right. A conditional variety of the theory might explain the "rule in practice" as being "stealing is never right except by a starving man from a wealthy one and 'in similar sorts of cases.'" Most restricted utilitarians assume the unconditional variety, although under pressure some switch to the conditional variety. Rawls suggests that the latter is the more defensible variety, but he seems half-heartedly to go on and associate it with the mixed variety. The mixed and the conditional varieties of restricted utilitarianism are occasioned by the difficulties with which a pure unconditional theory cannot deal.

Rawls defends restricted utilitarianism by taking the activities of punishment and promise-keeping as examples which illustrate how the restricted theory can meet difficulties fatal to extreme utilitarianism. The following example brings out the nature of these difficulties as they may arise in respect to punishment.

Suppose that a sheriff were faced with the choice either of framing a Negro for a rape that had aroused hostility to the Negroes (a particular Negro generally being believed to be guilty but whom the sheriff knows not to be guilty)—and thus preventing serious anti-Negro riots which would probably lead to some loss of life and increased hatred of each other by whites and Negroes—or of hunting for the guilty person and thereby allowing the anti-Negro riots to occur, while doing the best he can to combat them. [469] In such a case the sheriff, if he were an extreme utilitarian, would appear to be committed to framing the Negro. Stubborn, extreme utilitarians try to avoid this sort of embarrassing conclusion, but such is the dissatisfaction generally felt with their moves here that Rawls is rightly able to commend the restricted theory on the grounds that it, by contrast, offers a plausible utilitarian solution.

Rawls points out that we must distinguish between justifying a practice as a system of rules which are applied and enforced and justifying a particular action that falls under these rules. Utilitarian arguments, he contends, are appropriate with regard to questions about practices, while retributive arguments fit the application of particular rules to particular cases. As he reasons, "So firstly we should explain that A is put in jail because he is guilty, and that it is the practice to punish and put into jail those found guilty after a fair legal trial; and secondly, we should justify *the practice* of putting people found guilty in jail on utilitarian grounds."

This move, besides doing justice to the two important components in punishment—guilt of the punished and utility in the allocation of the punishment—seems to get over the difficulty that utilitarianism appears to involve unjust, illegitimate punishment of the innocent, because, as Rawls shows, punishing the innocent is condemned on utilitarian grounds as being contrary to a general utilitarian institution. The defense of utilitarianism on this point is not complete, however, until it is shown that the system of punishment is a better utilitarian institution than any comparable possible institution.

Arguing to this conclusion, Rawls sets out a contrast between the institution of punishment and an institution corresponding to that which critics of utilitarianism claim to be presupposed by the utilitarian theory. This institution Rawls refers to as *"telishment."* It consists in the infliction of suffering on innocent and guilty individuals alike for the sake of the general well-being, the victims being selected by senior state officials. Rawls argues of such an institution that it does not have the utilitarian justification punishment has, and from this he moves to the more general conclusion that "it happens in general that as one drops off the defining features of punishment one ends up with an institution [470] whose utilitarian justification is highly doubtful." Rawls's point is that the critics of utilitarianism do not seem to see that their criticisms presuppose the setting up by utilitarians of an alternative institution to that of punishment, and that once this is appreciated and once the new institution of telishment is described in detail, this institution is seen not to have the same utilitarian justification that is possessed by the institution of punishment.

Rawls's reply to criticisms of the type urged by W. D. Ross and others of the extreme utilitarians' defense of promise-keeping is in effect that these criticisms hold only against extreme utilitarianism and not against utilitarianism as such.[4] Restrcted utilitarianism acknowledges that not all promises which

---

[4] See W. D. Ross, *The Right and The Good*, (Oxford, 1930), esp. chs. i and ii, and *Foundations of Ethics* (Oxford, 1939), esp. ch. v.

ought to be kept produce the best possible results. This, it is explained, is so because it is the practice and not the individual action falling under it which has a utilitarian justification. Since the practice which has this justification is one which involves the abdication of the right to weigh individual promises on the utilitarian principle, there is no difficulty over the obligation to keep particular promises which do not have the best possible consequences. Bringing out the nature of the practice of promise-keeping Rawls writes:

> What would one say of someone who, when asked why he broke his promise, replied simply that breaking it was best on the whole? . . . It would be said of someone who used this excuse without further explanation, that he didn't understand what defences the practice, which defines a promise, allows to him. . . . The point of having the practice would be lost if the practice did allow this excuse.

It is quite clear from the examples of promise-keeping and punishment that the restricted theory does escape some of the more usual objections urged against the extreme utilitarian theory. The former theory is able to offer reasons, within the utilitarian framework, for punishing only the guilty and for keeping those promises which it is generally felt should be kept, even when acting otherwise might produce valuable results. The restricted theory cannot deal with all the more usual objections urged against the extreme theory, however; and it itself is exposed to new [471] objections. In brief, it fails to give reasons for keeping *all* those promises (and other obligations) which ought to be kept, but which on the extreme theory appear not to be obligatory; it implies obligations (for example, to keep promises)

which in fact are not real obligations; it fails to assist
the utilitarian position in meeting objections arising
in respect of many activities, such as killing, the
wrongness of which does not depend upon the existence of any institution; it involves a very paradoxical
form of ethical relativism; and at key points the
theory is vague and confused, and necessarily so.
These objections may now be developed in detail.

(1) If the value of the institution or rule in practice
is assessed on a utilitarian calculus, then it must be
asked: Why should there not be exceptions to the
institution also on utilitarian grounds in those situations in which the exception is not going to damage
the institution? Exponents of the restricted theory
speak as if to make exceptions on utilitarian grounds
is to set up a different practice; but to punish an
innocent person when and only when to do so is not
to weaken the existing institution of punishment and
when the consequences of doing so are valuable is
not to set up what Rawls calls an institution of
telishment. So even were it true that telishment is an
institution that cannot be justified on utilitarian
grounds—and this is by no means clear—it would still
not follow that we should never telish. Similarly with
promise-keeping and promise-breaking. The most
that the restricted utilitarian can seriously contend
is that if we knew that most people were going to
treat promises as utilitarians are said to be in consistency bound to treat them and that the general
practice and all the valuable results that accrue from
having a practice of promise-keeping were to be
thereby endangered, then the individual promise
which has bad consequences should nonetheless be
kept: whereas if we know that the practice will not
be endangered, that most people anyway are not
utilitarians, and that there can be a general expectation that people can be counted on to act in certain
ways in the future, then surely it is unreasonable to

insist that even here the utilitarian principle itself cannot be invoked and that the promise should be kept. Yet if this point is allowed it follows that in our society, or at [472] least in a society predominantly of nonutilitarians, utilitarians should not keep promises of which the consequences on the whole are bad. The only defense for conforming with the rule when the consequences of such conformity are bad would seem to be a causal one—that lack of conformity on this occasion weakens the practice, and so on. But this defense is possible only in rare, particular cases. Hence either there must be admission that very many promises need not be kept after all and that the restricted version is little better off than the extreme theory, or we get the absurd insistence on conformity with the rule, with no good reason for this being offered. The latter absurdity can be illustrated by amending an analogy used in another context by J. D. Mabbott and applying it in the context of restricted utilitarianism. The analogy then runs:

> The following dialogue at a bridge table will illustrate the fallacy. I am the third player on the first trick; the second player has played the ace. I hold the king. I remember that I have been told that the third player should play high. I whisper to my mentor behind me (the mentor representing the restricted utilitarian), "What do I play?" He says, "The king." "But it will do no good; the ace has been played." "Never mind that. You must play your king, that is the rule and you must conform with the rule."[5]

If the restricted utilitarian nonetheless denies this absurdity and insists that the rules of a practice should

---

[5] Mabbott, "Interpretations of Mill's Utilitarianism," *Philosophical Quarterly*, Vol. VI (1956), 115.

be kept where a breach will not harm the practice
and will produce good results—that is, if he insists
firmly that utility is a first principle and not a rule or
secondary principle and that decisions must be
reached by reference to secondary principles, then it
follows from the pure variety of the restricted theory
that all promises should be kept, that the truth should
always be told, and that the consequences are irrelevant simply because the first principle is irrelevant.
And this conclusion is as objectionable as the other;
the more especially as it seems also to imply that
there are no duties where there are no rules in practice.

What seems to have happened in the development
of restricted utilitarianism is that the restricted utilitarians have become confused [473] between what are
in fact accepted as good reasons in morals and what on
their theory *should be* accepted as such. This is an
important point and an important criticism. It is quite
true, as the restricted utilitarians suggest, that we do
regard it as giving a good reason for an action to
point out that it is an instance of a general practice;
but it does not follow from this that these same
reasons should be regarded on the utilitarian theory as
good reasons. Clearly on the utilitarian theory—the
extreme or restricted version—to point to the fact
that an action is an instance of a general moral practice is not always to give a good moral reason.

These various arguments which make up this first
general objection to restricted utilitarianism would
seem to be fatal to the claims of all varieties of the
restricted theory.

(2) There are, of course, conflicts even between
rules in practice. Even the restricted utilitarian has
to face the conflicts of duties so commonly supposed
to be fatal to the Kantian theory. There are either of
two possible courses open to him. One is to argue
that we should judge between the conflicting duties

in particular situations on the grounds of the value of the consequences of the respective *actions*. But this either amounts to the extreme utilitarian position, or at least exposes it to extension along the lines of making the consequences always relevant, as after all they really are. Alternatively, the restricted utilitarian could choose between the practices on the basis of the value of the practices. This would seem to be the consistent move; but it leads to the absurdity of always preferring one practice to another. For example, if it were determined that truth-telling is socially more valuable as a practice than promise-keeping, then in any conflict between these two activities it would always be obligatory to tell the truth and break a promise. This clearly is absurd, and no serious moral philosopher, utilitarian or otherwise, would be happy to accept a theory which led to this sort of conclusion. Further, there would remain the problem of what happens when two instances of the one rule conflict; for example, when two promises are in opposition, or when the truth at one level is incompatible with the truth at another level.

(3) This problem concerning the resolution of conflicts of duties brings to our notice another difficulty for restricted utilitarianism, [474] namely, the problem of how one is to determine the utilitarian value of the various alternative practices. Take punishment, for example. Is it clear, as Rawls assumes, that an institution of telishment would be bad on utilitarian grounds? Something of the sort appears to have been the prevailing institution in Russia since the Revolution, and it is not clear that it has been contrary to the public good. While I am no admirer of the U.S.S.R.—on moral grounds—I am nevertheless disposed to believe that the very great advances in that country since the Revolution and the alleviation of human misery over such vast areas of the world would not have been possible without the aid of some such

institution. Its utilitarian justification seems now to be diminishing, and the Russians appear to be acting as good utilitarians should, modifying the institution as the principle of utility requires. I may be wrong in this belief that such an institution had a utilitarian justification in the U.S.S.R.; at least it is arguable, but it is not seriously arguable that such an institution was morally unjustifiable in Russia whatever the empirical facts prove to be.

Further, we do not have to go to Russia to see that a system like telishment is possible, and possibly justifiable on utilitarian grounds. The people of Australia, guided by their prime minister, the Rt. Hon. R. G. Menzies, came very close to approving the introduction of a significant body of retrospective legislation. Punishment under retrospective legislation is punishment under quite a different institution to that in which one is punished only for offenses which are offenses at the time of the act. Punishment under retrospective legislation is a possible institution. The prime minister of Australia thought that it was a socially valuable institution. I am not qualified to judge whether he was right; but I suspect that he was right on the point of utility. Whether he was right on the point of utility or not, however, he was not so clearly right on the question of morals. But this is something a restricted utilitarian cannot afford to admit.

Similarly, laws such as those relating to punishment of habitual criminals, as well as those forbidding loitering with intent, alter the system from the kind which Rawls describes and which he suggests that we can justify on utilitarian grounds. The same [475] sort of arguments would seem to be applicable concerning the institution of slavery in ancient Greece. The latter institution, for the greater part of the time it prevailed, seems to have had a utilitarian justification; but it did not have a moral justification.

What it is important to stress here, however, is the difficulty of settling a dispute of the following kind: Is punishment or telishment the more valuable institution? Such a question is not an a priori question but an empirical one for which apparently there are considerations supporting each alternative. I am quite uncertain as to the solution of the empirical question, and I suggest that if we are honest with ourselves we all must admit to such uncertainty; yet I, and I suspect most other people, am not uncertain in the same way about the moral wrongness of telishment, and this surely is significant. It suggests a direct insight into the obligatoriness and disobligatoriness of certain kinds of activities—direct insight that can give us the assurance in our moral judgments that we have, but which we could not have if they were dependent upon the findings of an empirical enquiry. Ross and other intuitionists have been accused of being dogmatists by utilitarian writers; but the charge is totally unwarranted in most cases and is much more appropriate when directed against the restricted utilitarian philosophers themselves, for they are dogmatic about empirical matters concerning which they have very little evidence. It is an amazing thing, when one considers the importance of morality, to find that restricted utilitarians do virtually nothing toward defending their assumption that the current moral conventions are, in terms of utility, the morally best conventions; and further that these same moral philosophers do nothing toward entering into a general empirical enquiry in this sphere. (Mill would be an almost isolated exception, if he could properly be regarded as a restricted utilitarian.)

So much for our third objection. It would hold equally well against all varieties of restricted utilitarianism.

(4) A fourth criticism relates to the vagueness of the key concept in the restricted utilitarian theory—

the concept which is variously designated "social practice," "rule in practice," "institution," "principle," or simply "rule." This vagueness is [476] an important feature of the theory, and once it is eliminated the theory becomes much less plausible.

Rawls explains the notion of "a rule in practice" thus:

> In the case of actions specified by practices it is logically impossible to perform them outside the stage-setting provided by those practices for unless there is the practice, and unless the requisite properties are fulfilled whatever one does, whatever movements one makes, will fail to count as a form of action which the practice specifies. What one does will be described in some *other* way.
>
> One may illustrate this point from the game of baseball. . . . No matter what a person did, what he did would not be described as stealing a base or striking out or drawing a walk unless he could also be described as playing baseball, and for him to be doing this presupposes the rule-like practice which constitutes the game. *The practice is logically prior to particular cases; unless there is the practice, the terms referring to actions specified by it lack a sense.*

Rawls is here giving a correct account of one of the concepts of a "rule" required by the restricted utilitarian theory. One of the telling arguments of the restricted utilitarians is that various moral activities have their possibility and reality only in the context of a practice. Hence the need arises to ensure that there is a practice by conforming with it, at least on the whole.

Now, if Rawls is right—that the concept of "rules in practice" makes the practice logically prior to the action specified by it—then restricted utilitarianism is of assistance to the general utilitarian position in overcoming only some of the difficulties which beset extreme utilitarianism. Clearly not all of the activities claimed to be obligatory in their own right are such that they presuppose a general practice *to exist* as activities of a certain kind; and certainly they do not presuppose a general practice to be obligatory. Restricted utilitarianism arose out of an attempt to deal with the difficulties associated with the obligations relating to promise-keeping, truth-telling, repayment of debts, stealing, and punishment, and these are the difficulties the theory does appear to help to resolve. But there are other difficulties for extreme utilitarianism—difficulties associated with the obligations to perfect one's talents, to treat others as ends and not as means, not to kill, and so on. Whether or not there is a practice of not [477] killing others whenever we wish to do so, it is still prima facie wrong to kill, although where there is widespread disregard of the obligation, it may be permissible to kill more than in a society in which the established practice is not kill others. Further, murder and abstinence from murder are activities *logically prior* to a general practice and have a reality independent of a general practice in a way that promise-keeping does not. The same is true in respect of the duty not to treat others as mere means and of the duty to perfect our talents. These do not depend for their moral bindingness on their consequences, nor upon there being a general practice; hence if we are to treat others as means— and it is frequently necessary to do so—we need to have good reasons for doing so. The model of "rules" talk is promise-keeping and contracts generally. The "rules" talk is less effective with other prima facie duties, and with others again quite irrelevant.

The concept of a "rule in practice" elucidated by Rawls, while appropriate to a great deal of restricted utilitarian theory, is inappropriate for other parts of the writings of its exponents. A much vaguer concept is used. Clearly the sense in which the principle of utility can be thought of as a rule among rules cannot be the sense outlined by Rawls. The games analogy, popular with restricted utilitarians, brings out this confusion in the concept. It is a rule of football that if the ball is kicked between the center two posts at the end of the field it counts as a goal; and that a goal equals six behinds; that it is permissible to bump an opponent in the side but not in the back; that when a player is injured, and only when he is injured, he may be replaced by a reserve; and so on. It is a rule in practice, however, that a losing side replaces its weakest players in the last quarter, whether they are injured or not; that a team has a mascot; and so on. Now a careful consideration of the writings of restricted utilitarians brings out that there is an alternation between senses of rules corresponding roughly to these two senses of rule in football. For example, promise-keeping is a rule in practice in one sense; the next of kin caring for the aged is a rule in another sense of "rule"; and evading tax within the limits allowed by the law is a rule in practice in perhaps another sense again. Some points require one sense, some the other, and some, other senses again; but the theory requires a consistent sense. [478]

Another sense of "rule" to be noted here is such that a rule is simply equated with the principle of an action. Some utilitarians talk as if the practice aspect of the "rule in practice" is unimportant—that it is the principle of the action that is the relevant consideration, and further that there are some principles which on utilitarian grounds should be universalized. Hence, irrespective of the empirical fact as to whether an activity is practised or not, there are some principles, so it is argued, which, if they were generally practised, would be justifiable on utilitarian grounds, and these are those with which we should conform. The sole virtue of this contention is that it escapes the absurdity of implying that what is right or wrong and what is a good or a bad reason depends on the prevailing customs. To establish this kind of view—that it is the principle which counts, where the principle is one which would have utilitarian justification if it were a principle in practice—it has to be shown that conformity with the principle will help to bring about its general adoption and that the value of the act on this account is greater than the value of the consequences of a breach of the principle. This will not be the case very often, however; certainly it will not be the case often enough to permit a utilitarian theory to be established along these lines.

This means that the practice is what counts; *and it means that what constitutes a valid moral reason in support of an action depends on the cultural practice;* although it is true that it also means that what constitutes a valid reason in support of the practice itself is universal, unchanging, and objective. But the first conclusion is plainly false. The Spartan youths surely, while not morally blameworthy, were certainly mistaken in their moral conduct; and so too is the Soviet official who, in accord with the institution of "punishment" that prevails in Russia, frames an innocent individual; and so too were the Greek slave owners, the recent Nazi concentration-camp officers, and the contemporary Russian slave masters. To point to the practice is not to give a valid moral reason for holding another man in slavery.

The logic of the expression "valid moral reason" needs to be noted here. On the restricted utilitarian theory its logic would appear to run as follows: "X was a valid moral reason for owning [479] a slave in the fourth century B.C., but it is not a valid moral reason today." In fact the logic appears to be: "X was *thought to constitute a valid moral reason* for owning a slave by the Greeks of the fourth century B.C., but we see now that it was not a valid moral reason and that the Greeks were mistaken in the matter."

This point draws attention to a general difficulty for restricted utilitarianism, a difficulty which its exponents seem not to have considered because it has been concealed from them by the vagueness of their formulations of their theories. The difficulty springs from the fact that not all rules in practice are good utilitarian rules in practice nor the best utilitarian rules that could be rules in practice. What does the restricted utilitarian say about our duty in a society in which the rules in practice are not the best possible utilitarian rules, and perhaps not even rules justifiable at all on utilitarian grounds? The restricted utilitarian in fact seems to say nothing because he appears to have assumed that the rules in practice of Anglo-Saxon societies are the only rules that matter, and that these are good utilitarian rules in practice. On the whole they do seem to be good utilitarian rules, although many of them are by no means the best possible rules in practice. Examples of the latter probably include the prevailing rules relating to marriage, divorce, and sexual behavior generally; rules concerning the care of the aged by relations, if these may be called rules in practice; many systems of "punishment" in Anglo-Saxon countries; and the like. In any case, not all societies are Anglo-Saxon societies. Russia has its institutions of slave labor and "telishment"; Japan and the East their unutilitarian rules in practice. What is the moral agent's duty in these societies? The impression one gets from the writings of restricted utilitarians very strongly suggests conformity with the practice; and, after all, this is the impact this general account of ethics does have. Two answers are possible in terms of restricted utilitarianism, however, and both may be considered here.

We may consider first societies in which there are

both rules in practice which have no utilitarian justification and other rules which should positively be condemned on utilitarian grounds. To suggest that there should be conformity with such rules in practice and that to indicate the rule in practice is to give a good [480] moral reason for one's behavior would in most of these cases be to advocate blatant immorality. The Nazi rule in practice relating to treatment of Jews is a case in point; the Japanese practice of committing suicide to avoid dishonorable capture by the enemy is another case in point; and the many sacrificial practices of primitive religious groups are other examples. To point to the fact that one's action is in conformity with a rule in practice of one or other of these kinds is not to give an excuse or explanation which may exonerate the agent. Yet if it is suggested that the moral agent should not conform with these practices, what is the moral agent's duty in such a society? Should he be guided simply by the principle of utility itself, justifying his individual actions directly by reference to it? This is not an unreasonable answer, but it means that in such a society restricted utilitarianism is incapable of saving the general utilitarian position from attack along the lines indicated by critics such as Ross. Further, it means that it is up to the individual moral agent in each society to determine whether the various practices are justifiable utilitarian practices. Different conclusions will no doubt be reached by different agents about some of these practices.

Where the rules in practice are rules which have positive utilitarian justification but are nonetheless not the best rules in practice possible, the position is less clear. Some rules in practice are so much inferior to other possible rules in practice, even where the former have some utilitarian justification, that it is often positively immoral to condone the practice by conforming with it. Here the examples would depend on the sense of "rules in practice" used by the theory. On any usage examples are possible, but if the looser usage is adopted such that a rule in practice includes how people in fact behave and believe it to be clever to behave, then a multitude of examples becomes available. But quite apart from these cases, it is clear that conformity with the rule in practice, even where it is a good utilitarian rule or institution, such as telishment, is not necessarily the morally best action possible. If on the other hand it is maintained that conformity with the practice is only morally right where the rule in practice is the best possible utilitarian rule, then this same criticism may still be urged. In addition, two other criticisms become relevant. [481] If we should be right in conforming only when the practice is the best possible utilitarian practice, we should not often be able, in order to have a good moral reason, to point to the fact that we are conforming with a practice. That is to say, the move that characterizes restricted utilitarianism could seldom be made; and equally important, it could rarely be known that it could be made. It is unlikely, however, that any restricted utilitarian would maintain that we should conform only with the best possible practices.

Most of the points made here as our fourth objection to restricted utilitarianism may be well illustrated by reference to sexual morality. In the sphere of sexual behavior we find a clear distinction between the moral rule in practice and the behavior in practice. Further, we find, as modern investigators such as Kinsey have confirmed, that within one community there are different moral codes, or in the language of restricted utilitarianism, different rules in practice. The state in terms of its laws and sanctions recognizes one system of rules in practice; but this system may not coincide with those of any one group within the state. Which of these various practices is the restricted utilitarian's rule in practice? To which does one have to point to have a good moral reason for one's behavior? Some of these rules in practice have a better utilitarian justification than others; some have little utilitarian justification by contrast with others; but all have some utilitarian justification, because practically any code of sexual behavior is better than none. Is conformity the right thing, and does it or does it not matter which of these rules or set of rules is the set of rules in practice?

These objections apply with equal force against all varieties of the restricted theory, although the objection relating to the equivocation in the use of the expression "rule" is of special importance in respect to the mixed restricted utilitarian theories.

(5) Finally, it needs to be noted that it is difficult, in terms of the criterion used by restricted utilitarians, to distinguish in the way in which we do between *nonmoral* and *moral* practices. The test of a moral practice—that it is a *moral* practice and therefore a basis for valid moral reasons—would seem to be either that it is conducive to good consequences or that it is [482] thought so to be. If the former is the test, then many so-called nonmoral and even immoral practices, for example keeping to the left and possibly even slavery in the U.S.S.R., should be regarded as moral; and some so-called moral practices should perhaps be denied the name. If on the other hand the criterion is that the practice is generally thought to be productive of good consequences, then many important, genuinely moral practices would not qualify for the title, and some nonmoral practices would qualify. If we make the fact the criterion, we can seldom be sure that a practice is a moral practice; if we make the belief the criterion, then it would be surprising if many practices qualified. People just do not think or have opinions about the utilitarian value of institu-

tions like promise-keeping, truth-telling, and so on. Further, it would seem to follow from the theory that many principles—the so-called prudential maxims—should be elevated to the level of moral practices; but clearly whether so elevated or not, prudential maxims would remain of a significantly different moral status from the principles of promise-keeping, truth-telling, and so on.

Many other objections could be urged against restricted utilitarianism; but the objections already developed are sufficient to bring out that the distinction between justifying a practice and justifying an action falling under the practice will not do for utilitarianism what the exponents of restricted utilitarianism claim that it will do. It does not provide a means of saving utilitarianism as a tenable ethical theory.

As we have seen, most of the objections indicated above are fatal not only to the claims of the pure version but of all versions of restricted utilitarianism. It is worth while, however, to examine briefly the more complex varieties, since it may be thought that they have special merits which enable them to provide a more sure basis for utilitarianism.

The mixed version, as we have seen, admits the principle of utility as a secondary principle while putting it up also as the primary principle which provides the justification of the secondary principles. It will at once be noticed that this complicates the account of the relation between the primary and secondary [483] principles and obscures the concept of "rule" in the way already indicated. Clearly the sense in which promises are dependent for their reality upon the existence of the practice is different from the sense in which we can have a rule or practice of producing good. It is a theoretically possible version of utilitarianism, however, and one which escapes two absurdities to which the pure restricted theory leads, namely, that we should always conform with the rule and that we have no duties except those falling under the rules (in Rawls's sense of "rule"). Further, it is a version of which John Austin appears to have been an unwilling adherent and of which Toulmin is a lukewarm exponent. Toulmin's lukewarmness consists in the fact that while he is prepared to insist on the relevance of the principle of utility in all situations involving moral obligations, thereby treating it as a secondary as well as the primary principle, he is unwilling to treat it as a secondary principle of *duty*. Thus his particular theory is exposed to one of the absurdities of the pure theory—that there are no duties where there are no rules in Rawls's sense of "rule"—and also to the difficulties which are encountered by the mixed theory. These include the difficulties relating to the concept of rule and to the relation between the primary principle and the secondary rules. Toulmin suggests that this is the variety of utilitarianism he is adopting in various places, including the section in which he discusses the issue of conflicts of duties.[6]

It is difficult to argue against this variety of the theory except in terms of the general objections to restricted utilitarianism already noted. This is not because of any special virtue of this variety, nor for the reason wrongly advanced by Smart—that this version represents a collapse of restricted utilitarianism into the extreme theory—but simply because of its indefiniteness. In theory mixed restricted utilitarianism does represent a different theory from extreme utilitarianism. In practice it is difficult to determine whether the two have been assimilated. Unless we are told how to weigh the practice against the consequences and how much weight to attribute to the

---

6 Stephen Toulmin, *The Place of Reason in Ethics* (New York, 1950), pp. 147–148.

practice qua practice, it is difficult [484] to know how the mixed version works out in detail and whether its exponent has or has not fallen back into the out-moded extreme utilitarian calculus. Toulmin gives us no help in this matter, and the same seems to have been true of Austin. This means that no new objections relating specifically to this variety of utilitarianism can be developed here. Of those objections already indicated, however, 1, 3, 4, and 5 may effectively be pressed against it.

The conditional varieties of restricted utilitarianism are also difficult to appraise. This is because they too are so vaguely stated that they could imply anything at all. My impression is that if all the exceptions and conditions hinted at by some utilitarians as being part of the practice are indeed part of the practice, then there is little left of the practice at all. It is difficult to see that we can do justice to the special cases in which we break promises with justification on utilitarian grounds by saying, as is suggested by exponents of these varieties, that we are really not going against the practice. We *are* going against the practice. When we make a promise we are not accepting an obligation to act in a certain way except where there are good consequences resulting from an alternative action; and where we do break a promise on this sort of ground we think of ourselves as having and facing a conflict, and not of puzzling over what the practice is. The conditional amendment of the theory seems to detract from all that is introduced into utilitarianism by restricted utilitarianism, namely, by the admission of the moral significance of promises (and the like) which have no direct utilitarian justification and which would appear to be overriden by utilitarian considerations. These varieties are too vague and elusive to discuss in detail, however, and their rejection must be based on the general objections to restricted utilitarianism already noted. Nevertheless, once they are made more precise, additional specific objections could be urged against them. It is worth recording here that it is probably not without significance that the most notable utilitarians have not only not adopted the conditional variety but have in fact positively denied its central thesis.

It is now necessary simply to point out that some sort of synthesis of restricted and extreme utilitarianism will not provide [485] a solution to the difficulties which appear to be fatal to the claims of each theory. Extreme utilitarianism breaks down at points at which the restricted theory is unable to offer any assistance, for example, in respect to the duty to refrain from killing; and further, restricted utilitarianism, besides having fatal intrinsic defects, also has the defects of relating only to some duties and only to some societies, and then not to all the rules in practice in these societies. Utilitarianism therefore breaks down as an account of our moral obligations; and it breaks down because it is unsuccessful in accounting for the obligatoriness of those activities singled out by Ross as activities which are intrinsically obligatory.

TOWARD A CREDIBLE
FORM
OF UTILITARIANISM
Richard B. Brandt

Introduction

This paper is an attempt to formulate, in a tolerably precise way, a type of utilitarian ethical theory which is not open to obvious and catastrophic objections. It is not my aim especially to advocate the kind of view finally stated, although I do believe it is more acceptable than any other type of utilitarianism.

Utilitarianism is a topic discussed by contemporary moralists in either, or both, of two contexts. One of these contexts is that of traditional normative discussion of the correct answer to such questions as "What do all right actions have in common?" Many linguistically oriented philosophers do not believe such questions are a proper subject for philosophical discussion, but noncognitivists in metaethics can, as well as anyone else, consistently defend (or criticize) a

Reprinted from *Morality and the Language of Conduct* edited by Hector-Neri Castañeda and George Nakhnikian by permission of the Wayne State University Press. Copyright © 1963 by Wayne State University Press. Also used by permission of the author. The footnotes which originally occurred at the end of the article on pages 141–143 have been placed at the bottom of pages.

utilitarian normative ethic, not claiming that such a
theory is strictly true but nevertheless offering arguments of a kind.

Utilitarianism also plays a substantial part in contemporary [108] metaethical discussions. If you ask
some philosophers what can count as a good or valid
reason for an ethical judgment, you may be told that
some kind of utilitarian reason—inference from good
consequences to rightness—is one kind, or even the
only kind. This view may be supported by urging
that this is the kind of reasoning people actually do
use, or by saying that this is the kind of reasoning
used in reflective moments by people whom we
should count as reliable moral judges. Alternatively, it
may be argued that this kind of reasoning is the
kind that should be used—regardless of whether it is
used—in view of the function of ethical reasoning
and conscience in society, or in view of what counts
as a "moral judgment" or as "moral reasoning" or as
"justified ethical reasoning."

Discussions of utilitarianism in these two contexts are not as different as might at first appear. If
some kind of utilitarian reasoning can be shown to
be what reflective people do use, or if it can be
shown to be the kind all ought to use, then presumably utilitarianism as a normative position—as
the one "valid" principle in normative ethics—can be
established, in the way we can expect to establish
such things in ethics.

The formulation of utilitarianism I shall work out in
this paper, then, can be viewed in either of two
ways, corresponding with the persuasions of the
reader. It can be viewed as a candidate for the status
of normative "truth," or, for the noncognitivist, for
whatever status is in his theory the analogue of truth
in cognitivist theories. Or it can be viewed as a way
of thinking or reasoning, as a rule of valid inference—
the central theme either of considerations which play

a role in the ethical inferences of reliable moral judges, or of considerations which would play a certain role in ethical thinking if we thought as we ought to do, in view of the functions (etc.) of ethical discourse. One way of putting the contrast is this: we can view our formulation either as a candidate for the status of being a true principle of normative ethics or as a rule for valid inferences in ethics. I am not, incidentally, suggesting that it is a merely terminological matter which view we take of it; I think it is *not* merely this, since the kinds of reasoning used to support one view may be [109] quite different from those used to support the other view. My point is that the theory I wish to discuss may properly be considered in either light, and that the difficulties I shall raise are difficulties which must be taken seriously by philosophers who discuss utilitarianism in either of these contexts. Mostly, I shall talk for convenience as if utilitarianism were a normative principle; but everything I say, and all the difficulties I consider, can just as well be placed in the context of meta-ethical discussion.

The view to be discussed is a form of "rule-utilitarianism." This terminology must be explained. I call a utilitarianism "act-utilitarianism" if it holds that the rightness of an act is fixed by the utility of *its* consequences, as compared with those of other acts the agent might perform instead. Act-utilitarianism is hence an atomistic theory: the value of the effects of a single act on the world is decisive for its rightness. "Rule-utilitarianism," in contrast, applies to views according to which the rightness of an act is not fixed by *its* relative utility, but by conformity with general rules or principles; the utilitarian feature of these theories consists in the fact that the correctness of these rules or principles is fixed in some way by the utility of their general acceptance. In contrast with the atomism of act-utilitarianism, rule-utilitarianism is in a sense an organic theory: the rightness of individual acts can be ascertained only by assessing a whole social policy.

Neither form of utilitarianism is necessarily committed on the subject of what counts as "utility": not on the meaning or function of such phrases as "maximize intrinsic good," and not on the identity of intrinsic goods—whether enjoyments, or states of persons, or states of affairs, such as equality of distribution.

In recent years, types of rule-utilitarianism have been the object of much interest.[1] And for good reason. Act-utilitarianism, at least given the assumptions about what is valuable which utilitarians commonly make, has implications which it is difficult to accept.[2] It implies that if you have employed a boy

---

[1] In one form or another its plausibility has been urged by J. O. Urmson, Kurt Baier, J. D. Mabbott, Stephen Toulmin, R. F. Harrod, Kai Neilsen, A. MacBeath, C. A. Campbell, Jonathan Harrison, Marcus Singer, and, to some extent, John Rawls and P. H. Nowell-Smith. Mabbott has expressed the opinion that the essence of it is to be found in Francis Hutcheson.

[2] In this paper I propose to ignore that form of act-utilitarianism which proposes to close the gap between what seems to be right and the implications of act-utilitarianism, by asserting that such things as promise-keeping are intrinsically good. This form of theory has most recently been defended by Oliver Johnson in his *Rightness and Goodness* (The Hague: Martinus Nijhoff, 1959).

I am inclined to agree that there are some intrinsically good things which are not states of persons—for instance, equality of distribution of welfare. But act-utilitarians require to count further things—such as specific traits of character like truthfulness, or complexes like the-keeping-of-a-promise—as intrinsically good in order to square with reasonable convictions about what is right or wrong. But surely it is contrary to the spirit of utilitarianism to decide the issue, say, whether a promise should be kept by appeal to such intrinsic values. One

to mow your lawn and he has finished the job and asks for his pay, you should pay him what you promised only if you cannot find [110] a better use for your money. It implies that when you bring home your monthly pay-check you should use it to support your family and yourself only if it cannot be used more effectively to supply the needs of others. It implies that if your father is ill and has no prospect of good in his life, and maintaining him is a drain on the energy and enjoyments of others, then, if you can end his life without provoking any public scandal or setting a bad example, it is your positive duty to take matters into your own hands and bring his life to a close. A virtue of rule-utilitarianism, in at least some

---

would have thought the utilitarian would test the merits of traits of character like truthfulness by examining whether they have good consequences rather than decide that there is an obligation to tell the truth by considering the intrinsic goodness of truthfulness. Should not the issue of the intrinsic goodness of truthfulness wait upon reasoning to show that it is a good thing to tell the truth? One who denies this is far from traditional utilitarian thought. In any case, can we seriously claim that the-keeping-of-a-promise is an intrinsic good? It would be absurd to hold that we can add to the value of the world by the simple device of making promises and then keeping them, irrespective of what is effected by the keeping of them. Presumably, then, what is held is rather that the-breaking-of-a-promise is intrinsically bad. But how will it be shown that precisely this is intrinsically bad? Suppose I promise to do something no one wants done, and everyone is greatly relieved when I fail to perform. Is this intrinsically evil?

The kind of utilitarianism I propose here to discuss is one with narrower commitments about what is intrinsically good —one which does not claim that specific kinds of action or specific traits of character (like truthfulness or fidelity) are intrinsically good or bad. This kind of utilitarianism is worth assessment even if my reasons for ignoring other types are unsound.

of its forms, is that it avoids at least some of such objectionable implications.

In the present paper I wish to arrive at a more precise formulation of a rule-utilitarian type of theory which is different from act-utilitarianism and which is not subject to obvious and catastrophic difficulties. To this end I shall, after an important preliminary discussion, begin by considering two formulations, both supported by distinguished philosophers, which, as I shall show, lead us in the wrong direction. This discussion will lead to a new formulation devised to avoid the consequences of the first theories. I shall then describe three problems which the new theory seems to face, and consider how—by amendments or otherwise—these difficulties may be met.

I

Utilitarianism as a Theory About the Objectively Right

Before we can proceed there is a preliminary issue to be settled. It is generally agreed that utilitarianism is a proposal about which acts are *right* or *wrong*. Unfortunately it is also widely held—although this is a matter of dispute—that these terms are used in several senses. Hence, in order to state the utilitarian thesis clearly, we must identify which sense of these words (if there is more than one) we have in mind. Utilitarianism may be clearly false in all of its forms if it is construed as a universal statement about which acts are right or wrong, in some of the senses in which these words are, or at least are supposed to be, used. [111]

It is plausible to say that "wrong" is sometimes used in a sense equivalent to "morally blameworthy" or "reprehensible," in a sense which implies the propriety of disapproval of the agent for his deed. Now, if utilitarianism is understood as a theory about right and wrong actions in this sense, I believe it is an indefensible theory in all its forms. For we have good reason to think that whether an act is wrong in this sense depends in part on such things as whether the agent sincerely believed he was doing his duty, whether the temptation to do what he did was so strong that only a person of very unusual firmness of will would have succeeded in withstanding it, and whether the agent's action was impulsive and provoked, or deliberate and unprovoked. If whether an act is wrong depends in part on any one of these factors, then it is difficult to see how the utilitarian thesis that rightness or wrongness is in some sense a function of utility can be correct.

We can, however, construe utilitarianism as a thesis about which acts are right or wrong in some other sense. It may, for instance, be taken as a theory about which acts are right or wrong in a forward-looking sense, which I shall call the "objective" sense. But what is this sense? It is by no means easy to say; and we must be careful not to describe some alleged sense of these words which in fact they never bear in common speech at all. Let me explain this possible second sense by means of an example.

Consider Eisenhower's position at the summit conference in 1960. Khrushchev demanded that Eisenhower apologize, as a condition for negotiation. Let us suppose that Eisenhower proceeded to ask himself the moral question, "What is the morally right thing for me to do now? Is it my moral obligation to apologize or to refuse to apologize?" Clearly, it would seem, this is a question he might have asked himself, whether he did or not. Obviously, if he did try to answer this question, he must have considered many things. One thing he must have considered was the state of Khrushchev's mind. Did Khrushchev really think there had been a breach of faith, an affront to the Russian people, which in decency called for at least an apology? Was [112] Khrushchev really willing to negotiate for peace if only this—which might relieve some political pressures at home—were done? Everything considered, would an apology, however personally distasteful (and perhaps politically unfortunate, at home), markedly promote the cause of peace? Let us suppose that Eisenhower surveyed these points as carefully as possible with his advisers and came to a conclusion on them. And let us suppose that he then moved to a moral conclusion. Presumably his conclusion (if he raised the moral question) was that it was not his duty to apologize, that on the contrary it was his duty *not* to apologize. But surely in a complex situation of this sort he must have put his conclusion in a qualified way; he must have said something like, "*Probably* it is my duty not to apologize." And, conceivably, he might some day change his mind about this, and say to himself, "It was my duty to apologize; my judgment then was mistaken." I think we shall all agree that he might well have expressed himself in this qualified way and that he might later revise his judgment in the manner suggested.

The crucial thing about understanding the sense in which "duty" (or "wrong") is here being used is whether the qualifying "probably" is introduced or whether the revision conceding a "mistake" may be made, for one reason or for another. Does he say "probably" because he does not and cannot know Khrushchev's real state of mind? Does he say a "mistake" was made because, as it turns out, Khrushchev's state of mind was really different from what at the time he supposed it to be? If the answer to these questions is affirmative, then evidently duty depends, at least to some extent, on what the facts really are and not merely on what one thinks they are, even after careful consultation with advisers. But if the answer is negative, then it is open to one to say that the qualification and mistakes come in only because it is so difficult to *balance* different considerations, and that what is one's duty does not depend on what the facts really are, but only on what one thinks they are, at least after properly careful reflection and investigation.

If we answer these questions in the affirmative and consequently say that "duty" is sometimes used in a sense such that [113] whether something is one's duty depends on what the facts really are, then we are conceding that the word (and, presumably, "right" and "wrong" and "moral obligation") is sometimes used in an "objective" sense—the sense in which G. E. Moore thought it was sometimes used when he wrote *Ethics* and *Principia Ethica*. And if so, it is not entirely stupid to propose, as Moore did, that furthermore, an act is right, in that objective sense of "right," if and only if its *actual* consequences, whether foreseeable at the time or not, are such that the performance of the act produces at least as much intrinsic good as could be produced by any other act the agent could perform instead. It is this sense of these terms—the sense in which duty (etc.) depends on what the facts really are and not on what the agent thinks about them—which I am terming the "objective" sense. I shall construe utilitarianism as a proposal about which acts are right or wrong in this objective sense.

It would be foolish, however, to say that it is quite *obvious* that the answer to the above questions is in the affirmative; and consequently it would be foolish to affirm without doubt that there is a sense of "duty" in which duty depends on what the facts are and not on what the agent thinks they are—and much more foolish to affirm without doubt that there is *no* sense of "duty" in which duty depends, not on the facts, but on what the agent thinks the facts are, at least after properly careful investigation.

Philosophers who think these words have no "objective" sense at all, or who at least think there is still a third sense of these terms, over and above the two I have sketched, probably can mostly be said to think that these words are used in what we may call the "subjective" sense—and either that this is their only sense or that it is one ordinary sense. They do not agree among themselves about what this sense is. Some of them hold that "right" (etc.) is sometimes so used that—if I may identify their conception by my own terminology, which, of course, some of them would not accept—an act is right in that sense if and only if it would have been right in my objective sense, if the facts had really been what the agent thought they were, or at least [114] would have thought they were if he had investigated properly. What is one's duty, on this view, depends on what the agent thinks about the facts—or would think if he investigated properly—not on what the facts really are. Naturally, if one has this (alleged) sense of "duty" or "right" in mind when formulating the principle of utilitarianism, one will say the principle is that an act is right if and only if the agent *thinks*—or would think, if he investigated properly—it will maximize utility (or have some such relation to utility). Or, perhaps, the principle will say that an act is right if and only if it will maximize expectable utility, or something of the sort.

The question whether there is an objective sense, or a subjective sense, or perhaps both such senses, is a difficult one. Although I think it plausible to suppose there is an "objective" sense, I do feel doubt about the matter. I propose, nevertheless, to discuss utilitarianism as a theory about right and wrong in this sense. I do so for several reasons. First, there are many philosphers who think there is such a sense, and an examination of utilitarianism construed in this way "speaks to their condition."[3] Second, even if there were no such ordinary sense of "right," we could define such a sense by reference to the "subjective" sense of "right" (assuming there is one); and it so happens that we could say all the things that we have occasion to say in ethics by using this defined "objective" sense of "right" and also terms like "blameworthy" and "reprehensible." We could say "all we have occasion to say" in the sense that any statement we make, and think important, could be put in terms of this vocabulary. Third, it is important to see how types of rule-utilitarian theory fare if they are construed as theories about which acts are right or wrong in this sense. Doubtless sometimes writers on this topic have not kept clearly in mind just which sense of "right" they were talking about; it is useful to see what difficulties arise *if* they are to be taken as talking of what is right or wrong in the objective sense. Finally, an assessment of utilitarianisms as theories about which acts are objectively right will enable us to make at least some assessments of utilitarianisms as theories about which acts are subjectively right, in view of the logical connection [115] indicated above between "right" in the objective sense and "right" in the subjective sense.

---

[3] Notice that such philosophers are not refuted by the mere consideration that sometimes we say "is right" and not "is probably right" even when we know we lack evidence about some facts that might be relevant to what is right in the objective sense. It would be a mistake to infer from such usage that we are not employing "right" in the objective sense. For, in general, we are entitled to make any assertion roundly without the qualifying word "probable" if we know of no definite grounds for questioning the truth of the assertion.

2

Accepted Rules vs. Justifiable Rules
as the Test of Rightness

It is convenient to begin by taking as our text some statements drawn from an interesting article by J. O. Urmson. In this paper, Urmson suggested that John Stuart Mill should be interpreted as a rule-utilitarian; and Urmson's opinion was that Mill's view would be more plausible if he were so interpreted. Urmson summarized the possible rule-utilitarian interpretation of Mill in four propositions, of which I quote the first two:

A. A particular action is justified as being right [in the sense of being morally obligatory] by showing that it is in accord with [is required by] some moral rule. It is shown to be wrong by showing that it transgresses some moral rule.
B. A moral rule is shown to be correct by showing that the recognition of that rule promotes the ultimate end.[4]

Urmson's first proposition could be taken in either of two ways. When it speaks of a "moral rule," it may refer to an *accepted* moral rule, presumably one accepted in the society of the agent. Alternatively, it may refer to a *correct* moral rule, presumably one the recognition of which promotes the ultimate end. If we ask in which way the proposed theory should be taken, in order to arrive at a defensible theory,

---

[4] J. O. Urmson, "The Interpretation of the Moral Philosophy of J. S. Mill," *Philosophical Quarterly*, Vol. III (1953), 33–39 [reprinted in this volume, pp. 13–24].

part of the answer is that qualifications are going to be required, whichever way we take it. I think it more worthwhile and promising, however, to try to develop it in the second interpretation.

Various philosophers would make the opposite judgment about which interpretation is the more promising. And there is much to be said for their view, in particular the following points. First, we shall probably all agree that the moral rules accepted in a community often do fix real obligations on members of the community. For example, among ourselves it is taken for granted that primary responsibility for caring for an old man [116] falls on his children, although in special cases it could fall elsewhere. On the other hand, suppose that our social system contained the rule—as that of the Hopi actually does—that this responsibility falls primarily on the children of a man's sisters, again with exceptions for special cases. It seems clear that in a social system like ours the children do have responsibility for their father, whereas in a social system like that of the Hopi they do not—the responsibility belongs to the children of the sisters. There are complications, to be sure; but in general we must say that when an institutional system specifies that responsibility falls in a certain place, then on the whole and with some exceptions and qualifications, that is where it really does lie. Any theory which denies this is mistaken; and if our second theory is to be plausible, it must be framed so as to imply this. Second, I think we should concede that if two persons are debating whether some act is right and one of them is able to show that it infringes on the accepted moral code of the community, the "burden of proof" passes to the other party. The fact that it is generally believed that a certain kind of action is wrong is prima facie evidence that it is wrong; it is up to persons who disagree to show their hand. Third, if a conscientious man is

deliberating whether he is morally obligated to do a
certain thing which he does not wish to do, I believe
he will generally feel he must do this thing, even
if he thinks that a correct moral code would not
require him to, provided he concludes that many or
most persons in his community would conclude otherwise. The reason for this is partly, I think, that a
conscientious man will take pains to avoid even the
appearance of evil; but the reason is also that a
conscientious man will wish to make substantial al-
lowances for the fact that he is an interested party
and might have been influenced by his own prefer-
ences in his thinking about his obligations. He will
therefore tend to hold himself to the received code
when this is to his disadvantage.

Nevertheless, it is extremely difficult to defend
Urmson's rule interpreted in this way, even when we
hedge it with qualifications, as, for example, Toulmin
did. In the first place, people [117] do not *think* that
anything like this is true; they think they are assessing
particular cases by reference to objectively valid principles which they happen to know, and not simply
by reference to a community code. Notice how we
do not find it surprising that people with unusual
moral principles, such as the immorality of killing
and violence in all circumstances, come to distinctive conclusions about their own particular obligations, by no means drawing their particular moral
judgments from the code of the community. The
whole tradition emphasizing the role of conscience
in moral thinking is contrary to the view that socially
accepted principles are crucial for deciding what is
right or wrong. In the second place, we frequently
judge ourselves to have moral obligations either when
we don't know what the community "standards" are,
or when we think that in all probability there is
no decided majority one way or the other: for instance, with respect to sexual behavior, or to declara-

tion, to revenue officers, of articles purchased abroad or of one's personal income. Surely we do not think that in such situations the proper judgment of particular cases is that they are morally indifferent? Third, and perhaps most important, we sometimes judge that we have an obligation when we know that the community thinks we don't; and we sometimes think an act is right when the community thinks it wrong. For instance, we may judge that we have an obligation to join in seeking presidential clemency for a convicted Communist spy whom we regard as having received an unduly severe sentence because of mass hysteria at the time of his trial, although we know quite well that the communal code prescribes no favors for Communists. Again, we may think it not wrong to work on the Sabbath, marry a divorced person, perform a medically necessary abortion, or commit suicide, irrespective of general disapproval in our group. Were these things *ever* objectively wrong, in view of being proscribed—even unanimously—by the community of the agent? (It may be replied that the "code" does not legislate for complex matters of these sorts, but only for more basic things, like Ross's list of prima facie obligations. But it is not clear what [118] can be the basis for this distinction; the acts in question may be prohibited by law and would be reported by a visiting anthropologist as proscribed by the code.)

One might argue that the existence of an accepted moral rule is not sufficient to make particular actions wrong or obligatory but is a necessary condition. To say this, however, is to say that men have no obligation to rise above the commonplace morals of their times. Whereas in fact we do not think it right for men to be cruel to animals or to slaves in a society which condones this.

We cannot well say in advance that no thesis like Urmson's can play an important part in a defensible theory of morals, if it is interpreted in this first way. But the difficulties are surely enough to encourage experimenting with versions of the second interpretation. Let us turn to this.

For a start, we might summarize the gist of Urmson's proposal, construed in the second way, as follows: "An act is right if and only if it conforms with that set of moral rules, the recognition of which would have significantly desirable consequences." A somewhat modified version of this is what I shall be urging.

One minor amendment I wish to make immediately. I think we should replace the second clause by the expression, "the recognition of which would have the *best* consequences." This amendment may be criticized on the ground that the business of moral rules is with commanding or prohibiting actions whose performance or omission would be quite harmful if practiced widely, but not to require actions which just maximize benefits, especially if the benefit concerns only the agent. It may be said, then, that the amendment I propose is possibly a clue to *perfect* behavior but not to right behavior. But this objection overlooks an important point. We must remember that it is a serious matter to have a moral rule at all, for moral rules take conduct out of the realm of preference and free decision. So, for the recognition of a certain moral rule to have good consequences, the benefits of recognition must outweigh the costliness of restricting freedom. [119] Therefore, to recognize a moral rule restricting self-regarding behavior will rarely have the best consequences; rules of prudence should normally not be moral rules. Again, my proposal implies that moral rules will require services for other people only when it is better to have such services performed from a sense of obligation than not performed at all; so the amendment does not commit us to saying that it is morally obligatory to perform minor altruistic services for others.

But why insist on the amendment? The reason is that the original, as I stated it (but not necessarily as Urmson intended it), is insufficiently comparative in form. The implication is that a rule is acceptable so long as it is significantly better than no regulation at all. But the effect of this is tolerantly to accept a great many rules which we should hardly regard as morally acceptable. Consider promises. There are various possible rules about when promises must be kept. One such possible rule is to require keeping *all* promises, absolutely irrespective of unforeseeable and uncontemplated hardships on the promisee. Recognition of this rule might have good consequences as compared with no rule at all. Therefore it seems to satisfy the unamended formula. Many similar rules would satisfy it. But we know of another rule—the one we recognize—with specifications about allowable exceptions, which would have much better consequences. If we are utilitarian in spirit, we shall want to endorse such a rule but not both of these rules; and the second one is much closer to our view about what our obligations are. The amendment in general endorses as correct many rules which command our support for parallel reasons, and refuses to endorse many others which we reject for parallel reasons.

3
A Specious Rule-utilitarianism

I shall now digress briefly, in order to bring out the importance of avoiding a form of rule-utilitarianism which seems to differ only insignificantly from

our above initial suggestion, [120] and which at first
seems most attractive. It is worthwhile doing so,
partly because two very interesting and important
papers developing a rule-utilitarian theory may be
construed as falling into the trap I shall describe.[5] I
say only that they "may be" so construed because
their authors are possibly using somewhat different
concepts and, in particular, may not be thinking of
utilitarianism as a thesis about right and wrong in the
objective sense.

Suppose that we wrote, instead of the above suggested formulation, the following: "An act is right if
and only if it conforms with that set of moral rules,
general conformity with which would have best consequences." This phrasing is a bit vague, however,
so let us expand it to this: "An act is right if
and only if it conforms with that set of general
prescriptions for action such that, if everyone always
did, from among all the things which he could do on
a given occasion, what conformed with these prescriptions, then at least as much intrinsic good would be
produced as by conformity with any other set of
general prescriptions." This sounds very like our above
formulation. It is, however, different in a very important way: for its test of whether an act is right,
or a general rule correct, is what would happen
if people *really all did act* in a certain way. The
test is not the consequences of recognizing a rule,
or of acting with such a rule in mind; the test as
stated does not require that people do, or even can,
think of or formulate, much less apply the rule of a
moral code. What is being said is simply that a rule

---

[5] These articles are: J. Harrison, "Utilitarianism, Universalisation, and Our Duty to Be Just," *Proceedings of the Aristotelian Society*, Vol. LIII (1952–53), pp. 105–134 [reprinted in
this volume, pp. 25–57]; and R. F. Harrod, "Utilitarianism
Revised," *Mind*, n.s. XLV (1936), 137–156.

is correct, and corresponding conduct right, if it would have best consequences for everyone actually to act, for whatever reason, in accordance with the rule. Of course, one of the consequences to be taken into account may be the fact that expectations of conduct according to the rule might be built up, and that people could count on conforming behavior.

This theory is initially attractive. We seem to be appealing to it in our moral reasoning when we say, "You oughtn't to do so-and-so, because if everybody in your circumstances did this, the consequences would be bad."

Nevertheless, the fact is that this theory—however hard it may be to see that it does—has identically the same consequences [121] for behavior as does act-utilitarianism. And since it does, it is a mistake to advocate it as a theory preferable to act-utilitarianism, as some philosophers may have done. Let us see how this is.

Let us ask ourselves: What would a set of moral prescriptions be like, such that general conformity with it, in the sense intended, would have the best consequences? The answer is that the set would contain just one rule, the prescription of the *act-utilitarians:* "Perform an act, among those open to you, which will have at least as good consequences as any other." There cannot be a moral rule, conformity with which could have better consequences than this one. If it really is true that doing a certain thing will have the very best consequences in the long run, everything considered, of all the things I can do, then there is nothing better I can do than this. If everyone always did the very best thing it was possible for him to do, the total intrinsic value produced would be at a maximum. Any act which deviated from this principle would produce less good than some other act which might have been performed. It is clear, then, that the moral rule general conformity with which would produce most good is a rule corresponding to the principle of act-utilitarianism. The two theories, then, have identical consequences for behavior. I am, of course, not at all suggesting that everyone *trying* to produce the best consequences will have the same consequences as everyone *trying* to follow some different set of rules—or that everyone trying to follow some different set of rules may not have better consequences than everyone trying just to produce the best consequences. Far from it. What I am saying is that *succeeding* in producing the best consequences is a kind of success which cannot be improved upon. And it is this which is in question, when we are examining the formula we are now looking at.

To say that succeeding in producing the best consequences cannot be improved upon is consistent with admitting that what will in fact have the best consequences, in view of what other people in fact have done or will do, may be different from what would have had the best consequences if other people were to behave differently from the way in which they did or will do. [122] The behavior of others is part of the context relevant for determining the effects of a given act of any agent.

It may be thought that this reasoning is unfair to this rule-utilitarian view. For what this theory has in mind, it may be said, is rules forbidding classes of actions described in ways other than by reference to their utility—rules forbidding actions like lies, adultery, theft, etc. So, it may be said, the principle of act-utilitarianism is not even a competitor for the position of one of the rules admitted by this theory.

My reply to this objection is twofold. In the first place, it would be rather foolish to suppose that any system of moral rules could omit rules about doing good, rules about doing what will maximize utility. Surely we do wish to include among our rules one roughly to the effect that, if we have the opportunity to do a great deal of good for others at little cost, we should do it. And also a rule to the effect that we should avoid harming others. It is no accident that W. D. Ross's list of seven prima facie obligations contains four which refer to doing good, in one way or another. But the point would still stand even if we ignore this fact. For suppose we set about to describe a set of rules, none of which is explicitly to prescribe *doing good*, but general conformity with which will maximize utility. Now obviously, the set of rules in question will be that set which prescribes, by descriptions which make no reference to having good consequences, exactly that very class of actions which would also be prescribed by the act-utilitarian principle. And one can find a set of rules which will prescribe exactly this class of acts without referring to utility. We can find such a set, because every member of the class of acts prescribed by the act-utilitarian principle will have some other property *on account of which* it will maximize utility in the circumstances. Every act, that is to say, which maximizes utility does so because of some doubtless very complex property that it has. As a result, we can set up a system of prescriptions for action which refer to these complex properties, such that our system of rules will prescribe exactly the set of acts prescribed by the act-utilitarian principle. The set of rules may be enormously long and enormously complex. [123] But this set of rules will have the property of being that set, general conformity with which will maximize utility. And the acts prescribed will be identical with the acts prescribed by the act-utilitarian principle. So, again, the prescriptions for conduct of this form of rule-utilitarianism are identical with those of the act-utilitarian theory.

4
Rule-utilitarianism:
A Second Approximation

The whole point of the preceding remarks has been to focus attention on the point that a rule-utilitarianism like Urmson's is different from act-utilitarianism only when it speaks of something like "*recognition* of a rule having the best consequences" instead of something like "*conformity* with a certain rule having the best consequences." With this in mind, we can see clearly one of the virtues of Urmson's proposal, which we interpreted as being: "An act is right if and only if it conforms with that set of moral rules, *the recognition of which* would have the best consequences."

But, having viewed the difficulties of a view verbally very similar to the above, we are now alert to the fact that the formulation we have suggested is itself open to interpretations that may lead to problems. How may we construe Urmson's proposal, so that it is both unambiguous and credible? Of course we do not wish to go to the opposite extreme and take "recognition of" to mean merely "doffing the hat to" without attempt to practice. But how shall we take it?

I suggest the following as a second approximation. First, let us speak of a set of moral rules as being "learnable" if people of ordinary intelligence are able to learn or absorb its provisions, so as to believe the moral propositions in question in the ordinary sense of "believe" for such contexts.[6] Next, let us speak

---

[6] To say that a moral code can be learned by a person is not to say he can learn to *recite* it. It is enough if he learns it well enough to recall the relevant rule when stimulated by

of "the adoption" of a moral code by a person as meaning "the learning and belief of its provisions (in the above sense) and conformity of behavior to these to the extent we may expect people of ordinary conscientiousness to conform their behavior [124] to rules they believe are principles about right or obligatory behavior." Finally, let us, purely arbitrarily and for the sake of brevity, use the phrase "maximizes intrinsic value" to mean "would produce at least as much intrinsic good as would be produced by any relevant alternative action." With these stipulations, we can now propose, as a somewhat more precise formulation of Urmson's proposal, the following rule-utilitarian thesis: "An act is right if and only if it conforms with that learnable set of rules, the adoption of which by everyone would maximize intrinsic value."

This principle does not at all imply that the rightness or wrongness of an act is contingent upon the agent's having *thought about* all the complex business of the identity of a set of ideal moral rules; it asserts, rather, that an act is right if and only if it *conforms* to such a set of rules, regardless of what the agent may think. Therefore the principle is not disqualified from being a correct principle about what is objectively right or wrong, in Moore's sense; for it makes rightness and wrongness a matter of the facts, and totally independent of what the agent thinks is right, or of what the agent thinks about the facts, or of the evidence the agent may have, or of what is probably the case on the basis of this evidence.

An obvious merit of this principle is that it gives expression to at least part of our practice or procedure

---

being in a context to which it is relevant. Learning a moral code is thus like learning a complex route into a large city: we may not be able to draw it or explain to others what it is, but when we drive it and have the landmarks before us, we remember each turn we are to make.

in trying to find out what is right or wrong. For
when we are in doubt about such matters, we often
try to think out how it would work in practice to
have a moral code which prohibited or permitted various actions we are considering. We do not, of course,
ordinarily do anything as complicated as try to think
out the *complete* ideal moral code; we are content
with considering whether certain specific injunctions
relevant to the problem we are considering might
be included in a good and workable code. Nevertheless, we are prepared to admit that the whole ideal
code is relevant. For if someone shows us that a
specific injunction which we think would be an acceptable part of a moral code clearly would not work
out in view of other provisions necessary to an ideal
[125] code, we should agree that a telling point had
been made and revise our thinking accordingly.

In order to get a clearer idea of the kind of "set
of rules" (with which right actions must conform)
which could satisfy the conditions this rule-utilitarian
principle lays down, let us note some general features
such a set presumably would have. First, it would
contain rules giving directions for recurrent situations
which involve conflicts of human interests. Presumably, then, it would contain rules rather similar to
W. D. Ross's list of prima facie obligations: rules
about the keeping of promises and contracts, rules
about debts of gratitude such as we may owe to our
parents, and, of course, rules about not injuring other
persons and about promoting the welfare of others
where this does not work a comparable hardship on
us. Second, such a set of rules would not include
petty restrictions; nor, at least for the most part,
would it contain purely prudential rules. Third, the
rules would not be very numerous; an upper limit on
quantity is set by the ability of ordinary people to
learn them. Fourth, such a set of rules would not
include unbearable demands; for their inclusion would

only serve to bring moral obligation into discredit. Fifth, the set of rules adoption of which would have the best consequences could not leave too much to discretion. It would make concessions to the fact that ordinary people are not capable of perfectly fine discriminations, and to the fact that, not being morally perfect, people of ordinary conscientiousness will have a tendency to abuse a moral rule where it suits their interest. We must remember that a college dormitory rule like "Don't play music at such times or in such a way as to disturb the study or sleep of others" would be ideally flexible if people were perfect; since they aren't, we have to settle for a rule like "No music after 10 P.M." The same thing is true for a moral code. The best moral code has to allow for the fact that people are what they are; it has to be less flexible and less efficient than a moral code that was to be adopted by perfectly wise and perfectly conscientious people could be.

Should we think of such a moral code as containing only [126] prescriptions for situations likely to arise in *everyone's* life—rules like "If you have made a promise, then . . ." or "If you have a parent living, then treat him thus-and-so"? Or should we think of it as containing distinct sets of prescriptions for *different roles or statuses,* such as "If you are a policeman, then . . ." or "If you are a physician, then . . ."? And if the ideal code is to contain different prescriptions for different roles and statuses, would it not be so complex that it could not be learned by people of ordinary intelligence? The answer to these questions is that the rule-utilitarian is not committed, by his theory, to the necessity of such special codes, although I believe he may well admit their desirability —admit, for instance, that it is a good thing for a physician to carry a rule in his mental kit, specially designed to answer the question, "Shall I treat a patient who does not pay his bill?" In any case, our rule-

utilitarian theory can *allow* for such special rules. Nor
is there a difficulty in the fact that people of normal
intelligence could hardly learn all these special sets of
rules. For we can mean, by saying that a code can be
"learned" by people of ordinary intelligence, that any
person can learn all the rules relevant to the problems
he will face. A rule-utilitarian will not, of course,
have in mind a moral code which in some part is
secret—for instance, lawyers having a moral code
known only to themselves, a code which it would be
harmful for others to know about. For surely in the
long run it could not have best consequences for a
society to have a moral code, perhaps granting special
privileges to some groups, which could not stand the
light of public knowledge.

5
First Problem: Moral Codes
for an Imperfect Society

Our "second approximation" to a rule-utilitarian
principle has proposed that an act is right if and only
if it conforms with the requirements of a learnable
moral code, the adoption of which by *everyone* would
maximize utility—and meaning by "adoption of a
code" the learning and belief that the code lays down
the requirements for moral behavior, and conformity
[127] to it to the extent we may expect from people
of *ordinary conscientiousness*.

The italicized words in the preceding paragraph indicate two respects in which the proposed test of
rightness in a sense departs from reality. In actuality
moral codes are not subscribed to by everybody in
all particulars: there is virtual unanimity on some
items of what we call "the code of the community"
(such as the prohibition of murder and incest), but
on other matters there is less unanimity (in the United

States, the "code" permits artificial birth-control measures despite disapproval by many Catholics), and it is a somewhat arbitrary matter to decide when the disagreement has become so general that we ought not to speak of something as part of the code of the community at all. There is probably some measure of disagreement on many or most moral matters in most modern communities (and, surely, in at least many primitive communities). Furthermore, our proposal, in an effort to be definite about the degree of commitment involved in the "adoption" of a code, spoke of an "ordinary conscientiousness." This again departs from reality. Ordinary conscientiousness may be the exception: many people are extremely, perhaps even overly conscientious; at the other extreme, some people act as if they have developed no such thing as a conscience at all. It is characteristic of actual communities that there is a wide range in degrees of conscientiousness.

As a result of these departures from reality, our test for rightness savors a bit of the utopian. We are invited to think of different worlds, each populated by people of "ordinary conscientiousness," all of whom are inoculated with a standard moral code. We are to decide whether given types of action are right or wrong by considering which of these hypothetical communities would realize a maximum of value.

There is force in the proposal. In fact, if we are thinking of sponsoring some ideal, this conception is a useful one for appraising whatever ideal we are considering. Just as we might ask whether large military establishments or a capitalist economy would be suitable for the ideal community of the future, so we can ask whether certain features of our present moral code would [128] be suitable in such a community. It may be that such a conception should play a large role in deciding what ultimate ideals we should espouse.

Nevertheless, this conception may, from its very

framework, necessarily be unsuitable for deciding the rightness of actions in the real world. It appears that, in fact, this is the case with both of the features mentioned above.

First, the proposal is to test rightness by the desirability of a rule in a moral code among people of ordinary conscientiousness. Now, in a community composed of people of ordinary conscientiousness we do not have to provide for the contingency of either saints or great sinners. In particular, we do not have to provide for the occurrence of people like Adolf Hitler. In such a community, presumably, we could get along with a minimal police force, perhaps an unarmed police force. Similarly, it would seem there would be no value in a moral prescription like "Resist evil men." In the community envisaged, problems of a certain sort would presumably not arise, and therefore the moral code need not have features designed to meet those problems. Very likely, for instance, a moral code near to that of extreme pacifism would work at least as well as a code differing in its non-pacifism.

More serious is the flaw in the other feature: that the test of rightness is to be compatibility with the requirements of the moral code, adoption of which *by everyone* would maximize utility. The trouble with this is that it permits behavior which really would be desirable if everyone agreed, but which might be objectionable and undesirable if not everyone agreed. For instance, it may well be that it would have the best consequences if the children are regarded as responsible for an elderly parent who is ill or needy; but it would be most unfortunate if the members of a Hopi man's native household—primarily his sisters and their families—decided that their presently recognized obligation had no standing on this account, since the result would be that as things now stand, no one at all would take the responsibility. Again, if everyone recognized an obligation to share in duties pertaining to national defense, it would be morally acceptable [129] to require this legally; but it would hardly be morally acceptable to do so if there are pacifists who on moral grounds are ready to die rather than bear arms. And similarly for other matters about which there are existing and pronounced moral convictions.

It seems clear that some modification must be made if our rule-utilitarian proposal is to have implications consistent with the moral convictions of thoughtful people. Unfortunately it is not clear just what the modification should be. The one I am inclined to adopt is as follows. First, we must drop that part of our conception which assumes that people in our hypothetical societies are of ordinary conscientiousness. We want to allow for the existence of both saints and sinners and to have a moral code to cope with them. In order to do this, we had better move closer to Urmson's original suggestion. We had better drop the notion of "adoption" and replace it by his term "recognition," meaning by "recognition by all" simply "belief by all that the rules formulate moral requirements." Second, we must avoid the conception of the acceptance of all the rules of a given moral code by *everybody* and replace it by something short of this, something which does not rule out the problems created by actual convictions about morals. Doing so means a rather uneasy compromise, because we cannot sacrifice the central feature of the rule-utilitarian view, which is that the rightness of an act is to be tested by whether it conforms with rules the (somehow) general acceptance of which would maximize utility. The compromise I propose is this: that the test whether an act is right is whether it is compatible with that set of rules which, were it to replace the moral commitments of members of the *actual so-*

ciety at the time, *except where there are already fairly decided moral convictions*, would maximize utility.

The modified theory, then, is this: "An act is right if and only if it conforms with that learnable set of rules, the recognition of which as morally binding, roughly at the time of the act, by all actual people insofar as these rules are not incompatible with existing fairly decided moral commitments, would maximize intrinsic value."[7] [130]

The modification has the effect that whether an act is right depends to some extent on such things as (1) how large a proportion of the actual population is conscientious and (2) what are the existing fairly decided moral beliefs at the time. This result is not obviously a mistake.

6
Second Problem:
Conflicts of Rules

The objection is sure to be raised against any rule-utilitarian theory of the general sort we are considering that the whole conception is radically misconceived. For the theory proposes that what makes an

---

[7] This formulation is rather similar in effect to one suggested to me by Wilfrid Sellars. (I have no idea whether he now inclines toward it, or whether he ever did lean toward it strongly.) This is: "An act is right if and only if it conforms with that set of rules the *teaching of which* to the society of the agent, at the time of the action, would maximize welfare." This formulation is simpler, but it has its own problems. Teaching to which and how many individuals? By whom? With what skill and means? We should remember that it may be unwise to teach children the rules that are best for adults and that it may sometimes be desirable to teach ideals which are more extreme than we want people actually to live by, e.g., those of the Sermon on the Mount.

act right is its conformity to the set of rules, recognition of which would maximize utility; and it is proposed that if we are in serious doubt whether an action would be right, we should ask ourselves whether it would conform with a utility-maximizing set of rules. Now, the objection will run, the very conception of such a set of rules evaporates, or else appears to involve contradictions, when we try to get it in sharp focus. The very idea of a set of rules simple enough to be learned and different from act-utilitarianism, and at the same time sufficiently comprehensive and precise to yield directions for conduct in every situation which may arise, is an impossible dream.

The reason is that moral problems are often quite complex. There are pros and cons—obligations and counter-obligations—which have to be weighed delicately. For instance, a promise that has been made to do something is normally a point in favor of saying that doing it is obligatory; but just how much force the promise will have depends on various circumstances, such as when it was made, how solemnly it was made, whether it was fully understood by both parties, etc. The force of these circumstances cannot be stated and weighed by any set of rules. There is a moral to be drawn, it may be said, from W. D. Ross's theory of prima facie obligations: Ross could provide no general direction for what to do when prima facie obligations conflict; he had to leave the resolution of such conflicts to conscience or [131] intuition. So, in general, no code simple enough to be written down and learned (and different from act-utilitarianism) can prescribe what is right in complex cases.

The difficulty is obviously a serious one. If the very concept of a complete code, the recognition of which would maximize utility, cannot be explained in detail, then the proposal that the rightness of every action is fixed by its conformity with the provisions of such a code must be abandoned.

What must be done to meet this charge? Of course, it cannot be demanded that we actually produce the ideal moral code for our society, or even a complete code of which the correct code might be supposed to be a variation. What can be fairly demanded is that we describe classes of rules or elements which may be expected in the ideal code, and that we make clear, in the course of this description, that the rules constituting the classes are simple enough to be learned, and that a person who had learned the rules of the several classes would be in a position to give an answer to all moral questions—or at least as definite an answer as can reasonably be expected. We may suppose that, if the theory is to be plausible, these classes of rules will be familiar—that they will be rules which thoughtful people do use in deciding moral issues. Let us see what can be said.

It is clear that a complete moral code must contain rules or principles of more than one level. The lowest level will consist of rules devised to cover familiar recurrent situations, presumably rather like those proposed by Ross in his formulation of prima facie obligations. Thus, it will contain rules like "Do not injure conscious beings," "Do what you have promised to do," etc. On reflection, we can see that such rules must be qualified in two ways. First, each of them must conclude with an exceptive clause something like "except as otherwise provided in this code." But second, they must be more complex than our samples; as Ross well knew, such simple rules do not state accurately what we think are our prima facie obligations—and presumably such rules are not the rules it would maximize welfare to have recognized as first-order rules. Consider for instance the rule I have suggested about promises. It is too simple, for we do not [132] seriously believe that *all* promises have even a prima facie claim to be fulfilled; nor would it be a good thing for people to think they ought. For instance, we think there is no obligation at all to keep a promise made on the basis of deliberate misrepresentation by the promisee; and it is to the public interest that we should think as we do. Just as the law of contracts lists various types of contracts which it is against the public interest for the courts to enforce, so there are types of promises the fulfillment of which we do not think obligatory, and a moral requirement to fulfill them would be contrary to the public interest. The lowest-level group of rules, then, will include one about promise-keeping which will state explicitly which types of promises must be kept except when some more stringent obligation intervenes. And the same for the other basic moral rules.

I do not know if anyone would contend that it would be impossible to write down an exact statement formulating our total prima facie obligations—the kinds of considerations which to some extent make a moral claim on agents. I do not know if anyone would say that in principle we cannot state exactly the list of prima facie obligations it would maximize utility for everyone to feel. Whether or not anyone does say that a list of exact prima facie obligations cannot be stated, I know of no solid argument which can be put forward to show that this is the case. I do not believe a satisfactory list *has* been provided (Ross's statement being quite abbreviated), but I know of no sound reason for thinking that it cannot be. It would not, I think, be an impossible inquiry to determine what is the total set of distinct fundamental prima facie obligations people in fact do recognize in their moral thinking.

A set of first-level rules, however, is not enough. For moral perplexities arise most often where there are conflicts of prima facie obligations, where there would be conflicts of the first-level moral rules. If the rule-utilitarian theory is to work, it must provide for the resolution of such perplexities. How can this be done?

The problem can be partially met by supposing that a complete moral code will contain second-level rules specifically [133] prescribing for conflicts of the basic rules. One second-level rule might be: "Do not injure anyone solely in order to produce something good, unless the good achieved be substantially greater than the injury." In fact we already learn and believe rules roughly of this kind. For instance, Ross suggested in *The Right and the Good* that we think there is normally a stronger obligation to avoid injury to others than to do good or to keep one's promises. A moral code can contain some such second-order rules without intolerable complexity.

But such rules will hardly be numerous enough to solve all the problems. And the rule we stated was not precise: it used the vague phrase "substantially greater," which is clear enough, in context, to decide for many situations, but it is by no means precise enough to legislate for all. I think, therefore, that if the very conception of a set of rules simple enough to be learned and adequate to adjudicate all possible cases is to be intelligible, it must be possible to formulate a consistent and plausible "remainder-rule," that is, a top-level rule giving adequate directions for all cases for which the lower-level rules do not prescribe definitely enough or for which their prescriptions are conflicting. We are not here called upon to identify the correct remainder-rule—although we know that the rule-utilitarian theory is that the correct one is the one the recognition of which (etc.) would do most good. What we are called upon to do is to sketch out what such a rule might well be like.

It is worthwhile to mention two possibilities for a

remainder-rule.[8] First, such a rule might specify that all cases not legislated for by other clauses in the code be decided simply on the basis of comparative utility of consequences. For such cases, then, the remainder-rule would prescribe exactly what the act-utilitarian principle prescribes. Second (and I think this possibility the more interesting), the remainder-rule might be: "One is obligated to perform an action if and only if a person who knew the relevant facts and had them vividly in mind, had been carefully taught the other rules of this code, and was uninfluenced by interests beyond those arising from learning the code, would feel obligated to perform that action." Such a rule could decide [134] cases not legislated for by the remainder of the code only if the explicit rules were taught so as to be connected with different degrees of *felt obligation*. In some cases such an association could be established by the very content of the rule, for instance, in the case of a rule stating that there is an obligation not to injure others, and that the obligation increases in strength with the amount of injury involved. Another example is that of second-level rules about the priorities of first-level rules. In other cases the association might be fixed simply by the relative insistence or firmness of the teachers, with respect to the rule in question. As a result of the rules being taught in this way, conscientious people would have established in them hesitations, of different degrees of strength, to do certain sorts of things—in other words, a sense of

---

[8] It will probably be clear why the remainder-rule cannot simply be the rule-utilitarian principle itself. For the rule-utilitarian principle states that an act is right if and only if it conforms with the rules of a certain kind of code. If one of the rules of the code were the rule-utilitarian principle, it would contain reference to a code which presumably would itself contain again the rule-utilitarian principle, and so on ad infinitum.

obligation to do or avoid certain things, the sense
having different force for different things. Therefore,
when persons so trained were faced with a situation
in which lower-order rules gave conflicting directions
(and where no higher-order rule assigned an explicit
priority), they would hesitate to resolve the problem
in various ways because of the built-in sense of obligation. Now, the proposed remainder-rule would in
effect be a somewhat qualified prescription to take
whatever course of action would leave morally well-
trained people least dissatisfied. (I imagine that something like this is what Ross had in mind when he
said that in complex situations one must rely on one's
intuition.) The rule-utilitarian proposal is, of course,
that the correct degree of felt obligation to be associated with a rule is, like the order of priorities expressed in the second-level rules, fixed by the relative
utilities of the various possible arrangements—partly
the utilities of the adjudications of complex cases by
the remainder-rule.

It is after all possible, then, for a moral code different from act-utilitarianism to be simple enough to be
learned and still able to decide for all problems which
may arise. [135]

7
Third Problem:
Relativity to the Agent's Society

One final complication may be needed in the rule-
utilitarian proposal. In place of saying that the rightness of an act is fixed by conformity with the prescriptions of the moral code, the recognition of which
as morally binding by people (etc.) *everywhere*
would maximize intrinsic good, we might say that
the rightness of an act is fixed by conformity with
the prescriptions of that moral code, the recognition

of which as morally binding by people *in the agent's society* would maximize intrinsic good. This kind of complication should be avoided if possible, because it is difficult to assign a definite meaning to the phrase "in the agent's society." We should notice, incidentally, that it is *not* suggested that the test be the maximizing of intrinsic good only in the agent's society; such a thesis would promise quite dubious consequences.

A modification of this sort would admit a kind of relativism into ethics. For, while it is consistent with the rule-utilitarian principle itself being correct for everyone, it has the consequence that an act might be right in one society which would be wrong in another society. For instance, it might be a moral obligation for a man to support his elderly father in one society, but not his obligation in another society. Most philosophers, however, would probably view this kind of relativism as innocuous, since such differences in obligation could occur only when conditions in the two societies were different in such a way that recognition of one rule by one society would have best consequences, and recognition of a different rule by another society would also have best consequences.

But is there any reason for adopting this complicating feature? Why not say that, if a moral code is valid for anybody it is valid for everybody? Surely, it will be said, *some* moral rules are universally valid—perhaps, for instance, a rule forbidding a person from causing another pain merely in order to give himself pleasure. And if so, perhaps we can go on, with Ross, to [136] say that the fundamental principles of obligation are universally true, although their application in special circumstances may give rise to an *appearance* of society-bound rules. For instance, Ross would say that "Keep your promises" is universally a true and important first-level rule. But in some places a thing

is promised with certain mutually-understood but not
explicitly stated conditions, while in other places the
implicit conditions are different. As a result, the conduct required, in view of the explicit promise, by the
universally valid principle is different in different
societies. Or again, "Thou shalt not steal" or "Thou
shalt not commit adultery" might be construed as
universally valid injunctions, the first being not to
take property which, according to the institutions of
the society, is recognized as belonging to another,
and the second, not to have sexual relations with any
person if either party is, according to the custom of
the society, the marriage partner of another. All fundamental moral principles, then, may be thought to
have intersocietal validity; only the specific conduct
enjoined or prohibited may vary from one society to
another because of local conditions.

This view, however, faces serious difficulties. In
order to bring these into focus, let us consider an
example: the obligations of a father to his children.
In the United States, I believe, it is thought that a
father should see to it—within the limits of his fi-
nancial capacities—that his children receive a good
education, enjoy physical and mental health, and have
some security against unforeseeable catastrophes.
Contrast this with a society, like that of the Hopi,
in which responsibility for children falls primarily on
a household, "household" being defined primarily by
blood-ties with the mother. In this situation, responsibility for children is primarily a problem for
the mother and her blood relatives. (The factual
accuracy of these assertions is not, I believe, a material
consideration.) In the United States, the father is
generally charged with responsibility for bringing the
welfare, or prospects of welfare, of his children up
to a certain rough minimum; in the Hopi society this
responsibility falls roughly on other persons, although
the father may share in it as far as affection dictates.

Correspondingly, in the United States grown children have responsibility for their father, [137] whereas among the Hopi the responsibility for the father belongs elsewhere—not on a man's own children but on the household of the father, the one to which he belongs through blood-ties with his mother and siblings.

I take it nobody is going to argue that fathers in the United States do not have the obligations they are generally thought to have, or that Hopi fathers do have obligations which are generally thought to fall elsewhere. (There may be some exceptions to this.) Therefore, if there is to be a *universal* moral rule locating obligations for the welfare of children, it will be one which roughly places it, at least for the present, where it is recognized to be in these societies. What kind of rule might this be? It is hard to say. Very possibly there is uniformity of assignment of such responsibilities in societies with a certain kind of social structure, and hence one could conceivably state a general rule prescribing that fathers do certain things in societies of a specified sociological description. It is doubtful, however, whether such a rule is simple enough to be learned. Moreover, social structures may be too much organic wholes to permit even such generalizations; if so, in respect of some kinds of conduct there can be no general, intersocietally valid moral rule at all.

There is another way of putting much the same point. Instead of asking whether we can frame a general rule which will have implications for particular societies coincident with what we should want to say are the actual locations of responsibilities in these societies, we might ask whether any universal rules can be framed, recognition of which as morally binding would have consequences comparably as good as local rules, devised on the basis of examination of individual institutional structures as a whole. Is the universality of moral rules to be so sacrosanct that we shall not recognize a moral rule as binding on a given society unless it can be viewed as a special case of some universally valid rule? A person who wishes to make utility the test of moral rules will, I think, wish to make the utility of local rules his test.

It may be supposed that the example of family obligations is untypically complex. But to do so would be a mistake. The responsibilities [138] of physicians and teachers—or professional men in general—to the individuals whom they serve pose similar difficulties. So do the ethics of borrowing and the charging of interest. It is possible that the broad outlines of pro-hibited and required behavior will be rather similar in all societies. But when we come to the fine points —the exceptions, the qualifications, the priorities—we are in for difficulties if we must defend the view that stable universal rules are the best ones for every-body to feel bound by, or that they conform to serious opinions about the location of obligations in various types of society. This, I think, has been the conclusion of various "self-realizationist" philosophers like A. MacBeath and C. A. Campbell.

Let us then consider (without necessarily insisting that it be adopted) the view that the rightness of an act is fixed by conformity with the prescriptions of that moral code, the recognition of which as morally binding by people (etc.) *in the agent's society* would maximize intrinsic good. Can we propose a meaning of "in the agent's society" sufficiently definite that we can say the proposal is at least a clear one?

How shall we identify "the society" of the agent? This question could have been answered fairly simply in much earlier times when all societies were rather clearly demarcated atomic units, although when we remember the relationships of the *kula* reported by Malinowski, we can see that matters were not always so simple even among primitive peoples. The question is difficult in a modern civilization. What is a Columbia University professor who lives in the suburbs to count as his "society"? The faculty club? His suburb? New York City? The state of New York? Any choice seems a bit arbitrary. Or suppose Khrushchev makes a promise to Eisenhower. What society should we bear in mind as the one the utility of a set of rules in which sets the standard of right and wrong?

Very tentatively, I am inclined to suggest that we understand the "society of an agent" in the following way. An individual, I suggest, may live in several "moral worlds," and the rules for these several moral worlds may be different. For one thing, he is a member of a succession of local groups, each one more inclusive than the last: the local community, the [139] metropolitan area, etc. Now a good part of one's life is lived as a resident, a neighbor, a citizen. Insofar as moral problems arise as part of one's life in this capacity, the problem is to be settled by reference to the rules best for the geographical community. How wide a geographical community should we pick? The best answer seems to be: the largest area over which common rules can be adopted without loss of utility. If it were costly in utility to apply to a borough the rules which were the best for the metropolitan area, then we had better consider our case in the light of rules useful for the smaller group. But a person has other roles besides that of citizen and neighbor. One may be a member of groups which transcend the local community—perhaps nation-wide associations, class, or caste. Most important, perhaps, are transactions resulting from the institutional involvement of the participants; for example, business transactions involving corporations or unions, or the affairs of the church, or educational affairs, or the activities of the press or radio. In these cases a segment of the life-relations of the individuals involved consists in their interactions with others who have the same role or who participate in the same institution. In such cases, I suggest that the moral rules governing behavior should be the rules adoption of which by the relevant group (for example, the group participating in a given institution) would be best, as governing the transactions of that group. It may be, of course, that we do not need some of these complications, that there is no need to distinguish the rules for businessmen in dealing with each other or with a union from the ones properly followed in one's relations with wife and neighbor.[9]

8
Concluding Remarks

The principle with which we end is this: "An act is right if and only if it conforms with that learnable set of rules the recognition of which as morally binding—roughly at the time of the act—by everyone in the society of the agent, except for the retention by individuals of already formed and decided moral convictions, would maximize intrinsic value."[10] [140]

I wish to make three final comments on this principle.

First, one may ask whether a set of moral rules which would maximize intrinsic value in the way described would necessarily be a *just* set of rules.

---

[9] The above discussion shows that the theory that what is right is behavior conforming with the *accepted* rules of the agent's society has complications which have not been adequately discussed.

[10] As the principle now stands, a given individual might have to learn several codes, corresponding to his several roles in society.

Surely, if the rules are not just, conformity with them will by no means guarantee that an action is right. A further inquiry must be made about whether additional requirements are needed to assure that moral rules are just. It may be that, as I have suggested elsewhere, none is called for if equality of some sort is an intrinsic good.

Second, if the proposed principle is correct, we can give at least a partial answer to a person who asks *why* he ought to perform actions he is obligated to perform, if they conflict with his self-interest. Perhaps a person who asks such a question is merely confused, and his query not worth our attention. But we can say to him that one reason for meeting his obligation is that by doing so he plays the game of living according to the rules which will maximize welfare. And this will be, at least partially, a satisfying answer to a man who is activated by love or sympathy or respect directed at other sentient beings generally.

Finally, some reflections on the employment of the principle. It is, perhaps, obvious that it is not necessary to advocate that everyone always bear the rule-utilitarian principle in mind in deciding what he ought to do. Not that it would be harmful— beyond the waste of time—to do so; for it is obvious that the clear moral obligations are prescribed by the principle. For example, only an instant's thought is required to see that it is socially useful to recognize the rule that solemn promises should be kept—doubtless with some qualifications. The rule's employment is important, however, in analyzing more difficult cases, in making clear whether a given moral rule should be qualified in a certain way. Of course, it would be foolish to suggest that application of the principle is an easy road to the resolution of moral problems. It may very often be that after most careful reflection along the lines suggested, the most

that can be said is that a given action is probably
the one which the principle requires. If so, if we
accept the principle, we can go on to say that this
action is probably the right one.

IS THERE A CREDIBLE FORM
OF UTILITARIANISM?*

Alan Donagan

In his important essay, "Toward a Credible Form of Utilitarianism,"[1] Professor R. B. Brandt has shown convincingly that if utilitarianism is credible in any form, it is substantially in the version of rule-utilitarianism that he delineates. While conceding that, in that form, utilitarianism is plausible, I shall try to show that it is not credible.

Following Brandt, I take utilitarianism to be generically a theory about what acts are right, what wrong; and specifically a theory that the rightness or wrongness of an act consists *in some way* in whether its consequences are better or worse than those of other acts which the agent could have done instead. The modification "in some way" is important. The early utilitarians, Bentham and the Mills, did not treat it as the office of a moralist to calculate the consequences of individual acts, this murder or that lie,

---

* The original draft of this paper was read on 24 March 1964 at a colloquium at the University of Pittsburgh, and subsequently at a seminar at Indiana University. It was intended for discussion, not publication; and it is with misgiving that I have consented to the publication of this amended version of it.

[1] In H-N. Castañeda and George Nakhnikian (eds.), *Morality and the Language of Conduct* (Detroit, 1963), 107–43 [reprinted in this volume, pp. 143–186].

but only whether the consequences of classes of acts like murders or lies are better or worse than the consequences of the classes of alternative acts in which the agents refrain from murdering or lying.

Not all utilitarians have followed Bentham and the Mills in this. Professor J. J. C. Smart, for example, has argued that to "restrict" utilitarianism as in practice Bentham and the Mills did leads to absurdities; and that the only tenable form of utilitarianism is the "extreme" or "radical" doctrine that you ought never to do an individual act that will produce, on balance, more evil and less good than some alternative.[2] Following Brandt, I shall describe this position as "act-utilitarianism."

Act-utilitarianism has generally been put down as incredible, on the ground that in certain circumstances it enjoins as duties what virtually everybody considers to be criminal. To employ a hackneyed example: it might well be the case that more good and less evil would result from your painlessly and undetectedly murdering your malicious, old and unhappy grandfather than from your forbearing to do so: he would be freed from his wretched existence; his children would be rejoiced by their inheritances and would no longer suffer from his mischief; and you might anticipate the reward promised to those who do good in secret. Nobody seriously doubts that a position with such a consequence is monstrous.

To object that the conditions imagined in this example have never been fulfilled, even if the objection is true (which I doubt), would be beside the point. Moral theory is *a priori*, as clear-headed utilitarians like Henry Sidgwick recognized. It is, as Leibniz

---

[2] J. J. C. Smart, "Extreme and Restricted Utilitarianism," *Philosophical Quarterly*, Vol. VI (1956), 344–354 [reprinted in this volume, pp. 99–115].

would say, true of all possible worlds. A world in which some murders can be painless and undetected is certainly possible. And the notion that the reason why it would be wrong painlessly to murder your malicious, old, unhappy grandfather is that, in the actual world, you could not get away with it, if anything, is more monstrous than the view that such a murder would be permissible.

I therefore conclude that act-utilitarianism is incredible. And, while I am prepared to defend the common moral opinion that painless undetected murders of old unhappy people are wicked, no matter what benefits result, I take it that act-utilitarians will prefer to challenge my argument on some other point.

What, then, of the position suggested by the practice of Bentham and the Mills? It largely depends on how Mill's phrase, "to calculate the consequences of classes of actions"[3] is interpreted. Professor Singer has interpreted it as meaning to calculate what the consequences of acts of a certain kind "usually" or "generally" or even "frequently" are.[4] On this interpretation, to say that the consequences of the class of murders are bad simply means that the consequences of *most* murders are bad. But this does not entail that the consequences of any particular murder are bad; at best, it affords no more than "a guide to what the consequences are likely to be."[5] From a utilitarian point of view, if you have good reasons to believe that the consequences of refraining from a certain murder will be worse than those of committing it, the fact that you have good reasons

---

[3] J. S. Mill, "Dr. Whewell on Moral Philosophy," *Dissertations and Discussions* (London, 1859), vol. ii, 474.

[4] Marcus G. Singer, *Generalization in Ethics* (New York, 1961), 206–7. Cf. H. J. McCloskey, "An Examination of Restricted Utilitarianism," *Philosophical Review*, Vol. LXVI (1957), 471–473 [reprinted in this volume, pp. 123–126].

[5] Singer, *op. cit.*, 207.

to believe that the consequences of most murders
are bad can have no bearing on whether you ought
to commit *this* one. You draw upon your knowledge
about most cases only when you are in doubt about
a particular one.

One of the many virtues of Brandt's essay is that
it shows there to be a more credible form of "restricted" utilitarianism than the one Singer rejects.
Its germ is found in John Rawls's "Two Concepts of
Rules."[6] Brandt calls it "rule-utilitarianism."

Brandt's position, as I understand it, is as follows.
It is possible to ask, of any given moral system,
deontological or utilitarian, whether the consequences
of its general acceptance in a society would be better
or worse than the consequences of the general acceptance either of some other moral system or of
none. A moral system is generally accepted in a
society if most members of that society decide in
accordance with it what their obligations are, whether
or not they go on to discharge them. Moral systems
are seldom, if ever, accepted by making a social
compact, or indeed by performing any act or acts
of decision, whether collective or individual. The
acceptance of a moral system in a society is a matter
of the behavior dispositions of most of its members,
however those dispositions were acquired. Yet, even
though questions about the consequences of the general acceptance of a moral system are not about the
consequences of individual acts, they are questions a
utilitarian may legitimately raise; and they do not
appear to be any more difficult to answer than questions about the remote consequences of individual
acts.

Of the deontological moral codes that are practicable (that is, contain neither too many rules to

6 *Philosophical Review*, Vol. LXIV (1955), 3–32 [reprinted
in this volume, pp. 59–98].

be grasped in practice, nor rules that are too complicated) comparatively few have engaged the serious attention of moralists; nor will their number be much enlarged by adding any others that may be seriously considered in the future. If utilitarian methods are as powerful as all utilitarians must claim, it ought to be possible to establish, of any given member of the set of seriously considered deontological codes, whether the consequences of generally accepting some other member of the set would be worse than the consequences of generally accepting it. Hence it ought to be possible to establish, of some particular deontological code, that the consequences of generally accepting any other seriously considered deontological code would be worse than the consequences of generally accepting it. Having carried out these calculations, a utilitarian would be in a position to inquire whether the consequences of accepting some non-deontological moral system (e.g. act-utilitarianism) would be worse than the consequences of generally accepting the deontological code that is, on utilitarian grounds, preferable to all other seriously considered deontological codes. If he found that they would be worse, a utilitarian would be obliged, as a utilitarian, to embrace the preferred deontological code; and, having embraced it, he could not consistently raise the question whether, in a particular case, the desirable consequences of violating one of its rules (e.g., the prohibition of murder) would justify such a violation. *Ex hypothesi*, what is or is not morally permissible is a matter of the moral code; and if a code accepted on utilitarian grounds prohibits murder, the question whether this or that murder is permissible simply does not arise.

A utilitarian who scrupulously observes the rules of a deontological moral code which he has accepted because the consequences of its not being generally accepted would be worse than those of its being generally accepted, cannot justly be taxed with an idolatrous attitude towards rules.[7] He may find rules as irksome as any of us do. His acceptance of a morality of rules, far from being "superstitious rule-worship (easily explicable psychologically)"[8] is an answer, no worse supported than others of the kind, to a perfectly legitimate utilitarian question.

Some act-utilitarians have tried to do justice to the distinction between questions about the consequences of the general acceptance or non-acceptance of a moral code, and questions about the consequences of doing or not doing an individual act, by treating answers to the former as pertinent, not to questions about what to do, but to questions about what to praise. Sidgwick held that "in distributing our praise of human qualities, on utilitarian principles we have to consider primarily not the usefulness of the quality but the usefulness of the praise."[9] It may be wrong to do an act, because the consequences of not doing it are worse than those of doing it, and yet right to praise doing it, because the consequences of that praise would be to promote the tendency to do acts of the kind praised, and the consequences of that tendency are beneficial. Thus it may be, on utilitarian grounds, right to praise a certain act, e.g. one of refraining from tyrannicide, by saying that it is right, even when, as an act-utilitarian, you think it wrong: that is, it may be right to volunteer lies about certain questions of right and wrong.

Sidgwick remarked that such a conclusion is "of a paradoxical character,"[10] and added that "it seems

---

[7] Cf. I. M. Crombie, "Social Clockwork and Utilitarian Morality" in D. M. McKinnon (ed.) *Christian Faith and Communist Faith* (London, 1953).

[8] J. J. C. Smart, *loc. cit.*, 349 [reprinted above, p. 107].

[9] Henry Sidgwick, *The Methods of Ethics*, 7th ed. (London, 1962), 428.

[10] *Ibid.*, 489.

expedient that the doctrine that esoteric morality is expedient should remain esoteric."[11] Yet, while he perceived that another doctrine of act-utilitarianism, that "it may conceivably be right to do, if it can be done with comparative secrecy, what it would be wrong to do in the face of the world"[12] is one which it would be inexpedient to propagate, as having, among other bad consequences, "importantly injurious effects on the agent's habits of veracity,"[13] he appears not to have been apprehensive of the injury his theory of praise might do to an "enlightened Utilitarian's" habits of veracity. I cannot decide whether this was because he failed to observe that you cannot praise an act, from a moral point of view, without expressing or implying an opinion about its rightness, or because he did not think veracity on such moral questions desirable in an "enlightened Utilitarian."

Is rule-utilitarianism, as I have outlined it, and as Brandt has more fully elucidated it, credible? I have already conceded that one argument against it will not hold water, namely, that it degenerates in practice into act-utilitarianisms because its moral rules are no more than rules of thumb. Nor shall I urge the classical objection: that there is no scientific way of carrying out the calculations of comparative consequences that all forms of utilitarianism require. True, this objection is dismissed too lightly by utilitarians, who tend not to distinguish their awareness that their convictions about the consequences of socially recognizing this rule or that are strong from their persuasion that such convictions must somehow be scientific. Nor, finally, shall I argue that, in our society, a rule-utilitarian's moral conclusions would necessarily be

---

[11] *Ibid.*, 490.
[12] *Ibid.*, 489.
[13] *Ibid.*, 490.

wrong. But that his conclusions may well be right is beside the point. As we have seen, whether a moral theory is true or false depends on whether its implications for all possible worlds are true. Hence whether utilitarianism is true or false cannot depend on how the actual world is.

Is it possible to specify a possible world in which rule-utilitarianism would have implications that are false?

It must be acknowledged at once that in no possible world does rule-utilitarianism have implications of the kind that are fatal to act-utilitarianism: implications that acts which virtually nobody seriously doubts to be evil, and which not even "enlightened Utilitarians" will openly praise, may be right if they can be done secretly. In any possible world, rule-utilitarianism excludes esoteric moral principles, and enjoins observance of moral rules without regard to whether or not they can be secretly broken. Unlike act-utilitarianism, rule-utilitarianism is not a monstrous theory; and, if it can be shown to be false, the considerations by which it is shown will be delicate.

There appear to be at least two kinds of consideration that present difficulties for rule-utilitarians: (1) the distinction between duties and supererogatory acts; and (2) the distinction between duties and certain excusable or nearly excusable wrongs.

(1) Consider the following possible situation: a fifth of the members of a society are lazy, idle, and irresponsible; their behaviour causes them serious harm, yet coercing them to behave more responsibly would occasion grave evils; and, finally, if the rule, "It is the duty of every industrious and prudent person to set aside, according to his means, a small but appreciable portion of his income for the support of the lazy but needy," were adopted in the society in question, more good and less evil would result than if it were not adopted. I do not think that our society is of this

kind, but, since such a society is certainly possible, a rule-utilitarian living in it would have no choice but to consider himself morally obliged to recognize the proposed rule.

Now I think that many would reject such a rule. I do not mean that they would necessarily refuse to set aside part of their income for the undeserving poor, but only that they would vehemently deny that they were obliged to do it. And would they not be right? Is not their action a palmary example of a supererogatory rather than an obligatory act?

One possible reply must be briefly mentioned and dismissed. It may be held that to demand that the industrious and prudent work for the idle and irresponsible is evil in itself, and that its evil is so grave that it outweighs all the other good consequences of accepting that demand. It is true, of course, that to give up part of your income when you neither desire to nor have any inducement to is an evil according to utilitarianism. But if the part of your income that is given up, although appreciable, is small, utilitarianism cannot recognize it as a grave evil. Ethical theories, e.g. some theories of natural rights, according to which any rule depriving a man, without return, of any part of his earned income would be a very grave evil, all violate the sense of utilitarianism.

Let me offer a second example with a less conservative flavor. Suppose that you have a neighbor who is indiscreet and foolish, and who confides to you that he is mortgaging everything he can in order to make a speculative investment which you are convinced would be disastrous. You believe that, if you expend much time and effort, you can dissuade him from making the investment; that nobody else will even try to dissuade him; and that the disaster you anticipate for him would be out of all proportion to the inconvenience and embarrassment you will suffer in dissuading him. Are you morally obliged to dis-

suade him? I do not deny that you ought to express
your opinion that the investment he proposes would
be disastrous, and to express it strongly; but, beyond
that, is it your duty to embark on a lengthy and
possibly embarrassing attempt to change his mind?

There can be little doubt that there would be more
good and less evil in society as a whole if the rule
were to be adopted: "It is the duty of everybody who
has adequate reason to believe that the course of action which a neighbor proposes will be disastrous
to that neighbor, that he can without grave inconvenience or embarrassment dissuade that neighbor
from his proposed course, and that nobody else will,
to dissuade him." Hence there can be little doubt that
rule-utilitarianism entails that such a rule ought to be
adopted in the actual world. And even if the actual
world be not such that the consequences of adopting
such a rule are beneficial, it is evident that such a
world is possible. Yet I think that many would reject
such a rule. Once again, I do not deny that those
who reject it might set out to dissuade a foolish
neighbor in such a case. But I for one would deny
that I was morally obliged to do so; and would think
that, if I did so, my act would be supererogatory.

(2) A second consideration against rule-utilitarianism may be found in what it implies about certain
wrongs which are tempting and perhaps even excusable. Consider an example once unhappily employed
by Sir David Ross: Can it ever be expedient, as Caiaphas held, that one man should die for the people?[14]
Is a judge morally obliged to procure a judicial murder if it should be for the public good?

Although many rule-utilitarians maintain that their

---

[14] *The Gospel According to St. John,* xviii, 14. Sir David
Ross endorsed Caiaphas's dictum in *The Right and the Good*
(Oxford, 1930), 61, as P. T. Geach observed in "Good and
Evil," *Analysis,* 17 (1956–7), 41–2.

position implies the falsity of Caiaphas's doctrine, it can hardly be doubted that a world in which the good of the people sometimes would require it is *possible*, and that, in such a world, rule-utilitarians would be committed to the position of Caiaphas. Consider the rule: "Judges must conform to the prescriptions of their judicial calling, except when, by departing from them, but not in such a way as to bring about even worse consequences, they can avert major calamities to their nation or to the world," which I shall, for brevity, call "Caiaphas's rule."

The calamity which Caiaphas himself tried to avert was (on one version) a rebellion against the authority of the Sanhedrin, and (on another) a Roman persecution of the Jewish people. Whether Caiaphas's unjust judgment did in fact avert either calamity may be doubted; but there is no reason to suspect his sincerity. And it is at least conceivable, in a world in which large nations bully small ones as a matter of course, that a large nation might threaten a small one with bombing, military occupation, and the like, unless some innocent person whose conduct had given offence was tried and condemned on a capital charge.

A rule-utilitarian might object that, since general recognition of Caiaphas's rule would so discredit the judiciary that public life would be mortally injured, there could be no circumstances in which the public good would be served by recognizing that rule. But it is not at all evident that to recognize Caiaphas's rule as a moral rule (not, of course, as a legal one) would seriously impair confidence in the judiciary. It is even likely, as the remarks of some French anti-Semites about the Dreyfus case suggest, that some would sleep more quietly in their beds if they knew that their judges would not be overscrupulous in national emergencies. However that may be, it cannot seriously be denied that there could be a society in which the general recognition of Caiaphas's rule would not discredit the judiciary.

There seems to be no other reason for contesting the conclusion that, in some possible social situations, rule-utilitarianism would require that Caiaphas's rule be adopted. And although I do not pretend that we might not excuse or palliate the wrong done by somebody who acted on that rule, it seems to me that such an implication must ruin rule-utilitarianism. However much certain judicial murders may be excused or even defended, they are *not* morally right.

A dedicated rule-utilitarian might reject both considerations I have offered against it. He might simply reject my distinction between obligatory and supererogatory good acts, and maintain that a sound moral code must, so far as it is practicable, ordain that in any situation a man ought to do the best act that he can do. And he might reject, as a survival of rule-idolatry, my conviction that no circumstances can make judicial murder right.

It must be confessed that when, as with rule-utilitarianism, moral theory contradicts moral intuition only in a few farfetched cases, moral intuition is far from a safe guide. Against act-utilitarianism it suffices; for act-utilitarianism if I am right about its implications, outrages moral intuition at almost every turn. Rule-utilitarianism, on the other hand, provides so persuasive a theoretical basis for common morality that when it contradicts some moral intuition, it is natural to suspect that intuition, not theory, is corrupt. Moral theory must account for common morality, which act-utilitarianism does not do; but individual moral intuitions are not sacrosanct. One important reason for inquiring into moral theory is to purify our moral beliefs.

The intuitive considerations I have offered against rule-utilitarianism can stand only if they point to a theory that justifies them; and I think they do. I cannot here expound that theory, but it is incumbent on me at least to indicate it. It is manifestly Kantian, and its character is sufficiently exhibited in two principles, for the formulation of which I shall draw upon Sidgwick and Kant.

(i) "It cannot be right for A to treat B in a manner in which it would be wrong for B to treat A, merely on the ground that they are different individuals, and without there being any difference between the natures or circumstances of the two which can be stated as a reasonable ground for the difference of treatment."[15]

(ii) "[R]ational beings stand under the *law* that each of them should treat himself and all others, *never merely as a means*, but always *at the same* time as an end in himself."[16]

Of these principles, (i) is a principle of equity fundamental to any rational morality, and (ii) has to do with the substance and scope of moral rules.

Let me briefly sketch what these principles imply about the intuitive considerations I have offered against rule-utilitarianism. (1) *Supererogation.* Principle (ii) implies that, while one man is bound to respect the dignity and independence of another, he too is an "end in himself," and cannot be morally obliged to be merely a means of procuring for others what they are unwilling to procure for themselves. The mere fact that more good would accrue to society at large if the industrious were held to be obliged to provide for the idle cannot deprive the industrious of their character as ends in themselves. The cases of orphan children, of the sick, of the unjustly deprived, are of course different: here, respect for the dignity and

---

[15] Henry Sidgwick, *op. cit.*, 380.
[16] Immanuel Kant, *Grundlegung zur Metaphysik der Sitten*, 2nd edn. pp. 74–5; Pruss, Acad. edn., p. 433 (tr. H. J. Paton).

independence of human nature obliges others to furnish help. (2) *Wrongs done in the public interest.* To use any innocent man ill for the sake of some public good is directly to degrade him to being a mere means. Judicially to murder him, to deprive him at a stroke of life and good repute, is an extreme example of that fundamental wrong.

The consistency of my two principles with the moral intuitions that conflict with rule-utilitarianism is a point in their favor.[17] But it is not decisive. It is necessary also to show that they do not conflict with other moral intuitions, and that they are reasonable in themselves. The former I cannot even attempt here, but something ought to be said about the latter.

Let me acknowledge at once that my principles *are* principles: that is, that I do not think there to be any higher moral principle from which they can be deduced. However, that is not the end of the matter. There is an obvious objection to them. It runs:

    (a) The only valid reason why anybody should do anything is that it is for his own good.

    (b) To adopt either principle (i) or principle (ii) may, in certain circumstances, not be for a given man's own good.

    (c) Therefore, that man has a valid reason for rejecting both (i) and (ii) as moral principles (i.e., as valid in all circumstances), and can have no valid reason for accepting either as a moral principle.

This argument is, I think, valid, and premise (b) is clearly true. Whether its conclusion is sound will

---

[17] I have not formally established that consistency. To do so, it would be necessary formally to deduce the conclusions I have asserted to follow from my principles, i.e., to expound a moral system. That a formal system corresponding to my sketch can be elaborated I have no doubt, but I do not pretend to have elaborated it.

therefore depend on whether its first premise, which may be called "the Egoist Principle," is true.

Against it, it has been argued[18] that it is to nobody's interest, not even that of a successful man of violence, e.g. a racketeer who contrives to escape prosecution, to live in a society in which disputes are settled by fraud and cunning. That is true. And it is also true that nobody committed publicly to advocating a non-egoist morality can consistently denounce a moral principle on egoist grounds. These considerations, however, affect only a man's public political and social positions. Morality is private. A successful racketeer may be a Liberal in politics, and a traditionalist in his professed social morality, on the purely egoist ground that his violent and criminal enterprises flourish in such a society. It is true that such a man cannot consistently *profess* egoism; but he can consistently *be* an egoist, and moral philosophy is concerned with whether or not a man can have good reason for privately being an egoist.[19]

Yet there are considerations that court decisively against egoism. First, it entails that there are innumerable disputes which reason cannot decide, but which it would commonly be held that reason can decide. In a dispute between an armed robber who needs a boat to escape his pursuers, and a man who has just finished making the boat needed by the robber, the egoist principle entails that the robber has good reason to take the boat by violence, and the maker good reason to resist him by cunning. But it cannot decide who *ought* to have the boat. Secondly, egoism sanctions the settlement of such disputes by violence and cunning.

Arguments against objections to the principle can-

---

[18] E.g. by Kurt Baier, *The Moral Point of View*, abridged edn. (New York, 1965), 148–57.

[19] Egoism thus resembles Sidgwick's utilitarianism in being an esoteric doctrine.

not show that the principle is sound. What I have said about the egoist objection to my principles shows that there is something wrong with the Egoist Principle. But that is all.

In trying to support my two principles I should begin by investigating the presuppositions of the question, "On what principles does reason require you to act?" Such a question, we have seen, takes you beyond egoism. In asking it, you presuppose that you have characteristics by virtue of which rational claims can be made by others upon you and by you upon others. The primary moral claims arise from the acts of rational beings with respect to one another; and the principles of morality are concerned with how it is that the fact that two beings are rational should limit what is permissible for each to do with reference to the other. Since what gives rise to moral claims is rationality itself, not the degree in which it is present, from the point of view of morality, rational individuals will be equal as moral subjects, however they may differ in their characteristics. The value of each will be absolute. Hence my two principles.

Although I do not advance this sketch as a valid argument, I think that a valid argument of the kind sketched can be found. My reason for offering such a sketch, full of blunders though it doubtless is, was to elicit what is wrong with even the most plausible form of utilitarianism. Utilitarianism conceives our moral obligations to derive from the putative obligation to increase good and diminish evil, no matter what must be done to this or that individual. I wish to maintain, on the contrary, that moral obligations derive from the obligation to respect the independence and worth of every individual, no matter at what cost in good forgone and evil accepted. Violating the moral rights of this or that individual seldom in the end turns out well for others; but that is not why such violations are wrong.

RULES AND
UTILITARIANISM
B. J. Diggs

Although moral rules have had a prominent place in
recent moral philosophy, their character is not clear.
One reason for this is the vagueness and ambiguity
which infect the use of the term "rule": Philosophers
tend to conceive of moral rules on some particular
model, sometimes in a confused way, often innocently
and without a clear view of the alternatives. J. Rawls
called attention to one important instance of this: He
pointed out that the tendency to regard rules as convenient guides, or as summaries of earlier experiences,
seems to have blinded some philosophers ". . . to the
significance of the distinction between justifying a
practice and justifying a particular action falling under it. . . ."[1]

Partly as a consequence, utilitarianism has been interpreted in a special way, as asserting that the rightness and wrongness of particular acts is decidable on
general utilitarian grounds. This form of utilitarian-

FROM the *American Philosophical Quarterly*, Vol. I (1964),
32–44. Reprinted by permission of the author and the *American Philosophical Quarterly*.

[1] "Two Concepts of Rules," *Philosophical Review*, Vol.
LXIV (1955), 29–30 [reprinted in this volume, p. 94].

ism, so-called "act utilitarianism," is open to serious and well-known objections.[2]

The appeal of the recently more popular "rule utilitarianism" is that it is able to meet some of these objections, and still retain the tie between morality and "the general welfare," which is one of the most attractive characteristics of utilitarianism. I shall argue in this paper, however, that rule utilitarians (and some of their critics, and many others who view moral rules in the same general way) have also tended unwittingly to adopt a particular kind of rule as the model of a moral rule. When this kind of rule has been delineated, and alternatives noted, I think rule utilitarianism loses much of its initial appeal.

My object in this paper, however, is not so much to refute rule utilitarianism as to contribute to the clarification of moral rules. By distinguishing two kinds of rules I shall try to illuminate one of the fundamental options (as well as one of the fundamental confusions) open to moral theory. (1) The first kind of rule is exemplified by the rules which workers follow as part of their jobs; these rules may be used to describe a job. (2) The other kind of rule characterizes such common games as baseball, chess, and the like. Both kinds of rule define "practices," but the practices are very different. I think the easy tendency to confuse them may have blinded moral philosophers to significant distinctions between justifying a system of rules designed to contribute to some goal or product, justifying a system of rules which defines a "form of life," and justifying moral rules. Marking these distinctions should help clarify certain steps taken in recent moral philosophy: One should be able to appreciate more fully the point of Baier's assertion that although moral rules are "for the good of every-

---

[2] Cf. e.g., R. B. Brandt, *Ethical Theory* (Englewood Cliffs, N.J., 1959), chap. 15.

one alike," they are not designed to promote the greatest good of everyone.[3] One should also be able to see more clearly why Rawls maintains that the decision on the rules of justice is not properly conceived on the utilitarian model, as an administrative decision on how to promote the greatest happiness.[4] The analysis of rules is illuminating, moreover, not only because it helps mark major differences of this kind, but also because it shows what is behind some of the twists and turns of moral theory.

I

1.0 The first kind of rule which I shall describe belongs to a large class of rules which I call "instrumental." All rules in this large class are adopted or followed as a means to an end, in order to "accomplish a purpose" or "get a job done." The simplest of these rules is the "practical maxim" which one ordinarily follows at his own pleasure, such as "Be sure the surface to be painted is thoroughly dry" or "Do not plant tomatoes until after the last frost."[5][33]

The instrumental rule to which I call attention is more complex. On many occasions when one wants a job done, either he is not in a position or not able or not willing to do the job himself. If he is in a position of power or authority, or if he has money, he may simply order or hire others to "do the job" and leave it to them. In numerous cases, however, he

---

[3] K. Baier, *The Moral Point of View* (Ithaca, N.Y., 1958), pp. 200–204.

[4] "Justice as Fairness," *Philosophical Review*, Vol. LXVII (April, 1958), 164–194. It will be clear that Rawls's analysis in "Two Concepts of Rules" does not support a utilitarian theory.

[5] Cf. Max Black, "Notes on the Meaning of 'Rule'," *Theoria*, vol. 24 (1958), pp. 121–122; reprinted in his *Models and Metaphors* (Ithaca, N.Y., 1962), pp. 95–139.

himself lays down rules of procedure, and establishes "jobs" or "roles" in the institutional sense. A "job" in this latter sense is not a job to be "done," but a job to be "offered to" or "given" to a person. If a person "takes" or is "assigned" "the job" then we often think of him as under an obligation to "do his job," and this partly consists in his following rules. Instrumental rules of this kind, unlike practical maxims, have a social dimension: It *makes sense* to ask whether a job-holder (or role-taker) is *obligated* to follow a particular rule, or whether this is one of his *duties*, and the penalty attaching to a breach of the rules does not consist simply in his not "getting the job done."

Rules of this kind are found in very different institutions. Some are rules of a "job" in the ordinary sense. Others apply to anyone who voluntarily assumes a "role," such as "automobile driver." Others characterize a position which one is obliged to take by law, for example, that of private in the army. The goals which the rules are designed to serve may be ordinary products of labor, such as houses, steel beams, etc.; or fairly specific social goals such as "getting vehicles to their destinations safely and expeditiously"; or goals as general as "the national defense." In some cases the rules, differing from job to job, mark a division of labor, as the rules which say what factory workers, or the members of a platoon, are to do. In other cases, the same rules apply more or less equally to all, as in the case of (at least some) rules regulating traffic.

Notwithstanding their variety, these rules can be classified together because they share two fundamental characteristics: (1) The rules prescribe action which is thought to contribute to the attainment of a goal. This is the "design" of such rules, at least in the sense that if the prescribed action does not effectively contribute to the attainment of the goal, for the most part, then the rule itself is subject to criticism. (2) The rules are "laid down" or "legislated" or "made the rule" by a party which has power or authority of some kind; one cannot learn "what the rules are" simply by determining what general procedures most effectively promote the goal. This latter characteristic sharply differentiates these rules from what I have called practical maxims, although both share the first characteristic and are "instrumental."[6]

I shall now consider each of these two characteristics in turn.

---

[6] Practical maxims should not be dismissed, however, as "mere rules of thumb" on the one hand, or as "simply stating relations between means and ends" on the other. When one follows a maxim the rule *directs* action and is a *criterion* of certain kinds of rightness and wrongness in acting.

In passing note that Rawls's "summary conception," as a whole, does not properly apply to practical maxims, although several features of this conception do apply. Rawls's analysis, admirable as it is, is very apt to mislead. For the "summary view," as he calls it, is a blend of two quite distinct conceptions: In part it is a confused conception or a misconception of a rule, as a summary or report. In other respects it is an accurate conception of what I have called a practical maxim. This may account for an ambivalence of Rawls's article: Cf. ". . . it is doubtful that anything to which the summary conception did apply would be called a *rule*." [(p. 23) "Two Concepts . . ."] with "Some rules will fit one conception, some rules the other; and so there are rules of practices (rules in the strict sense), and maxims and 'rules of thumb'." (p. 29). [Reprinted above, pp. 85, 92.] The point is that maxims are rules in a *different* sense from other kinds of rules, whereas no rule, *qua rule*, is a summary or report.

The importance of this point is that there are two possible confusions here, not one: A person may conceive moral rules as summaries or reports, or he may conceive moral rules on the model of maxims. The texts of Austin and Mill, which Rawls cites, together with Rawls's discussion, suggest that the latter, more than the former, was their mistake. V., however, note 13 below.

1.1 Since rules of this kind are designed to serve a goal, the "best" set of rules is that set, *other things equal*, which is most effective in promoting the goal. The qualification is important: One ordinarily asks the question, "Is this a good rule?" in order to determine whether or not the action to be prescribed by the rule, together with other acts, will most efficiently produce the goal, without violating certain other rules, and in a way that harmonizes best with other aims, assuming persons can be persuaded to follow the rule.[7]

Consider a factory planner designing an assembly line, or an army officer considering platoon reorganization, or a traffic planning commission trying to decide whether a street should be made a throughway. In each case rules are proposed, but there is no contradiction in saying that action on the rules will not contribute to the goal. Within its context the question "Is this a good rule?" is one of practical fact and experience. This indicates one sense in saying that the goal is "over and beyond" the action and the rules. [34]

There is another sense in saying this: In practice a goal is often described in terms of rules or procedures which are thought to produce it (when, for example, a beam is to be built according to procedural specifications). Moreover, at the time of action one may not be able to say just what he wants in other terms. Nevertheless, there is no contradiction, explicit or implied, in saying that this person got the goal (in the sense that he can truthfully say "This has all the desirable features of what I wanted") without anyone's having laid down or followed rules. Although the beam was not constructed according to specifications, tests may now show that it is as strong as one could

---

[7] Cf. my "Technical Ought," *Mind*, vol. 69 (1960), July issue.

have wished for. In this sense it is *logically* possible for one to attain the goal which a set of instrumental rules is designed to serve without these rules having been followed. I shall refer to this characteristic by saying that the goal of any set of instrumental rules is "logically independent" of these rules.

Although an instrumental action is *properly* described in many ways, depending on the context, it can always be *truthfully* described in terms of a goal, as a "trying to get or produce G." For a goal is essential to such action, and to the rules which guide it. Nevertheless, it is clear that it is logically possible to act and follow instrumental rules without attaining the goal, and to attain the goal without following rules.

Moreover, although obviously one cannot act *on* a rule of any kind if there is no rule, one can act *in the way* specified by a set of instrumental rules (as well as attain a desired result) without *these* rules having been adopted. A group of workers, for example, may hit upon certain procedures which are so effective that they are made "the rule"; in such a case we may say, somewhat misleadingly, that one discovered a good rule by observing the actual results of a line of action. In complex cases it is very unlikely that men will act in the way rules would prescribe if the rules have not in fact been enacted. Nevertheless, there is no contradiction in saying that men acted in this way but there were no rules prescribing this course of action.[8]

Thus in the case of instrumental rules the action as well as the goal may be said to be logically independent of the rules.

1.2 Now consider the second major characteristic of rules of this kind, namely, that they are "laid down," "legislated," "made," or "adopted."

---

[8] Cf. Rawls, *ibid.*, p. 22 [reprinted above, p. 84].

It is clear enough that an employer, for example, who "informs" his employee of the rules, is not simply "giving information." Moreover, this act or performance is very different from one's "adopting" a practical maxim or making a rule "a rule for himself." Note that in the case of a maxim the adoption of the rule is "incomplete" so long as one simply resolves to follow it. Rules of the present kind, however, are normally made for others to follow: To make their adoption complete, one must get at least some of these others "to agree," in some sense, to follow the rules.

This is so in spite of our sometimes speaking, in the sense indicated earlier, of one's "discovering a good rule" of this kind. We also speak of an administrator's "thinking of a good rule," "deciding on a rule," and "informing an employee of the rules decided on." It is quite clear, however, that "thinking of a rule" and "deciding on it" are steps taken *in the direction of* adopting a rule; the latter corresponds roughly to the stage of "resolution" in the case of a maxim. They are only steps; the rule will not become effective, and strictly speaking, will not *be* a rule, until it is "put in force" or "made a rule."

Legislation is one way of putting such a rule in force. In this case parents and guardians "teach" their children what the laws are; they do not ask for consent. In other cases the members of a group, working co-operatively, "decide on the rules," or an employer or a sergeant "tells one the rules." By such an act those subject to the rules are "directed to follow them," and the rules are then "in force." The rules serve on the one hand as guides to action—they tell one what to do—and on the other as criteria of correctness of action—acts in accord with them are said to be *right* and breaches of them are said to be *wrong*. The rules thus tell one both *what* to do, and *that* he should do it. They are useful just on this account: One may lay down rules of this kind to make use of unskilled labor, or to gain the benefits of a division of labor, or simply to coordinate activity as in the case of an efficient traffic system.

The analysis of what the various cases of adopting a rule have in common, and what it is to be subject to rules, takes one to the difficult problem of what constitutes an authority. For our purpose the following will suffice: A party seems to be constituted as a *de facto* authority when one accepts the fact, that this party prescribes an act, as a *reason* for following the prescription (a rule of the present kind being one form of prescription). This indicates the somewhat technical sense of saying that the rule follower [35] "agrees to" follow the rules.[9] In the case of rules of the present kind authority is ordinarily constituted, and agreement to follow the rules obtained, by contract, law, convention, or the like. Some such arrangement is necessary to induce a person to follow rules of this kind, since persons other than the rule-follower "are interested in" the goal, and normally he himself does not get (more than a share of) the product of his labor. The contract, law, or convention both promises some reward to the rule-follower, and at the same time converts others' "being interested in" the goal to their "having an interest in it" —in a legal or quasi-legal sense. This, of course, is why one who follows rules of this kind, unlike one who adopts a maxim as his guide, is not free to alter or follow the rules "at his pleasure."

The point which needs particular emphasis here, however, is that the contract, law, or convention is essential to the rule's being a rule; it is not "external"

---

[9] Cf. Black, pp. 120–121. Black's analysis of the "laying down of rules" in terms of "promulgator activities" and "subject activities" (pp. 139–146) is illuminating, as is H. L. A. Hart's recent analysis of the complex idea of "acceptance" in the case of the law. V. *The Concept of Law* (Oxford, 1961), chaps. IV–VI, esp. pp. 107–114.

to the rule, since without it one's "laying down the rules" would be only so much rhetoric. When a contract is simply "to do a job," notice that the criterion of correctness is simply "getting the job done." If I hire a person to paint a house, he has done what he is supposed to do when the house is painted. On the other hand, to the extent to which a contract lays down rules specifying how the job is to be done, the rules are the criterion. If a painter contracts to follow certain procedures, and then fails to follow them, he has not done what he is supposed to do. This should make it quite clear that it is the contract, law, or convention which determines in a given case that rules will be the criterion of correctness. The "agreement" secured by contract, law, or convention thus makes a rule a rule, and without something like it there could be no rules of this kind.

1.3 The discussion of the two major characteristics of these rules reveals two criteria of correctness. On the one hand, there is the criterion of a "good" rule. On the other, there are rules *in force* constituting a criterion in certain respects of the *right thing to do*. In the case of these rules there is thus a clear distinction between the justification of a rule or practice and the justification of a particular action falling under it. Perhaps on this very account some have been led to view moral rules as rules of this kind.

1.3.1 Before going on to moral rules let us notice that this distinction is not important simply because acts are judged by rules which are judged in turn in another manner, in this case by reference to a goal. The significance of the distinction derives more from the fact that the two criteria are "independent" in the following way: One may do the thing which most contributes to the goal, yet violate the rules in force; and one may act according to the rule in force when the rule is a poor one.

Moreover, the rules *in force*, not the rules which

are *best*, constitute (at least under certain conditions) the criterion of right and wrong acts. This is evident in practice: A worker who does his job is *entitled* to his pay, whether or not the rules he follows in doing his job are *good* rules. This question, whether or not the rules in force are "good," ordinarily does not have to be settled for them to serve as a criterion of right action. Normally it does not even arise.

Of course, one might criticize the rules *in force* as "illegitimate" or as laid down by one who lacks rightful or proper authority, and *on this account* argue that they are not the "true" criterion of right action. However, the question of the "legitimacy" of the rules is not settled by determining which rules are best. To try to have it this way would be to invite disagreement concerning which rules *are* best, and to have no effective rule at all.[10] It would be wholly impractical to accept as authoritative or binding, and as the criterion of right action, only "the rules which are best." Who, for example, would lay down, or contract to follow under penalty, rules characterized only in this way?

Thus, even though rules of the present kind are explicitly designed to promote a goal, the rule follower is not generally at liberty to use the goal as his criterion of the right thing to do. The distinction between the two criteria so far remains firm.

1.3.2 Nevertheless, the independence of these two criteria can be overemphasized. For one thing, the criterion of a good rule, in virtue of its being used by those who adopt rules, is an indirect criterion of right action. The rules which are the criterion of right and wrong action do not prescribe action which

---

[10] Cf. Hume's remarks on the need of a "determinate rule of conduct," or "general rules," in his discussions of justice, both in the *Treatise* and *Inquiry*. Hume, however, does not make precisely the same point.

just *as a matter of fact* contributes or fails to contribute to the goal; the rules are *criticizable* if they
are not good rules. Thus it does not "just so [36] happen" that the right act *tends t*o contribute to the goal.
If it did not generally do this it would not be called
"right," for there would be no such rules.

Second, no statement of a rule includes reference
to all conditions pertinent to its application; one would
not wish so to encumber it, even if every contingency
could be foreseen. This implies that every rule follower is expected to know "what he is doing" in a
sense larger than "following the rules"; and if the
rules are instrumental he is often expected to know
the goal to which his rule-directed action supposedly
contributes—to know "what he is doing" in this sense.
Not always, to be sure, but often he could not make
a sound judgment of when and how to apply the
rule without this knowledge.

For both of these reasons it is a mistake to say,
in a pedestrian and casuistical way, that "the criterion
of right acts is the rules." It is a mistake to think
of *every* exception and *every* case as somehow included in the rule. The motive for doing so, presumably to preserve the authority of rules, is mistaken: There is an important difference between interpreting a rule, or violating it *in special circumstances*,
and deciding each individual case just as if there
were no rules. A person subject to rules who follows
the latter course merits a special kind of criticism.
Although it is difficult to specify conditions in which
the violation of an instrumental rule is proper, surely
the bare fact, "that by doing so one can better promote
the goal," is not sufficient. The rule follower is not
the sole or final authority on the propriety of breaking
a rule, even when it is for the benefit of the other
party.

This brings us back to the independence of the
two criteria. However, it should now be clear that

these criteria are interrelated and operate together. Moreover, since there are two criteria in the case of rules of the present kind, it always *makes sense* to ask if an action right by the rules is also right in the respect that it is good that a rule prescribes it. It not only *makes sense* to speak of its being proper to violate a rule, "successful violations" tend to be commended.

II

2.0 As soon as rules of the foregoing kind have been described it is rather obvious that many moral theorists, intentionally or not, have cut moral rules to their pattern. Anyone who regards the standard of morally right action as itself a means to an end will have this tendency, and this is typically true of rule utilitarians: The distinctive characteristic of their theory is that a system of rules is the criterion of morally right action, and these rules in turn are to be judged good or bad according to the consequences which action on the rules either generally produces as a matter of fact, or would produce if people could be persuaded to follow them.[11] The consequence which has been thought to be critical

[11] See, for example, J. O. Urmson's "The Interpretation of the Moral Philosophy of J. S. Mill," *Philosophical Quarterly,* Vol. III (1953), 33–39 [reprinted in this volume, pp. 13–24]. By and large I agree with this interpretation of Mill, although Mill showed other tendencies, not only toward a more radical utilitarianism but, in the opposite direction, toward the ethics of Bradley. John Austin is sometimes said to be a good representative of this point of view, but his conception of moral rules as commands, learned in the way we learn practical maxims, is a hodgepodge (see *The Province of Jurisprudence Determined,* Lectures I–III). In *some* respects Hume's discussion of the artificial virtues, especially justice, is a much

in assessing the soundness of a system of rules has been variously identified, as "the happiness of all," "public utility," "security," "the general welfare," etc. Nevertheless, in spite of the difference in name and even in conception, this has been taken to be a consequence, real or possible, and as an end or goal which a good system of rules would first promote and then ensure. The question of which system of rules will be most successful in this respect generally has been thought to be, at least broadly speaking, empirical: Fact and practical experience will decide which system is best. The theory thus implies that the goal, and goal promoting action, both, in senses indicated earlier, are *logically* independent of any system of rules. This fundamentally instrumental and telic character of the system of rules, and indirectly of rule-directed action as well, is a distinctive feature of utilitarianism.[12] Moreover, as [37] I pointed out

---

better (and perhaps the best) classical example of this type of theory.

Among contemporaries (and apart from useful textbook presentations: see Brandt, *loc. cit.*, and J. Hospers, *Human Conduct*) S. Toulmin in *The Place of Reason in Ethics* and P. H. Nowell-Smith in *Ethics* have come closest to an explicit statement of the theory.

An examination of actual cases of this kind of theory, with all the proper qualifications, especially if the theory is extended beyond utilitarianism, would require considerable space. I do not undertake the historical investigation here. In my judgment, the theory has a popularity which exceeds its merit, and some tendencies which are pernicious (see Section IV below). By isolating the germ, the disease may be better understood—its valuable antibodies notwithstanding.

[12] It would be a mistake to say that utilitarians maintained this deliberately, after considering alternatives, or even that they did so consistently. John Stuart Mill, in Chapter IV of *Utilitarianism*, seems to have been unaware of the issue when he discussed happiness as "a concrete whole" and virtue as one of its "parts." Cf. below 4.5.

above, it is an essential feature of rules of the fore-going kind that persons other than the rule follower are "interested" in the product; this "interest" is expressed in some kind of contract, convention, or law which gives the rules authority. In utilitarian theory the "party-in-authority" tends to be "the people"; directly or indirectly they enter conventions, "adopt" rules, then enforce them, so that all may share the fruits of the rule-directed action. The product is shared, the goal is the good of all.

2.1 Moral rules on the rule utilitarian view thus have the basic characteristics of the rules which I discussed in (1). When the two are compared, and the analysis in (1) is brought to bear, it quickly reveals that rule utilitarianism is faced with a fundamental problem. If the position is to have the advantage over act utilitarianism that is claimed for it, then the criterion of right action must be a system of rules and not general utility. Rules are a criterion of right action, however, only on condition that they are "rules-in-force" and in some sense "agreed to." But obviously the rules which are "in force" or "agreed to" may or may not be the rules which maximize utility; and to the extent that they are not, then the "best rules" by the utilitarian standard, not having been "adoped," are not the criterion of right action. The best rules may not even be known. The "rules" and the "utilitarianism" in "rule utilitarianism" thus constitute two independent criteria, and they may not be in much accord.

2.1.1 The analysis in (1) not only clearly shows the nature of this difficulty, but also helps one to understand some of the directions in which utilitarianism has moved in an effort to avoid it. Some good utilitarians, mindful of evil in ordinary conventions, tend to say that just as men *ought* to adopt a rule only if it maximizes utility, so one is *obligated* to follow a rule only if it maximizes utility. This

doctrine implies that one may freely disregard a rule
if ever he discovers that action on the rule is not
maximally felicific, and in this respect makes moral
rules the "practical maxims." It deprives social and
moral rules of their authority and naturally is in
sharp conflict with practice. On this alternative rule
utilitarianism collapses into act utilitarianism.[13]

2.1.2 Other rule utilitarians, equally concerned to
avoid an ethical conventionalism, either close their
eyes to the difficulty or else overlook it. They either
just declare an ideal set of rules to be the criterion,
or else say that the criterion of right action is the
system of rules which, *if* adopted, *would* maximize
utility, or something of the sort. Such a formulation
clearly does not acknowledge that rules must be
adopted if they are to be rules: The "if adopted"
is only a way of describing the ideal and actually
obscures the necessity of a rule's being adopted.

The fact that it is commonly the case that some
moral principles and rules to which a person sub-
scribes are not "in force" in his society raises important issues for *any* moral philosophy of rules. I
cannot even try to do them justice here. Nevertheless,
surely it is a mistake to maintain that a set of rules,
thought to be ideally utilitarian or felicific, is the
criterion of right action. If the rules are simply
described in this way, and are not enumerated, we
so far do not have any rules and are not likely to
get any.[14] On the other hand, if we are presented
with a list, but these are not rules in practice, the
most one could reasonably do is to try to get them

---

[13] For a clear recent statement of this position, see J. J. C.
Smart, "Extreme and Restricted Utilitarianism," *Philosophical Quarterly*, Vol. VI (1956), 344–354 [reprinted in this
volume, pp. 99–115]. Notice that Smart argues explicitly
that moral rules are "rules of thumb."

[14] Cf. above, 1.3.1.

adopted. A manager in the quiet of his office may dream of a system of rules which will maximize production, and a utilitarian may build a theory around the set of rules which will maximize utility. Surely the latter would be as foolish as the former if he said that these ideal rules are the criterion of right and wrong acts. As previous analysis has shown, acts are not judged by proposed rules, ideal rules, and rules-in-theory: for these do not fully qualify as rules.[15]

2.1.3 Other rule utilitarians show a finer appreciation of the logic of their position: They interpret moral rules on analogy with the rules in (1), even [38] if it forces them to admit that the criterion of right action is not the set of rules which maximizes utility. This alternative seems to be popular with those whose primary allegiance is to a "morality of rules," and who are utilitarian only because they suppose that "welfare" *must* have something to do with morality. (After all, what else *can* serve as a criterion of rules?)

---

[15] See 1.2 and 1.3.1 above. Since utilitarianism is rather often associated with reform, it tends to be formulated in ideal terms. See, for example, J. S. Mill's most explicit statement of his position in Ch. II, paragraph 10 of *Utilitarianism* ". . . the standard of morality, which may accordingly be defined 'the rules and precepts for human conduct', by the observance of which an existence such as has been described might be, to the greatest extent possible, secured to all mankind . . ." In this passage, how is "possible" to be taken? Does it mean "possible, within the framework of existing institutions?" For one attempt to avoid in this way the difficulties inherent in an ideal formulation, see R. B. Brandt, *op. cit.*, pp. 396–400. This attempt goes only part of the way in meeting the difficulty. On the difficulty itself cf. H. J. McCloskey, "An Examination of Restricted Utilitarianism," *Philosophical Review*, Vol. LXVI (1957), esp. pp. 475–481 [reprinted in this volume, pp. 128–136]; and J. Austin, *op. cit.*, Lecture III.

On this alternative it always makes sense to ask whether or not a "moral or social convention" subscribed to in practice is best, and this gives sense to the question, sometimes asked, whether a people who follow their conventions act in the best way they could. At the same time the question, whether an individual ought to do something in particular—for example, repay money borrowed—is quite a different question, to be answered by referring, at least in part, to the practices and conventions of that society. Such a view does not make the blunder of taking an ideal system of rules as the criterion of which particular acts are right, and yet it does not endorse conventions which are obviously questionable. One may seek earnestly to reform the moral conventions of a people, and yet insist that these conventions, some of which are in need of reform, are the general criterion by which a man must decide what in particular he ought to do, and by which his acts are to be judged. At the same time, such a view need not dichotomize the two criteria. As we found above, rules of this kind have an open texture which permits the criterion of the rules to enter into their proper interpretation. I think we may presume, moreover, that there are instances in which one should violate the letter of a moral rule when following it would clearly be to the detriment of the general welfare, or the welfare of all parties concerned. Rule utilitarians could no doubt take instances of this sort to support their theory. As we also found above, one may admit this without depriving rules of their authority.[16]

---

[16] I think this is the most favorable interpretation which can be given to the utilitarianism of the nineteenth century reformers: They framed a theory which would make sense of reform, but at the same time had too much practical (if not always philosophical) sense to advocate the use of the criterion

III

3.0 A careful development and criticism of rule utilitarianism, as just outlined, would be worth while, but it is outside the range of this paper. Even without this development, however, it can be shown that rule utilitarians, by using the kind of rule in (1) as a model, have exercised a definite option, and I want to indicate the general character of this option. To do this, I shall first consider briefly the rules of certain kinds of games.[17]

3.1 Rules of common competitive games, such as baseball, chess, and the like, say how a game is to be played. They state the "object of the game," "the moves," "how the counting should go," etc. Often they are stated in "rule books," and sometimes they

of rules as the criterion of acts. It is as if they perceived the importance of moral rules and practices but were unable fully to accommodate these to their theory. I think that the presence of the two criteria, which the analysis of the rules in (1) clearly reveals, explains for example the "tension" between chapter two of Mill's *Utilitarianism* on the one hand, and chapters three and five on the other.

[17] I can be brief because rules of this kind have been discussed by others. I shall mostly confine myself to points not previously mentioned, or at least not emphasized. I am perhaps most indebted to Rawls's acute analysis of what he calls the "practice conception," and on the whole agree with it. The name is misleading since very many "practices," as we ordinarily think of them, are defined by rules (e.g. by job rules) which are quite unlike those to which his "practice conception of rules" properly applies. Although unimportant in itself, it is just this kind of thing, I suspect, which has led moral philosophers into serious error. One can sympathize since it is almost impossible to find a conventional expression which is not misleading in some important respect.

are enforced by referees appointed by an acknowledged authority. These formalities, however, are not
at all necessary. The rules must be "laid down" or
"adopted" in some sense, but all that is required
(in the case of those games being discussed) is that
a group of players "agree" on a set of rules. This
agreement may consist simply in their following and
enforcing rules which they all have learned: Think,
for example, of a group of small boys playing baseball, and think of the difference between one's knowing the rules and playing the game. In such cases
there is no formally agreed-upon authority; each
player—in principle—is both rule-follower and rule-
enforcer. No player has the authority to modify the
rules at will, but the players together can change
them in any way they see fit. As one should expect,
there are many variations.

In the latter respects game rules of this kind are
quite like the rules in (1). These game rules, however, noticeably lack the first major characteristic of
those rules: They are not designed to yield a product. More precisely, they are not adopted to promote
the attainment of a goal which, in the [39] senses indicated earlier, is "over and beyond" the rules.[18]
They do not serve a goal which is "logically independent" of the game which they define.

3.1.1 Of course people who play games do so with
various motives, and some of the goals which motivate
them are logically independent of the game; for example, exercise, recreation, the opportunity to talk
to friends or make a conquest. Undoubtedly games
are popular because they serve so many ends. Nevertheless, motives and goals of this kind are not es-

---

[18] Some games have become instruments to such a considerable degree, and some instrumental activities have become so
much like games, that no description will prevent the intru-
sion of dubious and borderline cases.

sential. Many players participate (so far as can be determined without psychoanalyzing them) "just because they want to" or simply "from love of the game." Actually this kind of motive, even if it is not typical, is that which is most distinctive of players: One who "loves a game" commonly regards another, who lacks the motive, as poorly appreciating "the quality of the game." This is apt to be missed just because games have been turned into instruments, for exercise, diversion, etc., to such a great degree. The point is, they *need* not be.

Moreover, games *qua* games do not seem to have a design or goal *different* from the motives of the rule-followers, in the way rules of jobs commonly do. What is this goal? One who most appreciates a game speaks about it rather as if it were an aesthetic object, worth playing on its own account and apart from any product or result; and if he is asked to justify his claim that it is good, he seems to have a problem analogous to that of justifying an aesthetic judgment.[19] Sometimes, to be sure, the rules of games are changed, and in particular instances violated, in order to change the consequences. Many official rules, for example, have been changed in order to lessen player injuries; and particular persons may find a game played by the official rules too strenuous, or pursuit of the ball after a bad drive too troublesome. These facts, however, do not imply that the rules are designed to produce consequences, such as the right amount of exercise or exertion, or the good health of the players. Changes of the kind

---

[19] This reminds one of the ancient distinctions between "doing" and "making," and between (what the medievals called) "immanent" and "transitive" activity. I do not mean to deny that some jobs are worth doing "on their own account," but even when "one enjoys a job," there is a discernible purpose which it is designed to promote.

mentioned simply indicate that the rules of a game, like the rules of a job, are adopted in a context by persons who have many desires and many obligations other than "to play the game" and "follow its rules." Games are often altered to make them harmonize better with such contextual features. It is true, of course, that persons who have turned games into instruments change or violate the rules more readily. As we say, these people do not take the game as seriously.

Some philosophers are inclined to say that even when one plays a game "just because he wants to" or "for love of the game," the game is still an instrument—to "his enjoyment" or "pleasure." This stand depends for its cogency on our being able to describe this pleasure or enjoyment without referring to the game, which should be possible if the pleasure or enjoyment really were something separate from playing the game. However, although it is clearly possible to play a game and not enjoy it, the converse does not appear plausible. To be sure, one sometimes says that he gets about the same enjoyment from one game as another, especially when the two are similar. But this is apt to mean that he has no strong preference for one game over another, that he likes one as well as the other, not that there is a kind of pleasurable feeling which in fact results from both, more or less equally, and which *conceivably* could be had from very different activities or even from being acted *on* in some way. (Similarly, when one says that he "likes to talk to one person about as much as another," this clearly does not mean that talking to the two persons produces the same kind of pleasure in him.) Moreover, when we speak of getting about the same enjoyment from two games, sometimes the "enjoyment" does not appear to be, strictly speaking, the enjoyment "of playing the game," but rather the enjoyment of exercising, talking to friends, etc. I do not deny, however, that games can become instruments. I want to argue that they need not be, often are not, and that in calling them games we do not imply that they are instruments.

The kind of goal the pursuits of which to some degree *is* essential to the playing of the game is the "object of the game," as defined by the rules, and the various sub-goals which promote this object according to the rules. Such goals as these, for example, "to score the most runs," "to get the batter out at second base," obviously are not logically independent of the rules of the game—if there were no rules it would be logically impossible to try to do these things. It is just nonsense to speak of [40] changing the rules so that one can better attain the object of the game.

3.1.2 Since the action within a game is designed to attain goals defined by the rules, the action as well as the goal logically depends on the rules: In important respects a move in the game has the consequences it has because the rules say it has; *in these respects* the rules define the consequences and determine the character of the action.[20] Since the character of instrumental action is fixed at least partly by the goal which the action is designed to serve, the action can be described in this essential respect, as a "trying to get the goal," without referring to or presupposing rules. In the case of play in a game, unless the game has become an instrument, this is not possible; if one describes the action in a game apart from the rules, as a "trying to catch a ball," he leaves out the design. On account of this difference one may feel inclined to say that whereas rules of the kind described in (1) *may* be used to describe

---

[20] This is the point which Rawls emphasized.

an action, game rules by defining new kinds of action just constitute "forms of life."[21]

3.2 However, this is but one side of the story, and if it were the only one it is not likely that the two kinds of rules would be confused. To see the other side, which is equally important, one should attend to the fact that the play in a game is not wholly defined by the rules of the game. "The kind of game he plays" ordinarily does not refer to the game as defined by the rules; "to play a game" ordinarily means more than following the rules. The point is that although the object of the game is defined by the rules, since the action in a game normally consists in "trying to attain that object," and since the game rules do not determine success in this respect, the action in this *respect* is instrumental. Players often develop tactics and strategies and skills in playing. Sometimes they follow what I have called practical maxims, and at other times they follow team rules agreed on among themselves or laid down by the "manager." The latter are, of course, examples of the rules described in (1). Obviously they should not be confused with rules of games, as I have described them. For one can be said to play a game without his following any particular set of instrumental rules.

The point of greatest importance here is that although game rules are not themselves instruments, they support, as it were, a considerable amount of instrumental activity, much of which logically could not be carried on without them. To play a game is typically to follow the rules of the game *and* engage in this instrumental activity; a "good player" does more than just follow the rules. Even one who "loves the game for its own sake" derives his satis-

---

[21] Cf. A. I. Melden, "Action," *Philosophical Review*, Vol. LXV (1956), 523–541.

faction from the kind of *instrumental* activity which the rules of the game make possible. Games make new goals, new pursuits, and new skills available to men.

In this situation it is not surprising that some should regard games themselves as instruments. To regard them in this way, however, would be to confuse their function.

IV

4.0 The rules of games just considered differ most significantly from the rules described in (1) because they are, by our criterion, "non-instrumental." This point of difference between the two kinds of rules is one of the most important to be found. I have been concerned to mark it here to focus attention on the thesis, maintained by many utilitarians, that moral rules and social institutions are instruments designed to promote a goal logically independent of the rules and institutions. The thesis is only rarely discussed, and I think that failure to discuss it helps account for the recurrent popularity of utilitarianism. However, morality is obviously not a game, and if the thesis is to be fully assessed, moral rules must be carefully analyzed and alternatives considered. This is out of the question here. In the remainder of this paper I shall note a complexity which is too often overlooked, and just indicate the critical force of certain recently developed lines of argument. However, the fundamental issue here is not at all new.[22]

[41]

---

[22] Historically one perhaps first senses the issue in his reading of Plato and Aristotle. Is man's end somehow "writ in his nature" in such a way that it can be determined apart from a determination of virtue? If so, it might be reasonable to regard virtue as a *means* to the end, and instruction in virtue

4.1 Consider the rule "Do not cheat." Often it is
taught in the context of a game, and it acquires a
rather specific sense in this context. The rule in this
use can be paraphrased as "Do not violate the rules

---

as a matter of learning from practical experience the best
means. On the other hand, if man's end cannot be determined
without the determination of virtue—if man's end is properly
defined in terms of virtue, as activity in accordance with it,
and man's nature is defined as potentialities for this end—then
virtue is not a means and its discovery in practical experience
must be understood differently. Although the second interpretation is the sounder, there were tendencies in medieval
thought to favor the first—undoubtedly deriving from the fact
that God, who is certainly different from man, was said to be
man's end. Moreover, the desire of God was said to be im-
planted in man's nature. This inclination was said to be a natural participation of the eternal law, and natural virtue was
said to be an insufficient means to [41] God. I think myself,
however, that the second interpretation gives a sounder
account of the ethics not only of Augustine but also of
Aquinas. Yet it is not surprising that out of this tradition there should have come the contrary (Lockian) doctrine
that natural law applies to man in a "state of nature," and that
men by compact make societies as a remedy for natural evils
and as a means to natural goals. This doctrine in turn, by way
of reaction, stimulated theories according to which the distinction of right and wrong is not founded in nature, but in
contract, convention, or rules. In the nineteenth century the
opposition between the two general points of view assumed
more of its original form when idealists worked out their own
interpretation of the social contract, and opposed utilitarianism. (See, for example, Bradley's "Pleasure for Pleasure's Sake"
in *Ethical Studies* and Bosanquet's *Philosophical Theory of
the State*.) Very recent philosophy in some respects strongly
resembles idealism, undoubtedly because it itself is a reaction
to a kind of philosophy which arose in reaction to idealism.
For one example, cf. Bosanquet, *op. cit.*, with A. I. Melden,
Rights and Right Conduct (Oxford, 1959).

This is, of course, only a fragmentary account of the historical origins of the issue.

of the game in order to gain an advantage for yourself." In this use the rule logically presupposes games as social institutions; if there were no games, the rule could not have this use and this meaning.

The same general point applies to many other moral rules, such as "Keep your promises," "Do not steal," and "Do not lie." Each of these logically presupposes institutions and practices, such as "promising," "a system of property," "a language." Since these moral rules presuppose such practices, they cannot be understood apart from them; the practice, constituted by its own rules, makes the moral rule meaningful. Philosophical analyses which have attempted to clarify moral rules apart from institutionalized practices have surrounded them with theoretical perplexities and turned them into "mere forms" of morality.[23]

However, the fact that these moral rules presuppose institutions or practices does not *in itself* decide the question whether or not they are instrumental and utilitarian. In some respects the rules "Do not cheat," "Do not lie," etc., are like the rules "Do not violate traffic lights," "Do not drive on the wrong side," etc. These rules obviously presuppose practices, and the rules and practices appear to be primarily instrumental and utilitarian. We can easily conceive of the practices being changed in order to provide a more effective system of traffic control.

On the utilitarian view moral rules and the institutions which they presuppose are rather like a system of this kind. The assumption is that men have various destinations which they want to reach and the social aim is to provide the system of institutions which will be most effective in helping them along.

---

[23] This misinterpretation accounts for some criticisms of a morality of rules. Cf. A. Macbeath, *Experiments in Living* (London, 1952), Lecture XIII.

As men together devise such public instruments as roads and bridges, which no one alone could construct, and then regulate the use of these instruments for the "public good," so on this view men together have developed such institutions as "promising," "a system of property," etc. These institutions may not have arisen through deliberate design, although (there often seems to be the assumption that) if an institution or practice has arisen, then it *must* have been rewarding, and consequently *must* have served some purpose. The instrumental character of these institutions is evidenced more directly, however, by the fact that persons hold and dispose of property, make promises, and, quite generally, engage in the life of their institutions with goals in mind. If these reasons are decisive, moreover, one's language, too, should be viewed as a social tool.[24] Certainly men have purposes in speaking.

As in the case of a traffic system, however, on occasion it is to a person's advantage to break the rules of their institutions. Men must be taught not to; they must be made to realize that temporary advantage is far outweighed by the more permanent benefits to be gained if all can be depended on to follow the rules. Moral rules, such as "Keep your promises," "Do not steal," "Do not lie," like the rules "Always obey traffic signals," "Do not drive on the wrong side," seem to be conceived as deriving from the occasional but recurrent conflict between private advantage and public institutions. Utilitarians commonly make the point that if a person in his own interest is sometimes led to violate a rule, he will nevertheless insist, also in his own interest, that others follow the rule: The "security" which derives from a system of public institutions is given an important place in moral theory.

---

[24] Cf. Hume's *Treatise*, III, II, II. Esp. p. 490 in Selby-Bigge edition.

Moral rules of this kind thus seem to be conceived as supports for and ancillary to the public institutions which they presuppose. If these rules could only be made to serve a system of truly [42] *rational* (i.e., utilitarian) institutions, the aforementioned conflict would be minimized, as the happiness of all was promoted. The negative morality of rules would be lost in liberal affection for the general welfare.

4.2 Moral rules of this kind in a sense do *tend* to support the institutions and practices which they presuppose: They *tend* to receive their effective interpretation from the character of the institutions, and they are both taught and reaffirmed most vigorously when persons from self-interest show an inclination to violate the rules of the institutions. As a consequence (and for an additional reason which will soon be apparent[25]) these institutions and practices have, as it were, a "moral dimension" or a "moral part." Nevertheless, in assessing rule utilitarianism it is important to distinguish moral rules on the one hand from other rules which also define and characterize the underlying institutions and practices. For it is possible to learn the rules of a game, and to play the game, without being tempted to cheat, without grasping the concept of "cheating," and without learning the moral rule "Do not cheat." It is not uncommon for children to do this. Children ordinarily also learn to speak correctly, in the sense of learning many rules of the language, without learning the rule "Do not lie," thus without grasping the moral concept of a lie. It may not be so evident, but it is also the case that one can learn many rules governing property, can learn to make a promise, etc., without grasping the moral force of the rules "Do not steal," "Keep your promises," etc. There are surely legal experts on property and

---

[25] See 4.5 below.

contract who have, as we say, very little moral understanding.[26]

In considering the soundness of rule utilitarianism,
there are thus two interrelated questions. The first
is whether or not the institutions of promising, property, language, etc., are instruments serving goals logically independent of these institutions. This bears on
the question of the soundness of utilitarianism not
only as a *moral* but as a *social* theory. Then there
is the more restricted question whether rule utilitarianism offers a sound account of moral rules.

4.3.1 Several lines of thought, some recently developed, bear on these questions. To take one example,
primarily as it applies to the first of the questions:
Utilitarians, as already indicated, have put considerable emphasis on "security," if not as *the* goal, nevertheless as an important "part" of the goal. A person
cannot be "secure," however, without being able to
count on others to act and refrain from acting in a
variety of ways. His counting on others, moreover,
is in a great many cases not "an expectation" based
on an ordinary induction. For most often the expec-

---

[26] Although an adequate description of property and promising in a sense implies that theft and promise-breaking are
morally wrong, a person may fail to "see" the implication.
When we teach a child what property and promising are, we
commonly say that it is wrong for him to take what belongs
to another and wrong for him not to do what he has promised
to do. So far, however, the child is not guilty of theft or
promise-breaking, and until he has witnessed them, or an inclination thereto, in himself or another (since he has not yet
had occasion to *use* the rules "Do not steal" and "Keep your
promises"), he will have little practical understanding of these
rules. Before he reaches this point, however, he may have
learned enough of the underlying rules to exchange property,
make promises, etc. Growth in moral understanding is long
and complex and participation in ordinary practices does not
wait upon it.

tation involved in one's counting on another is based on the fact that the action or restraint in question is governed by rules which define right, obligations, duties, etc.: One can count on another because the other (presumably) is acting on such rules.[27] For this reason the expression "counting on another" in many occasions of its use makes no more sense apart from rules than "deciding to act" or "acting" makes apart from reasons for acting. There is also the related point that the action which one counts on another to do, itself, in many cases presupposes rules; for example, just as one could not count on a person to "play first base" if there were no game of baseball, so one could not count on another to "keep his promise" or "respect property" if there were no practice of promising or institution of property.[28] Although "security" is an ambiguous term, in the sense in which it refers to a significant social goal it could not mean what it does without rules which define institutions and practices.

For both these reasons "security" just does not appear to be a goal which is logically independent of the rules of institutions and practices like property, promising, language, etc. Moreover, it would seem very strange to think of the greatest number having the greatest happiness or pleasure or welfare without being fairly secure. The utilitarian position thus appears to be quite vulnerable, even apart from the fact that its proponents have [43] notoriously failed to give "happiness," "pleasure," "welfare," and the like the clarity of meaning which they must have to function as goals.

4.3.2 Furthermore, as the earlier analysis of games revealed, the fact that one does many things as a

---

[27] Cf. Hart, *op. cit.*, pp. 54–7.

[28] Cf. Hume, *loc. cit.* Black and many others make the same point.

means to an end when engaging in a practice gives
no support to the claim that the practice itself is a
means. The fact that one uses various devices to win
a game does not imply that the game is an instrument,
and similarly, the fact that one uses words as tools,
or makes a promise or deals in property for some
purpose, does not support the view that institutions
and practices such as language, promising, and property are instruments for the promotion of goals logically independent of these institutions and practices.
Nor does this appear plausible: It seems rather to be
the case that institutions and practices create or establish most of the goals which men pursue, in the sense
that these goals, like the object of a game, would be
logically impossibe without the institutions and practices. It also appears that persons who engage in business, or make speeches, or follow intellectual pursuits ultimately because "they just enjoy doing these
things" are rather like players who enjoy a game for
its own sake—in the respect that they derive their
enjoyment from instrumental activity which is also
made possible by institutions and practices.

At this point, however, it becomes apparent that
much requires to be worked out before one can replace the utilitarian view of social institutions with
another which is more adequate.

4.4 When one turns to consider utilitarianism as a
theory of moral rules, *to some extent* the same arguments apply. For some moral rules *are* in some respect ancillary to the practices and institutions which
they presuppose, and in so far as this is the case,
then generally speaking moral rules are just as utilitarian as, and no more utilitarian than, these practices
and institutions. Notice that the most common uses
of the moral rules "Do not lie," "Do not steal," and
the like presuppose not only underlying institutions
and practices, but also, as suggested above, a tendency
or inclination of some persons at some times not to

conform to the institutions and practices. This seems to explain why persons living in a law-abiding community use these moral rules so little. This in turn suggests that moral rules are "protective devices," rather like a police system, which also is little used in a law-abiding community and which also presupposes both institutions and an inclination on the part of some persons to violate them. The "police" view of moral rules is partial, but it is also partly true: It helps one see why moral rules are so often conceived as "external" to an individual, imposing restraints on him (and why some philosophers tend to pattern moral rules on rules in a prison!) At the same time it helps one understand why some people "internalize" moral rules in the way they do. For some insist on the importance of following moral rules only because they value a system of institutions and the "happiness and security" which the institutions afford. Seeing that valued institutions would cease to exist if people generally did not act in the way moral rules prescribe, they teach these rules—although morality for them is primarily a matter of promoting individual or public welfare, and it would be better if moral rules had little use. This interest in morality is epitomized in the person who regards moral rules as a protector of life, liberty, and property; breaking the rules breeds fear, ruins business, and disrupts the game. This is the internalization of moral rules as ancillary to institutions; it tends to characterize utilitarians past and present.

4.5 Moral rules, however, may be internalized in quite another way, and on this account utilitarianism as a *moral* theory is open to an additional criticism specific to itself.

For a person who values an institution constituted by rules may come to see that rules by nature apply to all members of a class. One who sees this may then be led to look upon the rules which characterize some particular institutions and practices not simply as "applying to all," but at the same time as constituting "a common standard of correctness." And in this way one may be led to the abstract but practical conception of "a community of men living under the idea of law," of which particular institutions afford so many possible examples. In so far as one thinks that others as well as himself act under this conception, he will no doubt value a particular game or language or any other such institution not only *qua* game, *qua* language, etc., but also as a particular instance and a particular form of such a community.

When the idea of such a community is attained and made to govern practice (as it seems to have been, for example, by the Socrates of the *Crito*) then the moral rules "Do not lie," "Do not steal," etc., will appear in a new light. One who acts under such an idea will teach these rules neither as primarily negative and restraining, nor primarily as supports or protections for particular institutions. For although he may view the rules in these [44] ways, he will regard them primarily as affirming in so many different ways the fundamental principle "Live under the idea of law." The principle may be stated negatively, in the form "Do not make an exception of oneself," but his primary aim in teaching the rules will be to raise one to the conception of a moral community. Since such a community potentially includes all men, part of the challenge may be to find particular institutions in which the conception can be realized.

Moral rules regarded in this way of course still presuppose particular institutions and practices. However, they are no longer, properly speaking, "ancillary to" the institutions and practices: They now "add something" to the institutions and practices which they presuppose; the institutions and practices now have a new dimension. Cheating comes to be deplored not primarily because it tends to disrupt a game but because it detracts from the quality which a game can have. If there is cheating, one may simply prefer not to play. In a similar way, lying may be deplored because it detracts from the quality of speech, theft because it detracts from the quality of exchange, etc. Put affirmatively, the idea of a moral community is realizable analogically—only in a variety of forms— in sportsmanship, morally mature speech, honest argument, etc. It should be evident that common institutions and practices are often not in fact logically independent of morality; one has to form a limited or abstract conception of them to make them so.

When moral rules are regarded in this way,[29] then obviously they do not serve a goal logically independent of themselves. In the language of Mill, virtue has now become a "part" of the end, a "part of happiness." Only it is clear that when Mill said this, with his usual willingness to sacrifice theory to good sense, he deserted utilitarianism. The instrumental and utilitarian pattern just will not fit.

V

Further discussion of moral rules is beyond the aim of this paper. My primary purpose has been to contribute to the clarification of moral rules by clarifying a fundamental option open to moral theory. To this end I have both analyzed the general utilitarian view of social rules and practices, along with some variations, and I have tried to lay bare the (largely implicit) utilitarian view of moral rules. I have analyzed moral rules, however, only to the point where

[29] Cf. K. Baier, *op. cit.*, pp. 200–204, and W. D. Falk's comments on "natural obligation" and "mature moral thinking" in "Morality and Convention," *Journal of Philosophy*, vol. 57 (1960), p. 675–685.

the character and significance of the option, and the force of some of the arguments which apply, will be fairly clear. I do not want to suggest that all moral rules are like those which I have considered. The analysis of games, in distinguishing the moral player from the good player, may remind one that there are two traditions in the history of ethics, one emphasizing an exoteric ethic and a moral law known to all, the other an esoteric ethic and a virtue reserved for the wise. I have been concerned, almost exclusively, with the former, and not all of that.

In the course of the discussion attention has been called to the fact that moral rules can be (and thus tend to be) conceived as summaries, reports, practical maxims, rules designed to promote a goal, rules which define institutions, rules which protect institutions, and as particular forms of the fundamental principle of justice.[30] Marking the important differences between these alternatives should remove more than one confusion and at the same time provide *some* of the subtlety which will be needed if the discussion of moral rules is to make genuine advances in the future.

---

[30] The list is not meant to be exhaustive. Cf. e.g., D. S. Shwayder, "Moral Rules and Moral Maxims," *Ethics*, vol. 67 (1957), pp. 269–285.

A NON-UTILITARIAN
APPROACH
TO PUNISHMENT
H. J. McCloskey

Although the view that punishment is to be justified on utilitarian grounds has obvious appeal, an
examination of utilitarianism reveals that, consistently and accurately interpreted, it dictates unjust
punishments which are unacceptable to the common moral consciousness. In this rule-utilitarianism
is no more satisfactory than in act-utilitarianism.
Although the production of the greatest good, or
the greatest happiness, of the greatest number is
obviously a relevant consideration when determining which punishments may properly be inflicted, the question as to which punishment is just
is a distinct and more basic question and one which
must be answered before we can determine which
punishments are morally permissible. That a retributivist theory, which is a particular application
of a general principle of justice, can account more
satisfactorily for our notion of justice in punishment is a positive reason in its support.

FROM *Inquiry*, Vol. VIII (1965), 249–263. Reprinted by permission of the author and the editors of *Inquiry*. The footnotes which originally occurred at the end of the article on
page 263 have been placed at the bottom of pages.

I. Introduction

At first glance there are many obvious considerations
which seem to suggest a utilitarian approach to punishment. Crime is an evil and what we want to do is
not so much to cancel it out after it occurs as to prevent it. To punish crime when it occurs is, at best,
an imperfect state of affairs. Further, punishment, in-
voking as it does evils such as floggings, imprisonment, and death, is something which does not commend itself to us without argument. An obvious way
of attempting to justify such deliberately created evils
would be in terms of their utility.

  This is how crime and punishment impress on first
sight. A society in which there was no crime and no
punishment would be a much better society than one
with crime and resulting punishments. And punishment, involving evils such as deliberately inflicted suffering and even death, and consequential evils such
as the driving of some of its victims into despair and
even insanity, etc., harming and even wrecking [250]
their subsequent lives, and often also the lives of their
relatives and dependents, obviously needs justification.
To argue that it is useful, that good results come from
such punishment, is to offer a more plausible justification than many so-called retributive justifications.
It is obviously more plausible to argue that punishment is justified if and because it is useful than to
argue that punishment is justified because society has
a right to express its indignation at the actions of the
offender, or because punishment annuls and cancels
out the crime, or because the criminal, being a human
being, merits respect and hence has a right to his
punishment. Such retributive type justifications have
some point, but they are nonetheless implausible in a
way that the utilitarian justification is not. Yet I shall

be concerned to argue that the key to the morality
of punishment is to be found in terms of a retributive
theory, namely, the theory that evils should be dis-
tributed according to desert and that the vicious deserve to suffer. In so arguing, I shall be bringing
together and adding to a number of arguments I have
set out elsewhere.[1]

II. How Our Common Moral Consciousness Views Punishment

Is the punishment which commends itself to the moral
consciousness always useful punishment? And is all
punishment that is useful such that we should consider
it to be morally just and permissible? Punishment
which we commonly consider to be just is punishment
which is deserved. To be deserved, punishment must
be of an offender who is guilty of an offence in the
morally relevant sense of 'offence'. For instance, the
punishing of a man known to be innocent of any
crime shocks our moral consciousness and is seen as
a grave injustice. Similarly, punishment of a person
not responsible for his behaviour, e.g. a lunatic, is
evidently unjust and shocking. Punishment for what
is not an offence in the morally significant sense of
'offence' is equally unjust. To punish a man who
has tried his hardest to secure a job during a period
of acute and extensive unemployment for 'having insufficient means of support', or to punish a person
under a retroactive law is similarly unjust. So too,
if the offence for which the person punished is one
against a secret law which it was impossible for him

---

[1] 'An Examination of Restricted Utilitarianism', *Philosophical Review*, Vol. LXVI, 4 (Oct., 1957) [reprinted in this volume, pp. 117–141]; 'The Complexity of the Concepts of Punishment', *Philosophy*, Vol. XXXVII, pp. 307–325 (Oct., 1962).

to know of, the punishment is gravely unjust. Similarly, punishment of other innocent people—e.g. as scapegoats—to deter others, is [251] unjust and morally wrong. So too is collective punishment—killing all the members of a village or family for the offences of one member. Whether such punishments successfully deter seems irrelevant to the question of their justice. Similarly, certain punishments of persons who are offenders in the morally relevant sense of 'offenders' also impress us as gravely unjust. We now consider to have been gravely unjust the very severe punishments meted out to those punished by hanging or transportation and penal servitude for petty thefts in the 18th century. Comparable punishments, e.g. hanging for shoplifting from a food market, would be condemned today as equally unjust. It is conceivable that such unjust punishments may, in extreme circumstances, become permissible, but this would only be so if a grave evil has to be perpetrated to achieve a very considerable good.

In brief, our moral consciousness suggests that punishment, to be just, must be merited by the committing of an offence. It follows from this that punishment, to be justly administered, must involve care in determining whether the offending person is really a responsible agent. And it implies that the punishment must not be excessive. It must not exceed what is appropriate to the crime. We must always be able to say of the person punished that he deserved to be punished as he was punished. It is not enough to say that good results were achieved by punishing him. It is logically possible to say that the punishment was useful but undeserved, and deserved but not useful. It is not possible to say that the punishment was just although undeserved.

These features of ordinary moral thinking about just punishment appear to be features of which any defensible theory of punishment needs to take note.

Punishment of innocent people—through collective punishments, scapegoat punishment, as a result of inefficient trial procedures, corrupt police methods, mistaken tests of responsibility, etc., or by using criteria of what constitute offences which allow to be offences, offences under secret and retroactive laws—is unjust punishment, as is punishment which is disproportionate with the crime. Thus the punishment which we consider, after critical reflection, to be just punishment, is punishment which fits a retributive theory. It is to be noted that it is just punishment, not morally permissible punishment, of which this is being claimed. Sometimes it is morally permissible and obligatory to override the dictates of justice. The retributive theory is a theory about justice in punishment and tells only part of the whole story about the morality of punishment. It points to a very important consideration in determining the morality [252] of punishment—namely, its justice—and explains what punishments are just and why they are just.

Before proceeding further, some comment should be made concerning these allusions to 'what our common moral consciousness regards as just or unjust'. Utilitarians frequently wish to dismiss such appeals to our moral consciousness as amounting to an uncritical acceptance of our emotional responses. Obviously they are not that. Our uncritical moral consciousness gives answers which we do not accept as defensible after critical reflection, and it is the judgements which we accept after critical reflection which are being appealed to here. In any case, before the utilitarian starts questioning this appraoch, he would do well to make sure that he himself is secure from similar criticism. It might well be argued that his appeal to the principle of utility itself rests upon an uncritical emotional acceptance of what prima facie appears to be a high-minded moral principle but which, on critical examination, seems to involve grave moral evils. Thus the problem of method, and of justifying the use of this method, is one which the utilitarian shares with the non-utilitarian. It is not possible here to argue for the soundness of this mode of argument beyond noting that whether an intuitionist or non-cognitivist meta-ethic be true, this sort of appeal is what such meta-ethical theories suggest to be appropriate.

III. What Utilitarianism Appears to Entail in Respect of Punishment

Is all useful punishment just punishment, and is all just punishment useful? Here it is necessary first to dispose of what might not unfairly be described as 'red herring'. A lot of recent utilitarian writing is to the effect that punishment of the innocent is logically impossible, and hence that utilitarianism cannot be committed to punishment of the innocent. Their point is that the concept of punishment entails that the person being punished be an actual or supposed offender, for otherwise we do not call it punishment but injury, harm-infliction, social quarantining, etc. There are two good reasons for rejecting this argument as nothing but a red herring. Not all unjust punishment is punishment of the innocent. Much is punishment which is excessive. Thus even if punishment of the innocent were not logically possible, the problem of justice in punishment would remain in the form of showing [253] that only punishments commensurate with the offence were useful. Secondly, the verbal point leaves the issue of substance untouched. The real quarrel between the retributionist and the utilitarian is whether a system of inflictions of suffering on people without reference to the gravity of their offences or even to whether they have committed offences, is just and morally permissible. It is immaterial whether we call such deliberate inflictions of sufferings punishment, social surgery, social quarantining, etc. In any case, as I have elsewhere tried to show, the claim is evidently false. We the observers and the innocent victims of such punishment call it punishment, unjust punishment. In so referring to it there is no straining of language.

To consider now whether all useful punishment is just punishment. When the problem of utilitarianism in punishment is put in this way, the appeal of the utilitarian approach somewhat diminishes. It appears to be useful to do lots of things which are unjust and undesirable. Whilst it is no doubt true that harsh punishment isn't necessarily the most useful punishment, and that punishment of the guilty person is usually the most useful punishment, it is nonetheless easy to call to mind cases of punishment of innocent people, of mentally deranged people, of excessive punishment, etc, inflicted because it was believed to be useful. Furthermore, the person imposing such punishment seems not always to be mistaken. Similarly, punishment which is just may be less useful than rewards. With some criminals, it may be more useful to reward them. As Ross observes:

> A utilitarian theory, whether of the hedonistic or of the 'ideal' kind, if it justifies punishment at all, is bound to justify it solely on the ground of the effects it produces. . . . In principle, then, the punishment of a guilty person is treated by utilitarians as not different in kind from the imposition of inconvenience, say by quarantine regulations, on innocent individuals for the good of the community.[2]

----

[2] W. D. Ross, *The Right and the Good*, Oxford University Press, Oxford 1930, p. 56.

What is shocking about this, and what most utilitarians now seek to avoid admitting to be an implication of utilitarianism, is the implication that grave injustices in the form of punishment of the innocent, of those not responsible for their acts, or harsh punishments of those guilty of trivial offences, are dictated by their theory. We may sometimes best deter others by punishing, by framing, an innocent man who is generally believed to be guilty, or by adopting rough and ready trial procedures, as is done by army courts martial in the heat of battle in respect of deserters, etc; or we may severely punish a person not [254] responsible for his actions, as so often happens with military punishments for cowardice, and in civil cases involving sex crimes where the legal definition of insanity may fail to cover the relevant cases of insanity. Sometimes we may deter others by imposing ruthless sentences for crimes which are widespread, as with car stealing and shoplifting in food markets. We may make people very thoughtful about their political commitments by having retroactive laws about their political affiliations; and we may, by secret laws, such as make to be major crimes what are believed simply to be anti-social practices and not crimes at all, usefully encourage a watchful, public-spirited behaviour. If the greatest good or the greatest happiness of the greatest number is the foundation of the morality and justice of punishment, there can be no guarantee that some such injustices may not be dictated by it. Indeed, one would expect that it would depend on the details of the situation and on the general features of the society, which punishments and institutions of punishment were most useful. In most practical affairs affecting human welfare, e.g. forms of government, laws, social institutions, etc., what is useful is relative to the society and situation. It would therefore be surprising if this were not also the case with punishment. We should reasonably expect to find that different punishments and systems of punishment were useful for different occasions, times, communities, peoples, and be such that some useful punishments involved grave and shocking injustices. Whether this is in fact the case is an empirical matter which is best settled by social and historical research, for there is evidence available which bears on which of the various types of punishments and institutions work best in the sense of promoting the greatest good. Although this is not a question for which the philosopher *qua* philosopher is well equipped to deal, I shall nonetheless later briefly look at a number of considerations which are relevant to it, but only because the utilitarian usually bases his defence of utilitarianism on his alleged knowledge of empirical matters of fact, upon his claim to know that the particular punishments and that system of punishment which we regard as most just, are most conducive to the general good. J. Bentham, and in our own day, J. J. C. Smart, are among the relatively few utilitarians who are prepared—in the case of Smart, albeit reluctantly—to accept that utilitarian punishment may be unjust by conventional standards, but morally right nonetheless.

Against the utilitarian who seeks to argue that utilitarianism does not involve unjust punishment, there is a very simple argument, [255] namely, that whether or not unjust punishments are in fact useful, it is logically possible that they will at some time become useful, in which case utilitarians are committed to them. Utilitarianism involves the conclusion that if it is useful to punish lunatics, mentally deranged people, innocent people framed as being guilty, etc., it is obligatory to do so. It would be merely a contingent fact, if it were a fact at all, that the punishment which works is that which we consider to be morally just. In principle, the utilitarian is committed to saying that we should not ask 'Is the punishment deserved?'

The notion of desert does not arise for him. The only relevant issue is whether the punishment produces greater good.

IV. What Utilitarianism in Fact Entails in the Light of Empirical Considerations

What is the truth about the utility of the various types of punishments? As I have already suggested, it would be astonishing if, in the sphere of punishment, only those punishments and that institution of punishment we consider to be just, worked best. To look at particular examples.

In an article cited above, I argued that a utilitarian would be committed to unjust punishment, and used the example of a sheriff framing an innocent negro in order to stop a series of lynchings which he knew would occur if the guilty person were not immediately found, or believed to have been found.[3] I suggested that if the sheriff were a utilitarian he would frame an innocent man to save the lives of others. Against this example, it is suggested that we cannot know with certainty what the consequences of framing the negro would be, and that there may be other important consequences besides the prevention of lynchings. Utilitarians point to the importance of people having confidence in the impartiality and fairness of the legal system, a belief that lawful behaviour pays, etc. However, as the example is set up, only the sheriff, the innocent victim and the guilty man and not the general public, would know there had been a frame-up. Further, even if a few others knew, this would not mean that everyone knew; and even

---

[3] 'An Examination of Restricted Utilitarianism', *op. cit.*, pp. 468–469 [reprinted above, pp. 120–121].

if everyone came to know, surely, if utilitarianism is thought to be the true moral theory, the general body of citizens ought to be happier believing that their sheriff is promoting what is right rather than promoting non-utilitarian standards of justice. Since complex factors are involved, this example is not as decisive as is desirable. It can readily be modified [256] so as to avoid many of these complications and hence become more decisive. Suppose a utilitarian were visiting an area in which there was racial strife, and that, during his visit, a negro rapes a white woman, and that race riots occur as a result of the crime, white mobs, with the connivance of the police, bashing and killing negroes, etc. Suppose too that our utilitarian is in the area of the crime when it is committed such that his testimony could bring about the conviction of a particular negro. If he knows that a quick arrest will stop the riots and lynchings, surely, as a utilitarian, he must conclude that he has a duty to bear false witness in order to bring about the punishment of an innocent person. In such a situation, he has, on utilitarian theory, an evident duty to bring about the punishment of an innocent man. What unpredictable consequences, etc., are present here other than of a kind that are present in every moral situation? Clearly, the utilitarian will not be corrupted by bearing false witness, for he will be doing what he believes to be his duty. It is relevant that it is rare for any of us to be in a situation in which we can usefully and tellingly bear false witness against others.

We may similarly give possible examples of useful punishments of other unjust kinds. Scapegoat punishment need not be and typically is not of a framed person. It may be useful. An occupying power which is experiencing trouble with the local population may find it useful to punish, by killing, some of the best loved citizen leaders, each time an act of rebellion occurs; but such punishments do not commend them-

selves to us as just and right. Similarly, collective
punishment is often useful—consider its use in schools.
There we consider it unjust but morally permissible
because of its great utility. Collective punishments
of the kind employed by the Nazis in Czechoslovakia
—destroying a village and punishing its inhabitants
for the acts of a few—are notorious as war crimes.
Yet they appear to have been useful in the sense of
achieving Nazi objectives. It may be objected that
the Nazi sense of values was mistaken, that such
punishment would not contribute towards realizing
higher values and goods. But it is partly an accident
of history that it was the Nazis who, in recent times,
resorted to this method. If we had had to occupy a
Nazi territory with inadequate troops, this might have
been the only effective way of maintaining order.
As with human affairs generally, it would depend on
many factors, including the strength of our troops,
the degree of hostility of the occupied people, their
temper and likely reaction to this sort of collective
punishment, etc. Punishment of relatives could also
be useful. [257] It would be an interesting social experiment in those modern democracies which are
plagued by juvenile delinquency, for parents as well
as the teenage delinquents to be punished. Such
punishment would be unjust but it might well be useful. It would need a number of social experiments to
see whether it is or is not useful. It is not a matter we
can settle by intuitive insight. If it did prove useful, it
is probable people would come to think of such punishment of parents as punishment for the offence of
being a parent of a delinquent! This would obscure
the awareness of the injustice of such punishment,
but it would nonetheless be unjust punishment.

Similarly with punishment for offences under secret
and retroactive laws. Such laws, it is true, would be
useful only if used sparingly and for very good reasons
but it is not hard to imagine cases where the use

of a retroactive law might be useful in the long as well as in the short run. That a plausible case could have been made out for introducing retroactive laws in post-war Germany on utilitarian grounds as well as on the other sorts of grounds indicated by legal theorists, suggests that such cases do occur. They may be the most useful means, they may, in the German case, even have been morally permissible means and the means of achieving greater total justice; but they are nonetheless means which in themselves are unjust. Retroactive laws are really a kind of secret law. Their injustice consists in this; and secret laws, like them, seem useful if used sparingly and with discretion. The Nazis certainly believed them to be very useful but again it will no doubt be said that this was because their system of values was mistaken. However, unless the system of values includes respect for considerations of justice, such secret laws are possibly useful instruments for promoting good.

In our own community we define 'offence' in such a way, with various laws, that we condone unjust punishment because of its utility. The vagrancy law is a very useful law but what it declares to be an offence is hardly an offence in the morally relevant sense. And it is not difficult to imagine countries in which it would be useful to have a law making it an offence to arouse the suspicions of the government. Suppose there were a democratic revolution in Spain, or in Russia, which led to the perilous existence of a democratic government. Such a government might find that the only way in which it could safely continue in existence was by having such a law and similar laws involving unjust punishments. It would then have to consider which was morally more important—to avoid the unjust punishments which such a law involves, or to secure and make permanent a democratic [258] form of government which achieved greater over-all injustice. That is, it would face conflicting claims of justice.

In an ignorant community it might well be useful to punish as responsible moral agents 'criminals' who in fact were not responsible for their actions but who were generally believed to be responsible agents. The experts suggest that many sex offenders and others who commit the more shocking crimes, are of this type, but even in reasonably enlightened communities the general body of citizens do not always accept the judgements of the experts. Thus, in communities in which enlightened opinion generally prevails (and these are few) punishment of mentally deranged 'criminals' would have little if any deterrent value, whereas in most communities some mentally deranged people may usefully be punished, and in ignorant, backward communities very useful results may come from punishing those not responsible for their actions. Similarly, very undesirable results may come from not punishing individuals generally believed to be fully responsible moral agents. Yet, clearly, the morality of punishing such people does not depend on the degree of the enlightenment of the community. Utilitarian theory suggests that it does, that such punishment is right and just in ignorant, prejudiced communities, unjust in enlightened communities. The utility of such punishment varies in this way, but not its justice. The tests of responsible action are very difficult to determine, although this need not worry the utilitarian who should use the test of utility in this area as elsewhere. However, to make my point, we need not consider borderline cases. The more atrocious and abominable the crime, the more pointless its brutality is, the more likely it is that the criminal was not responsible and the more likely that the general public will believe him to be fully responsible and deserving of the severest punishment.

Utilitarians often admit that particular punishments may be useful but unjust and argue that utilitarianism becomes more plausible and indeed, acceptable, if it is advanced as a theory about the test of rules and institutions. These utilitarians argue that we should not test particular punishments by reference to their consequences; rather, we should test the whole institution of punishment in this way, by reference to the consequences of the whole institution.

This seems an incredible concession; yet rule-utilitarianism enjoys widespread support and is perhaps the dominant version of utilitarianism. It is argued that particular utilitarian punishments may be unjust but that useful systems of punishment are those which are just [259] systems in the judgment of our reflective moral consciousness. This modification of utilitarianism involves a strange concession. After all, if the test of right and wrong rules and institutions lies in their utility, it is surely fantastic to suggest that this test should be confined to rules and institutions, unless it is useful so to confine its application. Clearly, when we judge the utility of particular actions, we should take note of the effects on the institution or rule, but surely, it is individual acts and their consequences which ultimately matter for the utilitarian. There are therefore good reasons for believing that the half-hearted utilitarianism of rule-utilitarianism involves an indefensible compromise between act-utilitarianism and Ross's theory of a plurality of irreducible prima facie duties.

To consider now the implications of rule-utilitarianism. As with act-utilitarianism, it would be surprising if what was useful was also at all times just, and that what was the most useful institution of punishment was the same under all conditions and for all times. For example, what we in Australia regard as useful and just, fair trial procedures—and these are an important part of justice in punishment—

for example, rules about the burden of proof, strict limitation of newspaper comment before and during the trial, selection of the jury, provision of legal aid for the needy, etc., differ from those found useful in dictatorships. Also, obviously a country emerging from the instability of a great revolution cannot afford to take risks with criminals and counter-revolutionaries which a stable, secure, well established community can afford to take. In Australia we can take the risk of allowing a few traitors to escape deserved punishment as a result of our careful procedures directed at ensuring that the innocent be not punished in error. During a war we may take fewer risks but at the expense of injustices. In an unstable community, immediately after a revolution, a more cavalier approach to justice is usually found to be the most useful approach. And there are differences within any one community. What is useful for civil courts is not necessarily what is most useful for military courts, and the most useful 'institution' for the whole community may be a mixture of different systems of justice and punishment. Thus not only particular punishments but also whole institutions of punishment may be useful but of a kind we consider to be gravely unjust. It is these difficulties of utilitarianism—of act- and rule-utilitarianism—and the facts which give rise to these difficulties which give to the retributive theory, that the vicious deserve to suffer, its initial plausibility. [260]

V. Positive Considerations for a Retributive Theory of Punishment

There are many positive considerations in support of the retributive theory of punishment, if it is constructed as the theory that the vicious deserve to suffer. Firstly, it is a particular application of a general principle of justice, namely, that equals should be treated equally and unequals unequally. This is a principle which has won very general acceptance as a self-evident principle of justice. It is the principle from which the more celebrated, yet opposed accounts of justice, are derived. It is a principle which has wide application and which underlies our judgements of justice in the various areas. We think of it as applying—other things being equal—to fair prices, wages, and treatment generally. It is in terms of such a principle that we think that political discrimination against women and peoples of special races is unjust, and that against children, just. Justice in these areas involves treating equals equally, unequals unequally—where the equals are equal in the relevant respect, and the unequals unequal in the relevant respect. Hence it is that we think it just to deny women some jobs because of their weaker physique, but unjust to exclude a woman from a post such as librarian or violinist if she is more proficient as such than other candidates for the post. So too with justice and punishment. The criminal is one who has made himself unequal in the relevant sense. Hence he merits unequal treatment. In this case, unequal treatment amounts to deliberate infliction of evils— suffering or death.

We need now to consider whether our retributive theory implies that there is a duty to punish with full, deserved punishment. Look at the other areas of justice, for example, wage justice. If it is just, say, to pay a labourer £20 a week, there is no breach of justice if the employer shows benevolence and pays £25, whereas there is a grave breach if he pays only £15. Similarly with retributive justice, but in a reverse way. We do not act unjustly if, moved by benevolence, we impose less than is demanded by justice, but there is a grave injustice if the deserved punishment is exceeded. If the deserved punishment is inflicted, all we need to do to justify it is to point out that the crime committed deserved and merited such punishment. Suppose that the just punishment for murder is imprisonment for 15 years. Suppose also that the judge knows that the murderer he is about to sentence will never be tempted to commit another murder, that he is deeply and [261] genuinely remorseful, and that others will not be encouraged to commit murders if he is treated leniently. If the judge imposed a mild penalty we should probably applaud his humanity, but if he imposed the maximum penalty we should not be entitled to condemn him as unjust. What we say in cases like this is that the judge is a hard, even harsh, man, not that he is an unjust man.

Is only deserved punishment morally permissible? Obviously not. Here we might take an analogy with other parts of morality. It is wrong to lie, to break promises, or to steal. This is not to say that we are never obliged to lie, break promises, steal, etc. What it means is that we need to have another, conflicting, more stringent duty which overrides the duty to tell the truth, keep our promise, or not steal, if we are to be justified in lying, breaking our promise, or stealing. Similarly with justice in punishment. The fact that a punishment is just entitles the appropriate authority to inflict it, but that is not to say that it must be inflicted nor that more cannot properly be inflicted. Many considerations may weigh with the relevant authority and make it morally right to inflict more or less than is strictly just; and not all such considerations will be utilitarian considerations—some may be other considerations of justice. We determine what punishment ought to be inflicted by taking into account firstly what punishment is deserved, and then other considerations. Relevant here are considerations such as that the criminal's wife and children may be the real victims of the punishment, that the criminal would be unable to make restitution to the person whose property he has stolen; of benevolence, e.g. in not imposing the punishment because the criminal has already suffered greatly in blinding himself in attempting to blow a safe; of the general good, as in making an example of the criminal and inflicting more than the deserved punishment because of the grave consequences that will come about if this type of crime is not immediately checked, etc. Production of the greatest good is obviously a relevant consideration when determining which punishment may properly be inflicted, but the question as to which punishment is just is a much more basic and important consideration. When considering that question we need to determine whether the person to be punished committed an offence in the morally relevant sense of 'offence' and what punishment is commensurate with the offence.

It is important here to note and dismiss a commonly made criticism of this retributive theory, namely, that there is no objective test of the gravity of a crime except in terms of the penalty attached to the crime. [262] If the penalty is hanging, then, it is argued, the crime is a serious one; if the penalty is a £2 fine, it is a trivial offence. This criticism is often reinforced by the contention that if all the people in any given group were to make out lists of crimes in order of their gravity, they would give significantly different lists such that what appear as grave crimes on one list are minor crimes on other lists. Obviously, if this criticism were sound, it would mean that one very important element of the retributive theory would be nullified, for punishment could not be other than commensurate with the offence. However, this criticism is unsound and rests on a number of confusions.

It is true that we speak of a crime as serious if

the penalty is hanging, but this is not to say that it is therefore a grave crime in the morally significant sense of 'grave crime'. The fact that hanging was the penalty for stealing a loaf of bread made that a serious offence in one sense but not in another, for we speak of the punishment as gravely disproportion-ate and as treating the offence as much more serious than it really is. It is on this basis that we can and do speak of penalties as being too light or too heavy, even where similar offences have similar penalties. It is unjust that the theft of a loaf of bread should meet with the same punishment as murder. Further, the fact that we reach different conclusions about the relative gravity of different crimes constitutes no dif-ficulty for the retributive theory. Most of us would agree that murder is a very serious crime and that shoplifting a cake of soap is a considerably lesser offence. We should perhaps differ about such ques-tions as to whether kidnapping is more or less serious than blackmail, whether embezzlement should be treated as a lesser crime than housebreaking, whether stealing a car worth £2,000 is less serious than steal-ing £2,000 worth of jewelry. We do disagree, and most of us would have doubts about the right order of the gravity of crimes. This shows very little. We have the same doubts—and disagreements—in other areas of morality where we are uncertain about which duties are more stringent, and where we differ from others in our ordering of duties. Similarly, utilitarians differ among themselves about goods such that if a group of utilitarians were asked to list goods in their order of goodness we could confidently expect dif-ferent lists of different goods and of goods listed in different orders. But this would not show that utilitarianism is therefore a theory to be discounted. It shows simply that whatever theory of punishment is adopted, there will be disagreements and uncer-tainties as to precisely what it dictates. With the utilitarian theory, the uncertainty and doubts arise concerning [263] the assessments of the value of the goods and the determination of which goods should be promoted by punishment. With the retributive theory the difficulties arise in determining the relative gravity of offences; and there, clearly, the appropriate method of seeking to resolve our doubts is neither to look at what punishments are in fact imposed, nor at what punishments will produce the greatest good, but rather to look at the nature of the offence itself.

A UTILITARIAN REPLY
TO DR. McCLOSKEY
T. L. S. Sprigge

A theory of punishment should tell us not only
when punishment is permissible but also when it
is a duty. It is not clear whether McCloskey's retributivism is supposed to do this. His arguments
against utilitarianism consist largely in examples of
punishments unacceptable to the common moral
consciousness but supposedly approved of by the
consistent utilitarian. We remain unpersuaded to
abandon our utilitarianism. The examples are often
fanciful in character, a point which (*pace* Mc-
Closkey) does rob them of much of their force. If
there was no tension between utilitarian precepts
and those which come naturally to plain men, utilitarianism could have no claim to provide a critique
of moralities. The utilitarian's attitude to such tensions is somewhat complicated, but what is certain
is that there is more room in his system for the
sentiments to which McCloskey appeals against him
than McCloskey realizes. We agree with McCloskey, however, on the absurdity of substituting rule-
utilitarianism for act-utilitarianism as an answer to
his attacks. The distinction itself may represent a

FROM *Inquiry*, Vol. VIII (1965), 264–291. Reprinted by permission of the author and the editors of *Inquiry*.

conceptual confuson. In our view, indeed, unmodified act-utilitarianism provides the best moral basis
for thought about punishment.

I.   Introduction

Dr. McCloskey's article* is an impressive presenta-
tion of many of the main arguments against utilitarianism as a theory of punishment, and in favour
of retributivism. As one who favours the utilitarian
view I am very pleased at this opportunity to see
whether I can find satisfactory rejoinders. Moreover
I am struck by the fact that McCloskey has a better
grasp of the essentials of the kind of moral attitude
which utilitarianism presents than do many of its opponents or even proponents.

The order of my comments will follow his article.
[265]

Now utilitarianism exists both as a general theory
and as one specifically about punishment. The general
theory entails the specific theory, but the converse
does not hold. However, one who was a utilitarian
about the particular kind of action called punishment,
but not about every kind of action, might run into
difficulties if an act of punishment was also one of
those acts to which he applied non-utilitarian criteria.
My discussion is doubtless applicable to utilitarianism
simply as a theory of punishment, but I shall be
assuming for the most part that the theory of punish-

---

* Page references in brackets refer to 'A Non-Utilitarian
Approach to Punishment' by H. J. McCloskey in this same
issue of *Inquiry* [reprinted in this volume, pp. 239–259; the
original page numbers referred to by Sprigge are given in
brackets in the text of McCloskey's article as reprinted in
this volume].

ment is just one application of the general ethical theory.

McCloskey does not specify the kind of utilitarianism he is attacking. Is it hedonistic or ideal utilitarianism? I shall take it that it is the former which is in question, though here again my remarks would doubtless serve as well in defence of the latter. I concentrate on hedonistic utilitarianism partly because it is my own view, partly because the issue between the ideal utilitarian and the non-utilitarian lacks sharpness, seeing that by adopting certain views regarding what is intrinsically good, and using the principle of organic unities, the ideal utilitarian can accept the substance of any non-utilitarian judgement. (Cf. A. C. Ewing's article in *British Philosophy in the Mid-Century*, ed. C. A. Mace.)

There is no time to be very nice in our formulation of hedonistic utilitarianism. This formulation will have to do: An act is wrong or bad if and only if *either* it produces more unhappiness than happiness, *or* although it produces more happiness than unhappiness, the unhappiness it produces is not required for the production of that happiness. Other acts are morally permissible, and if they produce a great deal of happiness actually *good*.

My reasons for favouring this rather than some more familiar formulations will have to go unstated here, as will some points of clarification. One may remark, however, that the happiness or unhappiness in question is such as is reasonably predictable as a consequence of the action, and has a weight according to its degree of probability. Moreover one must include the prevention of unhappiness in the term 'happiness' and of happiness in 'unhappiness'. This last point, however, can lead to paradoxes unless certain restrictions are introduced.

So much by way of introduction. [266]

II. Some Distinctions

a) *Unjust and Undeserved Punishment*

A preliminary question arising from page 251 of
McCloskey's article is this. Just how does he think
the two terms 'deserved punishment' and 'just punishment' are related? Are they supposed to be syn-
onyms?

Perhaps his view is this. The terms 'just' and
'unjust' apply to activities of many sorts, though in
each case they make the same sort of contrast. In
the case of punishment the contrast they make is the
same as that made by 'deserved' and 'undeserved'.
The two pairs are not, however, exactly synonymous,
because of this fact, that 'just' and 'unjust' make
similar but other contrasts in cases where 'deserved'
and 'undeserved' do not apply, and we don't want
to say that 'just' and 'unjust' have different meanings
in these other cases.

Perhaps this is McCloskey's view. At any rate it
seems a plausible one.

b) *Just, Right and Permissible Punishment Distin-guished*

McCloskey emphasizes the distinction between just
punishment and morally permissible punishment (p.
251). I shall argue that this distinction is acceptable
to the utilitarian and even useful to him in meeting
some of McCloskey's criticisms. But first I want to
turn to another distinction, that between morally permissible and morally obligatory punishment. Although McCloskey recognizes this distinction, I think
he pays it insufficient attention.

Both these terms are in a certain sense relative.

That is one cannot properly say that the punishment of Smith for a certain offence in a certain manner is itself morally permissible or morally obligatory, one must specify the person for whom it is so. It might be morally permissible (or obligatory) for a father to punish a child in a certain manner, but not for a neighbour to do so. But in a general discussion one need not always specify the potential punishment-imposer to whom these terms are relative, provided it is understood that they are thus relative.

It is presumably sometimes not only morally permissible to punish but actually morally obligatory to do so. A magistrate who never punished would probably be failing in his duty. McCloskey pays great attention to the justice of a punishment as the main reason for its being morally permissible, but he would surely allow, indeed even insist, [267] that it was also on many occasions the main reason for its being morally obligatory.

It is, above all, on page 261 that I find a certain unclarity on this point. He there raises the question whether *only* deserved (= just) punishment is morally permissible, which is equivalent to the question whether unjust punishment is not sometimes morally permissible. He answers it in the negative, drawing an analogy with other parts of morality. For he points out that although it is wrong to lie, break promises or steal, it is sometimes (morally) obligatory to do so. His point can be put in the terminology of W. D. Ross. There is always a prima facie duty to refrain from lying (breaking a promise, stealing) but sometimes another prima facie duty which on this particular occasion is more stringent conflicts with this duty, and our final duty involves lying (breaking a promise, stealing). It is similar with punishment.

The analogous point concerning punishment which this most obviously suggests is that although there is a prima facie duty to refrain from unjust punish-

ment, another prima facie duty which is on this
occasion more stringent may dictate such punishment as our final duty. So far our concern seems
to be with the prima facie moral character of an
unjust punishment, rather than with that of a just
punishment. But it is rather to this latter that attention must turn when he says: 'The fact that a
punishment is just entitles the appropriate authority
to inflict it . . .' Now is the main prima facie character
of a just punishment moral obligatoriness or moral
permissibility? The quotation suggests the latter. But
he says later: 'We determine what punishment ought
to be inflicted firstly by taking into account what
punishment is deserved, and then other considerations.' To determine that a punishment ought to be
inflicted is to determine that it is morally obligatory,
and not simply that it is permissible. Here justice
(= deservedness) comes in *first* apparently, which
is to say surely that it bestows prima facie obligatoriness, not merely permissibility. For in general, if
one wonders what one ought to do in a given situation
one concerns oneself *first* with such (prima facie)
duties or obligations as the situation may impose, not
with what it merely allows.

It is true that one of its recent proponents has
urged that retributivism does not state positive
grounds for punishing, but simply specifies conditions which must hold if other grounds for punishing
are to be acted on. (See 'The Retributivist Hits Back',
by K. G. Armstrong in *Mind*, October 1961.) But
however this may be, it seems clear that on any
reasonable definition of Justice, it is something which
there is [268] a positive duty to promote, and not
something which it is merely morally permissible to
promote. It would be odd if this did not extend to just
punishment.

So I think we may take it that the fact that a
punishment is just implies its prima facie obligatori-

ness, not merely its permissibility. It is not, however, enough to establish its final or actual permissibility, let alone its obligatoriness, for other considerations might show that infliction of the punishment was actually wrong in the circumstances.

This conclusion is not inconsistent with McCloskey's article, and I should expect him to accept it. But it seemed desirable to point out the need not only for distinguishing the terms 'just punishment' and 'permissible punishment', but for distinguishing each of these from 'obligatory punishment'.

On page 251 McCloskey emphasizes the point that retributivism 'tells only part of the whole story about the morality of punishment. It points to a very important consideration in determining the morality of punishment—namely, its justice—and explains what punishments are just and why they are just'. But an unjust punishment may at times be morally permissible (or even obligatory?) for other reasons.

This admission blunts the force of certain of McCloskey's arguments against utilitarianism. To show that the utilitarian must classify as obligatory or permissible certain punishments which the common moral consciousness calls unjust is not of itself enough to show that the utilitarian diverges from this common consciousness. For the utilitarian might admit that they were *unjust*.

He can indeed only do this if he admits that although the principle of utility gives the criteria for morally permissible or obligatory punishment, the criteria for just punishment cannot simply be identified with this. Perhaps this sounds like the admission of conflicting moral criteria, but that would be a misunderstanding.

The utilitarian may allow that there are certain goods the promotion or diminution of which is likely to be the main way in which actions of certain recognized classes promote or diminish the general good.

That is, it will usually be true that when such an action promotes more than it diminishes goods of this type it promotes the general good more than it diminishes it, and usually true that when it diminishes more than it promotes goods of this type it diminishes more than it promotes the general good. In short, any reverse effects such actions have on goods of other types may be rather seldom sufficient to count for much against its effects on goods of this type. [269]

Of course, evils here are as relevant as goods, and one must understand such phrases as 'diminishing goods of this type' as covering also 'increasing evils of this type'.

If one is evaluating an action belonging to such a class the first question one will naturally ask will concern its effects on goods of this type. For the utilitarian consideration of the likely effects of an action will properly start with those effects most likely to be important. Life is normally too complicated for equal attention to be paid to the effects it may have in every field irrespective of any prior presumptions as to where effects of the greatest importance are to be found. This being so, what more sensible than a special term for an action of this class which increases rather than diminishes goods of this class, with an opposite term for the opposite case? Now I suggest that the utilitarian may find the words 'just' and 'unjust' ideally suited for such a role. To the extent that ordinary moral opinion and terminology is of a utilitarian character they seem to play this role already, but the utilitarian need not deny that they sometimes have a less utilitarian character in ordinary usage.

If this view is right, actions which come under the heading *imposition or infliction of punishment* are peculiarly calculated to increase or decrease goods (or evils) of a certain type, which we may call the goods (or evils) of justice, and usually their main effect on the common good (or ill) is determined by their effects on these goods (or evils) of justice. All such actions will be appropriately called 'just' or 'unjust' according as they increase or diminish the goods of justice. It will usually but not necessarily always be true that just actions are right or good from a utilitarian point of view, and unjust ones are bad or wrong.

A similar account might be given of 'just' and 'unjust' as applied to actions of other recognized types, but we must leave it an open question how far it would be the same goods of justice which would then be in question.

If it were my present purpose to expound a utilitarian view of justice in full there are various loose ends I should have to tie up. Moreover I should of course have to specify what these goods of justice are. But even without this I have said enough to show the kind of way in which the utilitarian may rebut some of McCloskey's criticisms. Actually Mill's account of justice falls more or less within the pattern described. One point to be noticed, however, is this. The goods and evils of justice need not themselves be pleasures or pains. They may simply be events with a special tendency to produce pleasure or pain. [270]

So the utilitarian need not assimilate the question whether a punishment is just or unjust to the question whether it is useful or harmful. The former question concerns only one specific set of utilities. Even if in theory utilitarianism can dictate the rightness of punishing an innocent man, it would not have to describe it as just. To argue against the utilitarian here, then, appealing to the admitted injustice of such punishment is not enough; it must be shown that the circumstances which on utilitarian theory would demand that we override the dictates of justice are not such as should be accepted as doing so. It is a great point gained for the utilitarian when a retributivist admits (as McCloskey does) that sometimes it is permissible (even desirable?) to override the dictates of justice.

III. Our Common Moral Consciousness

McCloskey comments briefly on the ethical method employed by him of critical reflection on our common moral consciousness (p. 252). He says (in effect) that utilitarians may hold it a poor way of determining a moral question (such as whether a certain punishment is morally permissible) to ask what our common moral consciousness tells us, for the question is: 'Is it permissible?' not: 'Do we ordinarily regard it as permissible?' He points out, however, that some such method as this is really the only way we have for deciding whether utilitarianism is itself acceptable, so that the utilitarian cannot afford to scoff at it. A similar point was made by Sidgwick when he said that the utilitarian cannot altogether scoff at moral intuitions, since the principle of utility can only be defended as one.

What McCloskey says is true, but the utilitarian needs to explain the matter more carefully.

His principle is often attacked on the ground that it has consequences which go against our ordinary moral views. To such attacks there are two quite different types of utilitarian rejoinder. One may try to show that there is no real conflict with ordinary morality. Alternatively one may say: 'So much the worse for ordinary morality.' (Cf. McCloskey p. 254.)

Now, on the one hand, it seems that something has gone wrong if a reply of the latter sort is never made. If the principle of utility is never capable of reversing views to which we would otherwise be inclined it has little point. It should surely guide our moral feelings, [271] not merely be provisionally adopted subject to its never giving them a shake-up.

On the other hand, although one might like to say that moral judgements which conflict with the dictates of utility represent mere feelings to be suppressed in the interests of a rational ethics, it is difficult to combine this with the (necessary) admission that the principle of utility itself represents simply a well weighed moral feeling. For we would then have a conflict between two moral feelings, and if after reflection the non-utilitarian one is left the stronger, there seems nothing the utilitarian can say.

We have a dilemma which I would resolve as follows.

For one inclined to the utilitarian point of view but not dogmatic about it, there is a subtle interplay between his ordinary moral sentiments and the principle of utility. The principle is accepted partly because it seems to supply a unitary basis to the existing moral sentiments, or to most of them, and is to some extent to be tested by its compatibility with these moral sentiments, but the moral sentiments are themselves under trial by the principle of utility. In cases of conflict, if such should arise, moral sentiments which are not too deeply felt will give way to the principle, but if they *are* deeply felt, then his utilitarian position comes up for review, and a choice must be made. The principle of utility does of course itself express a very basic moral sentiment. The utilitarian can hardly rule out the theoretical possibility that he may find a conflicting sentiment that he puts above it. But he will not lightly give up a principle which provides a unitary and substantial basis for ethical thought such as does no other principle which anyone (of good will) would dream of accepting. I am in fact inclined to doubt whether it really does stand in conflict with any moral sentiment which many men would continue to have if they were aware of this conflict, though of course if it was not in conflict with some less deeply rooted moral sentiments it would have little point, since it claims to be their guide and curb.

In talking of the ethical (not meta-ethical) method which a utilitarian will employ, one must distinguish between his discourse in support of the principle of utility, and his discourse in application of it. The method of the second type of discussion is that of empirical enquiry and deduction from the results thereof in conjunction with the utility principle. One may expect it on occasion to result in opposition to common moral sentiment. If the opposing sentiment is deep-rooted a temporary move back to discourse of the first type is normally indicated. [272] The method of this is indeed roughly what McCloskey calls critical reflection on our common moral consciousness. Discourse against the principle of utility belongs of course at this same level. At this level conflict of the principle of utility with other deeply held moral sentiments is important, but not necessarily decisive.

IV.   Actual and Fanciful Examples

Before going on to discuss McCloskey's actual examples of wrongful punishment supposedly justifiable on purely utilitarian grounds I want to discuss some more methodological points.

First, let me mention that I quite accept his dismissal of a certain 'red herring' on page 252.

Now McCloskey's main argument against a utilitarian theory of punishment lies in examples which he presents of moral judgements which he supposes would follow from utilitarian theory, and which clash with our common moral consciousness, even presumably when this has been altered to meet the demands of critical reflection. Such examples may be of two types. They may be moral judgements regarding situations of a kind which actually occur or they may regard situations of a kind which do not occur. Or, to put it another way, these moral judgements may be deducible from the utility principle and certain contingent truths (or from fictions akin to such truths) or they may be deducible from the utility principle in conjunction with contingent factual premisses which include falsehoods. Although McCloskey recognizes this distinction, he evidently does not think it of much importance. For he says: 'Against the utilitarian who seeks to argue that utilitarianism does not involve unjust punishment, there is a very simple argument, namely, that whether or not unjust punishments are in fact useful, it is logically possible that they will at some time become useful, in which case utilitarians are committed to them.'

Actually, I have a certain hesitation regarding the sense of this passage. Is there an especial significance in the future tense? Presumably if it is logically possible that they will become useful, it is logically possible that they are useful now. After all it is logically possible that Britain and the United States are now at war. Use of the future tense suggests that perhaps by its being logically possible that they will become useful, McCloskey really means the quite different thing that *for all we know* they may become useful one day. It is an important question which is meant. For it is very easy indeed to establish the [273] logical possibility that something like punishment of the innocent will be (is, or was) useful. One can for instance imagine the most basic facts of human nature altered for this purpose. But it is a more empirical task to establish that *for all we know* they will become useful one day. Since the 'we' presumably does not refer just to one perhaps ignorant person,

one must show that there are not (say) well confirmed principles of psychology which give us firm
reasons for saying that things will not develop that
way.

Situations instanced in which utilitarian judgements
are alleged to be offensive to our common moral
consciousness (understand henceforth: even when
purified by critical attention) may be of three kinds.
First, they may be actual or relevantly akin to actual
situations. Second, they may be situations not es-
tablishable as actual or akin to such, but not establish-
able either as such as will never have occurred.
Thirdly, they may be logically possible situations,
but ones which there is good reason to suppose will
never have occurred. Of course, this rough classification is capable of refinement.

McCloskey presumably would think a situation on
which a utilitarian judgement shocks our moral consciousness counts equally against utilitarianism to
whichever type it belongs (cf. p. 254). For this he
could argue as follows. The principle of utility is a
theory about what would be right and wrong under
any conceivable (i.e. logically possible) circumstances. Our common moral consciousness also provides us with principles about what would be right or
wrong under any conceivable circumstances. If
therefore they clash in their judgement on a conceivable situation, however out of the question such
a situation is, they do indeed clash, and one must be
discarded.

I accept this description of the principle of utility,
but not of our common moral consciousness. I do
not think the latter is thus thought of by most people
we might consider typical vehicles of it. Plain men
will probably admit that if the empirical nature of
the world had been very different then different
moral sentiments would often have been appropriate.
For instance, Christians who urge more or less

strongly the principle of turning the other cheek, are wont to support it with references to the contrary effects of love and hate. However basic such facts about love and hate are, they are in the last resort contingent. Similarly with the kind of support most people would give for our sentiments in favour of just rather than unjust punishment. Utilitarianism then is not eccentric in basing the rightness of some very fundamental moral sentiments on ultimately contingent facts. [274]

Now if one considers some fantastic situations of the third type one does of course consider them as a person with certain moral sentiments, the strength of which in society as it is, is an important utilitarian good. These sentiments are offended. A utilitarian will see no point in trying to imagine oneself looking with approval on the imaginary situation, since this is likely to weaken the feelings while not serving as a preparation for any actual situation. If in fact punishing the innocent (say) always is and always will be harmful, it is likewise harmful to dwell on fanciful situations in which it would be beneficial, thus weakening one's aversion to such courses. Thus the utilitarian shares (quite consistently so) in the unease produced by these examples. Although he may admit that in such a situation punishment of the innocent would be right, he still regards favourably the distaste which is aroused at the idea of its being called right.

Certainly, if one imagines the world as other than it is, one may find oneself imagining a world in which utilitarianism implies moral judgements which shock our moral sentiments. But if these moral sentiments are quite appropriate to the only world there is, the real world, the utilitarian is glad that moral judgements in opposition to them seem repugnant. He sees no need for moral acrobatics relevant only to situations which in fact are quite out of the question.

We must be very careful therefore in using the fact that strong and, we feel, right-minded antipathies are aroused at the thought of certain utilitarian type judgements on type three examples, as an argument against utilitarianism. For the utilitarian himself will commend this distaste as something to be kept alive in himself and others, and is perhaps claiming for the offended moral sentiments as much as, on reflection, most people would be prepared to do.

There is another reason for caution in discussing type three situations. Suppose one describes a case where punishment of an innocent man would yield a balance of good, and insures that this is so simply by stipulating certain striking benefits which will derive from it, and explicitly eliminating all the harms one can think of. If one finds oneself still half-inclined to call such punishment wrong, it may well be because one does not really succeed in envisaging the situation just as described, but surrounds it with those circumstances of real life which would in fact create a greater probability of unhappiness in its consequences than happiness.

We may conclude that it would be more convincing if examples of conflict between the common moral consciousness and utilitarianism [275] were looked for in type one situations rather than in type three, while situations of type two (clearly) have a degree of relevance here lying between the other two.

V. McCloskey's Examples

Let us now consider McCloskey's individual examples. I shall not dwell much on his first example, as he himself lays more weight on his second, which is a modified version of it. But I should like to comment on one oddity in his discussion of the first.

The sheriff is supposed to have framed an innocent

Negro to prevent a series of lynchings which he knows will occur if no one is 'punished' for the offence. It is urged that this is obviously the right course from a utilitarian point of view.

One line of objection to this conclusion appeals to the likelihood that the facts will become known. I may urge parenthetically that in the real world such a likelihood is likely (surely) to be pretty strong. The utilitarian may then insist on a variety of evils which would result from its becoming known, such as a loss of confidence in the impartiality and fairness of the legal system, of a belief that lawful behaviour pays, etc. Now McCloskey says that 'even if everyone came to know, surely, if utilitarianism is thought to be the true moral theory, the general body of citizens ought to be happier believing that their sheriff is promoting what is right rather than promoting non-utilitarian standards of justice' (p. 255). This strikes me as absurd. Let us consider first the white citizenry. It is quite obvious that they are not utilitarians, or that even if by chance some are in theory, their feelings are not in fact governed by utilitarian theory. For if they were utilitarians they would not be charging around the country lynching people. For who could seriously believe that this was the best way of creating the greatest happiness of the greatest number? If they were utilitarians (in practice) the sheriff would not be in the situation he is in. As it is, he has to think about them as they are. How they *would* react to the fact that the sheriff framed the Negro is a different matter, but for a utilitarian to expect their satisfaction because he has done the right thing from a utilitarian point of view would be absurd. You might as well suggest that a utilitarian penologist should urge that all prisons should be without bars, on the grounds that once it is explained to the offenders how useful it is for society that they should be punished they will see the wrongness of

escaping. Let us now consider the Negroes. There is
[276] not the same evidence within the very hypoth-
esis that their actions and feelings are opposed to utilitarian precepts. But one may take it that whatever
their ethical views, they are filled with bitterness at
white behaviour. They are hardly going to be over-
joyed at learning that a Negro up for trial is likely to
be framed in order to sate the fury of brutish whites.
Will not their incentives to law-abidingness be de-
creased when they learn that someone else's crime
may just as well get them punished as one of their
own? Is racial harmony really going to be advanced
by such an event?

But I shall now turn to the second supposedly
more forceful example (p. 256). Here a utilitarian
visitor from outside the area bears incriminating false
witness against a Negro so that his being 'punished'
for a rape will put an end to a series of riots and
lynchings. One main point of thus changing the example presumably is to eliminate such harms as might
be supposed to ensue from a local figure, especially
a legal authority, practising the deception.

Before commenting on this example in further detail I should like to ask the reader (or McCloskey
himself) to stand back for a moment and consider
the prima facie implausibility of what McCloskey
tries to show. Forget for a moment all question of
the rightness or wrongness of utilitarian theory, forget morality, and imagine simply that you are a
reasonable being with one overriding aim, to create
as much happiness as possible at the cost of as little
unhappiness as possible. Does it really seem on the
cards that in a situation where race riots are going
on as a result of a rape, you will find no more effective
way of forwarding your aim in this area than to bear
false witness against some unfortunate Negro, thus
ensuring that at least one human being is thoroughly
miserable? Does not a vague unanalysed sense of how

the world really works inform one that this is not a type of action which increases human happiness? People who lack this common-sense grasp of how the world runs are dangerous whatever moral backing they may claim for their actions.

Let us now turn to details. Our utilitarian is said to *know* 'that a quick arrest will stop the riots and lynchings'. How does he know this? How does he know that they aren't going to die down soon anyway? Even if he has good reason to think that they will go on unless such an arrest is made, does he know how intense they will be, how many people are actually going to get lynched? One thing he does know is that if he bears false witness (successfully) an innocent man is going to get punished. We are not told what the punishment will be, but it [277] is likely either to be death or a long term of imprisonment, which will mean the ruin of the man's life. Suppose he does not bear the false witness, that the riots go on as he expected, but that no deaths or permanent injuries take place. Isn't it likely that the suffering in this case is less than that of a man sentenced to execution (together with the sufferings of his family) or languishing for long years in prison?

Utilitarian judgement that the false witness would be right must be based on its foreseeable consequences. Now an event can be foreseen as a probable (or certain) consequence of a given action on two roughly distinguishable grounds. It may be a well confirmed generalization that actions of that broad type in that broad type of situation very often (or always) have such a consequence. But an action may (also) be characterized by features too unusual to figure in such generalizations. If these are to provide a basis for prediction it must be because of some hunch about the situation which will be no more rational than an indefinite number of other hunches. Reliance on such hunches is something which often leads people wildly wrong. (This is well confirmed, I suggest.) This suggests that a product (such as happiness) will be increased in the long run more by those who base their expectations on well confirmed generalizations than on hunches, and that therefore the utilitarian should stick to the former, especially where the amounts of happiness or unhappiness are large. The situation is quite different from that of scientific research. Here the hunches are needed for major advances, and can be put to the test and abandoned if necessary, with no harm done. And indeed in ethical decisions which do not have consequences of too great import, action on such hunches may be useful as a mode of experiment.

Now I suggest that the prediction of misery for the innocent man if he is successfully framed rests on well confirmed generalizations, but that the prediction that this will stop lynchings, etc., which would otherwise have occurred, will be based on a hunch about the character of the riots. In that case the sensible utilitarian will attach a predominating weight to the former prediction, and refrain from framing the man.

McCloskey may, however, insist that the utilitarian has the very firmest grounds for his beliefs about the duration and degree of the rioting if no punishment takes place, and concerning the preventability of all this by the means in question. I'm inclined to suggest then that a man with such a rich knowledge of the nature of these riots should devote himself fully to a documented study of them with a view to [278] putting his knowledge before such organizations as can arrange by propaganda and other means to alleviate their causes. If he has something to hide concerning his own illicit means of checking them, he will not be at ease in drawing up a report on the situation and will therefore not do his work properly, work which will stop more riot-caused suffering in the end than this isolated act.

If these last remarks seem somewhat fanciful I should urge that the situation in which a man *knows* that the riots will go on unless he tells this lie is also fanciful, and is an example of type two perilously close to type three. In an actual situation this would probably only be a hunch, of little weight besides the well supported belief that a successful frame-up will produce massive suffering for the innocent man and his family. There is also good reason for believing that facing a man and telling lies which will ruin his life will blunt one's sensibilities in a way which may well lead one to use such methods again with still less justification. I should suspect, moreover, that a utilitarian who persuaded himself that such an act was useful would be finding an outlet for harmful impulses which it would behoove him not to indulge; for instance an urge to exert power in a secret God-like manner, and without scruple. It is dangerously easy for someone who wants to do something for motives of which he is ashamed to persuade himself that the general good would be served by it. This gives another reason for suspicion of 'hunches'.

None of this has appealed to any such principle as that the suffering of an innocent man is a worse thing in itself than that of a guilty one. What of this principle? The utilitarian cannot consistently say that one is worse in itself if the degree of suffering is the same. But if there is reason to believe that more suffering is involved in a given punishment for an innocent man than for a guilty man this is something of which the utilitarian should take account.

There does seem some reason to believe this. An innocent man is liable to suffer more shock at being thus punished. He will suffer from an indignant fury as the guilty man will not. Whatever the utilitarian thinks of the appropriateness of such indignation (a matter too complicated for comment here) he must take it into account as a fact. But apart from the indignation, the punishment will come on him as much more of a surprise, and thus be something he is less able to cope with psychologically (accept) or even practically. The distress caused to his relatives will also probably be greater, since it is likely to come as more of a shock to them also. His wife may be ill prepared [279] in every way for life alone, and she will also be more likely to be dismayed if she now believes her husband guilty. Moreover punishment of the innocent (especially in a case like that described) is very likely to arouse emotions leading to anti-social action on the part of someone previously law-abiding.

Of course McCloskey can deal with each specific point by imagining a situation in which it would not arise. Let the innocent man be without family and a natural pessimist always prepared for the worst. But what sort of investigation prior to his false witness is our wily utilitarian to make into these matters? It is hard to believe that a man of such tenacity will not find less costly ways of advancing racial harmony.

It seems to me, then, highly unlikely that in a situation at all like the one described by McCloskey a man guided by a cool assessment of probabilities rather than by wild surmises will see such bearing of false witness as the most felicific act. This applies even if we ignore the effects on the utilitarian's own character, still more if we take these into account.

Still, I should not say it was absolutely *out of the question* that situations may arise where a sensible utilitarian would think it right to implicate an innocent man. As I have explained at length, he could still think the resultant punishment *unjust*, although his production of it was right or justified. In such a situation the good to be achieved by the punishment would presumably be predictable as near certain on well confirmed principles, and be great enough to outweigh harms of the sort we have described, and such other evils (especially evils of injustice) as might arise. It would also have to be unobtainable at less cost. I suspect that with such goods to be gained our utilitarian's action would be such as many plain men (not just official utilitarians) would condone or approve.

What plain men would feel, however, is an uneasiness at the situation, and a deep regret about it. Now sometimes one gets a picture of the utilitarian who can feel no regret at any overriding of conventional moral principles provided his sums come out all right. This is a travesty of the utilitarian outlook.

There is indeed a certain problematicness about regret on any ethical theory. Everyone must admit that on occasion the action which on balance one ought to do, has characteristics or consequences which considered in themselves suggest the wrongness of the act. A general fighting for a good cause may well regard the dead and injured on the field of battle with a terrible regret that he should have brought [280] this about, and yet think he acted rightly—although he always knew there would be a sacrifice like this. Moreover his regret may in a sense be a moral regret, different in character from the regret one feels at the sacrifice of one's own interests for the sake of duty. An unimaginative moral philosopher might say that such regret was inapposite, if he had really done the right thing. Most of us do not feel this way and utilitarianism offers at least two justifications for our attitude. First, a man who was not sad at producing suffering would lack the basic sentiment which inspires the utility principle, namely a revulsion at the suffering and a delight in the happiness of any sentient being. Second, sentiments such as the love of justice, respect for human life and so on, are sentiments which utilitarian considerations bid us cherish in ourselves and others. When the promptings of these sentiments have to be set aside in the interests of a greater good, the man who feels no regret can have them little developed, and the man who checks all regret will blunt them. Regret in such situations is therefore a desirable state of mind according to utilitarianism.

Feeling regret must not be confused with a judgement that it would be a good thing to feel regret. There is no such confusion here. Whether I feel regret is a psychological fact not normally in my control. All I have argued is that the utilitarian who feels regret need not think that his theory demands an attempt to set it aside as a weakness. Rather he should be troubled by his character if he does not feel it.

So even if on some rare occasion a greater good demands some such injustice as the punishment of an innocent man, the utilitarian will certainly accept this as an appropriate matter for regret.

VI. Further Examples

Among further examples which McCloskey gives of unjust but useful laws are scapegoat punishment and collective punishment. He does not make it very clear, however, what his own moral attitude to such punishments is, or what he takes to be that of the common moral consciousness. Certainly he thinks they are unjust even when useful—and that is something with which the utilitarian can agree—but does he think that they are sometimes justified nonetheless? He seems at least to leave it open that they may be, and in one case, collective punishment in schools, he goes further (p. 256). Now to say that they are unjust but all the same morally right or justified is a position which [281] the utilitarian who really believed they produced more good than evil would probably adopt.

Consider the type of scapegoat punishment he mentions (p. 256). It is within the bounds of possibility that a commander whose chances of victory demanded some sort of co-operation from the local people, and who had good reason to believe that without this victory the common good of humanity would suffer, finding this method of securing the population's co-operation the only workable one, would rightly consider that it was justified. I say that it is within the bounds of possibility, but it is also perhaps more probable that such a method is not even the most efficient for his end, or at least not more efficient than other means less damaging to the goods of justice. But if the circumstances really were as described most people who condone war at all would probably think the act was right.

In saying that such an undesirable means to a desirable end might possibly on rare occasions be justified, one is not giving one's general approval to such methods of gaining one's ends. There is, however, always the danger that when once one has allowed the justifiability of such means on one occasion, one will be ready to use them again on other occasions where although immediately convenient the same justifying conditions do not hold. The fact that an act may be a bad example to oneself and others (even if supposing this fact left out of account it would be justified) may often finally tip the balance against the rightness of doing it. As an example, I should like to take the bombing of centres of civilian population in wartime. For many such raids the British may well have had acceptable justification. This was certainly the belief of quite decent people in Britain. The victory of the allies really was an overwhelming good for humanity and this may have been an unavoidable means to it. But once moral scruples against such bombings were set aside in the interests of a greater good the capacity for moral reflection on the matter seems to have become blunted, and we have the bombing of Dresden which it is widely agreed served no essential purpose. In the same kind of way injustices in the treatment of an occupied country are likely to escalate, and this consideration should probably tip the balance in any cases (if there are such) where it might otherwise have been justified from a utilitarian point of view.

Just about the same can be said regarding collective punishments as scapegoat punishments.

In both cases one doubts whether these acts really ever are justified [282] from a utilitarian point of view. Anyone concerned to gain the co-operation of an occupied territory without making it a slave population will presumably be concerned to gain its good will, to which end these methods are hardly conducive. The purposes for which the occupation is undertaken are obviously relevant here. On the whole, the more immoral the purposes the more such methods will seem required.

Although I am not attempting in this reply any account of what constitutes the goods (and evils) of justice (and injustice), I should perhaps mention a good of this type which would be prevented by scapegoat and collective punishment. One of the great goods furthered by various legal and quasi-legal institutions when properly conducted is the increased chance they give to everyone to control their own futures (so far as these depend on human agency) within limits imposed by the common good. This can perhaps be called one of the goods of justice, when it is the result of such institutions. (A similar good arising from a different cause might not be so called.) But the good of justice with which I am concerned is rather the *maintenance* of institutions serving this purpose. This can be called a major good of justice. Among such institutions we may include various habits of people wielding authority even where they are not directed to act thus by some positive law. It should not be very controversial to urge that the maintenance of institutions which (or of those aspects of them which) increase a person's opportunities to plan his future is a great utilitarian good.

An institution which serves the purposes in question will ensure that such evils as may arise for a man through human agency and frustrate his plans, when they are also such that their attempted elimination (by—or in the case of punishment from—the institutions in question) would be predominantly harmful, are at least so far as possible predictable by him, and preferably dependent for their occurrence on circumstances within his control. Thus although customs which ensured that a man could never lose his job would doubtless be harmful on the whole, habits of employment according to which a man knows under what circumstances he will lose his job, especially if these circumstances are within his control, serve the purpose we have described and action which weakens such habits is so far unjust. Now we may accept that punishment (like the sack) is necessary evil, but granted that, we should try to preserve institutions according to which a man can predict and control the circumstances in which he will suffer it. Acts which weaken such institutions will be so far unjust, and be so even on those [283] rare occasions where they may effect a predominating good and so be right.

It is not difficult to see that the infliction of scapegoat or collective punishment will be unjust from this point of view. There are various rules adherence to which is generally regarded as a criterion of just punishment. A main one is the rule that a man should only be punished for an action if he knew before doing it that he was likely to be punished for it, and could have refrained from the act if he had chosen. Various departures from this rule are in fact countenanced without people feeling that there is an injustice. For instance it is accepted that a man may be punished if in some sense he should have known that punishment might be inflicted for something he has done, even if in fact he did not know this. That is a rather minor departure. But there are also cases such as some punishments of war criminals where the rule is departed from more strikingly, and yet not everyone regards such punishment as unjust. I think we may say, however, that a departure from this rule always gives some reason for talk of injustice.

Adherence to this rule is an institution such as I have been describing. So long as a person is only punished in conformity to it the evil he suffers is such as he could have anticipated and avoided. If we weaken this institution we are acting against the major good of justice I have mentioned, and forwarding the opposing evil.

Now infliction of a scapegoat or collective punishment represents a breaking of the rule in question. A collective punishment can hardly be a secret affair, and it is not very clear that a scapegoat punishment can be. (For we do not call such frame-ups as were discussed in the last section scapegoat punishments.) In acting against the rule we create a general sense that this institution (adherence to the rule) is breaking down, and this acts in various ways to bring about that result. Even if in some examples this result is supposed avoided, it is unrealistic to imagine it possible thus to act without weakening one's own tendency to abide by the rule. One's adherence to the rule represents a personal habit and sentiment, which when once broken for what seem good reasons is much more likely than before to be broken for bad reasons. It seems then that collective and scapegoat punishment will always weaken the institution in question, and will be so far *unjust*, using this word according to the utilitarian account I have adumbrated.

It is of course theoretically possible that a punishment of this sort will bring about more good than evil, even when the weakening of the [284] institution and the intrinsic evil of the punishment itself are both taken into account, and I would not care to insist that it was not sometimes a practical possibility. But there are two different possibilities here which must be distinguished. One is that the goods which outweigh these evils are other goods of justice. The other is that these goods are of a different type. In the former case we may wish to describe the punishment as on the whole just, in spite of seeming unjust when one aspect of the situation only is considered. Such might be the case with the punishment of war criminals. In the latter case, however, we will allow that the punishment was unjust, but urge that nonetheless it was justified by the special good it did. It seems likely that whatever other goods can be described as goods of justice besides that major one which we have considered, they will never be forwarded by scapegoat and collective punishment. So that the utilitarian can accept that such punishments are always unjust.

The possibility remains that these unjust punishments may on occasion be right and proper, because useful in some other way. This possibility seems, however, to be allowed by McCloskey. It is not at all clear in my judgement that occasions of this kind actually occur. At any rate the utilitarian has every reason for urging the serious damage done to the goods of justice on any likely occasion of scapegoat or collective punishment, and for insisting therefore on the extreme gravity of any decision to use them.

These remarks of mine have in effect already dealt with some further examples of supposedly useful but unjust punishment given by McCloskey. Punishment of relatives would be a form of scapegoat punishment. It would be a departure from an institution according to which punishment could only come as a result of circumstances within one's control. Retroactive laws represent a striking departure from the rule we have discussed. The utilitarian might perhaps accept that in some cases (such as in post-war Germany) punishments based on such laws are just, for he might see other goods of justice forwarded by such punishment, but inasmuch as they inflict damage on a major good of justice he may still insist that in an important respect they are unjust. This is rather close to what McCloskey says.

The next examples which McCloskey brings forward are of a rather different type. He talks of vagrancy laws and of laws making it an offense to arouse the suspicions of the government (p. 257). Now the prime issue here is surely whether these are not bad (perhaps unjust) laws. Discussion of these examples would need to raise the [285] question: Must punishment for an offence against an unjust law be unjust? There would seem to be a use for the phrases 'just punishment' and 'unjust punishment' where their applicability is independent of the question whether the 'offence' committed is an act which the authorities are justified in trying to prevent. It is perhaps best in a short discussion of the matter that we should stick to this latter use, and so I shall leave these examples aside, as rather beside our main point.

McCloskey's last example of useful but unjust punishment is the punishment of moral imbeciles in order to deter the morally sane (presumably from performing similar actions) (p. 258). His remarks raise issues we have no room to discuss, and I must confine myself to a few casual comments.

If workable criteria are available for distinguishing the sane and the insane, non-punishment of the insane will not encourage the sane to think that they can get away with things, because they will know that they will not meet those criteria. This demands that the workings of the law be widely known, but that would anyway seem to be a demand of justice. Thus deterrence of the sane need not be jeopardized, while deterrence of the insane is probably out of the question anyway. If, on the other hand, such criteria of insanity are not available, there will be no means of exempting the insane from punishment, and the question will not arise.

These remarks leave out of account various emotional factors, such as the indignation perhaps felt by the sane at those whom the authorities call insane getting away with it. But surely institutions which educate public emotion are more beneficial than those which pander to it?

It may be asked: Why not punish the insane? The utilitarian answer is, put briefly,—because it does no good, or no good not obtainable at less expense of evil. We must remember that for the utilitarian punishment is always an evil, to be dispensed with where possible without preponderant harm. The only good done by punishment of the insane is deterrence of the sane, and that we have remarked can be done as well without it.

To say that punishment of the insane does no good is to suggest that punishment of the sane does do good. This is the assumption of any utilitarian justification of punishment. The main goods in question are deterrence of other offenders and of the same offenders in the future. In some cases incapacitation of the offender from criminal action is also a major factor, but where this end alone is sought the disgracefulness of being 'punished' is supposed to be avoided, as in 'preventive [286] detention' and indeed in detention of the insane. Another good which should not be forgotten is the inhibition of acts of private revenge which can run riot, causing family feuds, etc., by substituting the depersonalized revenge of the law. (If people believe a man to be insane these revenge feelings are as a matter of fact to a great extent assuaged.)

How far punishment (of the sane) does achieve these goods, and how far other means to them involving less evil might not be substituted, is a question we shall touch on briefly at the end. The opinion of McCloskey to which we are replying is that utilitarianism entails too much punishment rather than too little, and therefore we have taken for granted rather traditional views of the efficacy of punishment. If the utilitarian of today decides that punishment can with advantage be largely dispensed with, he may have to consider the opposite line of attack from McCloskey, who may seek to show the desirability of inflicting useless punishment.

What I have tried to show is that to a great extent the utilitarian can agree with McCloskey that punishments of the sorts he describes are unjust, while the extent to which he may allow that they may nonetheless on occasion be justified may be no greater.

VII. Rule-utilitarianism

I have sought to defend utilitarianism against McCloskey's attacks, and what I have had in mind throughout has been 'act-utilitarianism', not 'rule-utilitarianism'. I entirely agree with McCloskey, however, that if his attacks on this are accepted, changing to rule-utilitarianism can hardly offer an acceptable remedy (pp. 258–9). There is indeed something absurd about rule-utilitarianism *if* it is thought of as in conflict with act-utilitarianism. If a rule is good precisely because action in accordance with it usually advances the general good, and this is the only reason, it is very odd to think that any value should be attached to action according to the rule in those exceptional cases where it hinders rather than advances the general good. When I talk of its hindering rather than advancing the general good, I mean that it does so even when such goods as that of keeping the rule in general respect are taken into account. For if the rule-utilitarian is only drawing attention to the need for keeping this particular highly important type of good in mind when evaluating an individual action, he is urging the value of general rules by the criteria of act-utilitarianism and is therefore not putting forward a rival view to it. If the rule-utilitarian [287] thinks that on occasion one should do an act which has a predominantly unfavourable hedonic effect, because it is an example of a kind of action which usually has a predominantly favourable hedonic effect, one wonders why he has suddenly lost the concern for the general happiness which made him favour the rule in the first place.

So I am at one with McCloskey in regarding rule-utilitarianism as absurd. However, the matter has another aspect, which suggests that the contrast between act-utilitarianism and rule-utilitarianism is somewhat confused conceptually.

Any intelligent utilitarianism will acknowledge that the rightness and wrongness of an act is determined by the consequences reasonably predictable beforehand rather than by the actual consequences. An example used by several writers to support this point is that of a doctor called in to save the life of a certain baby, which baby later became Adolf Hitler. His life-saving action one can be almost sure resulted in more suffering than happiness, when the later actions of Hitler are taken into account, as clearly they should be. But these were not among the reasonably predictable consequences of the act, and it would seem absurd for the utilitarian to call the action wrong or bad.

Now the reasonably predictable consequences of an act will normally be predictable as probable to a certain degree rather than as certain, and in any case this last can be treated as a special degree of probability. Moreover incompatible consequences can be predictable as each probable to complementary degrees. It is clear that the probability with which a consequence can be predicted affects the weight which a utilitarian ascribes to it, so that its weight in terms of the amount of pleasure it involves has to be multiplied by its probability represented as a fraction.

Suppose that one judges an action as 'right' because according to one's prediction before the event it had a greater weight of good probable consequences than bad probable consequences. I do not say that one cannot decide later that one's judgement was mistaken and that the act was *really* wrong. I only say that such a revision of one's view must depend on a realization that the original prediction was unreasonable, and must not depend upon actual consequences ensuing which were not reasonably predictable.

Once these points are acknowledged we see that the contrast between individual utilitarian judgement of each act and the application of general principles supposed to have a utilitarian basis is confused. To calculate the hedonic value of an act (before its performance or [288] non-performance) is to make an inductive assessment of probabilities. Essentially it is to take general characteristics of the act, and consider what has usually followed upon acts of this sort in the past. The characteristics which would show an act as prohibited by a *general* principle accepted because such acts usually do more harm than good are just such characteristics as would be taken in a utilitarian consideration of this individual action as indicative of its being *probably* more harmful than beneficial, and therefore bad. This suggests that only one type of utilitarian evaluation of acts can be seriously proposed. One considers the sort of act an act is, and considers what usually ensues upon acts of this sort. Reasonable prediction of consequences is always based upon general principles. It makes little difference in the end whether the utilitarian calls his principles scientific statements about the tendencies for weal or woe of certain types of action which can be used in making reasonable predictions about the probable effects on happiness of individual actions, or moral principles as to the rightness or wrongness of certain types of action based on their usual consequences for weal or woe.

Let us imagine a case where rule-utilitarianism and act-utilitarianism seem to conflict. Suppose it is accepted that F actions generally produce more unhappiness than happiness. The rule-utilitarian therefore accepts the rule that F actions are wrong. Now we consider a particular F action. The act-utilitarian who knows no more about it than its F-ness will agree with the rule-utilitarian that it is wrong, since the only evidence he has indicates its probable harmfulness. However, he studies it further and decides (let us suppose reasonably) that this F action will probably do more good than harm. This can only be because he notes some other characteristic of it, say G, such that the principle that F and G actions usually do more good than harm is acceptable. Now in view of this last, the rule-utilitarian can substitute for his original rule, this: 'F actions are wrong, except when they are also G.' This rule concerns a class of actions, F and non-G ones, which are more often harmful than these, the F actions, denounced in the original rule. The rules conflict, and it would surely be odd to prefer the original principle. But if the latter principle is chosen there is no occasion here for any conflict between act-utilitarianism and rule-utilitarianism. The latter only diverges from the former, if it is insisted that the rules must concern classes of act distinguished by predicates of a certain simplicity, such as F may be, but not *F and not-G*. Apart from being vague, this would be strangely arbitrary. [289]

So we come round to the same point that rule-utilitarianism can only be opposed to act-utilitarianism at the cost of making it absurd.

I should perhaps add that my insistence that utilitarian consideration of an individual act must turn on classification of it as of a certain type, is not derived from the view that ethical statements must be universalizable. Universalizability if required is obtained for the utilitarian by such facts as that if an act is wrong, then any act like it in having (on a reasonable estimate) more probable suffering among its probable consequences than probable happiness, will also be wrong. What is in question here is a fact about reasonable prediction, namely that reasons for expecting an individual act to have certain consequences must be reasons for expecting acts of a certain *type* to have certain consequences.

VIII. The Retributive Theory Considered

McCloskey rather gives the impression that the chief argument in favour of retributivism is that its main rival theory, the utilitarian, although initially more plausible, breaks down. So in arguing that the utilitarian theory does not break down in the way he suggests, I am endeavouring to remove one of the main supports he claims for the retributive theory. That is well, for there is no space for me to launch a counter-attack on the retributive theory. I shall merely comment on a few points McCloskey makes in his last section.

(1) The principle that equals should be treated equally is capable of so many mutually incompatible applications that the retributive theory cannot be defended as deducible from it. The utilitarian could say that all men were equally capable of suffering and should equally be protected from it, except where the general interest of the community precludes it.

(2) A last word on the topic of permissible and obligatory punishing: McCloskey says that the authority is entitled to impose a just punishment, but that does not mean that he is obliged to do so. But is McCloskey saying that he is never morally obliged to impose a just punishment? If the authority is sometimes so obliged and not merely so permitted, should not retributivism characterize the circumstances in which this is so? A theory of punishment should surely say something on this. If he is never so obliged, or if the justness of the punishment never plays any part in producing such obligation (so that, e.g., it is not producible except by utilitarian considerations) it seems that [290] every imposition of punishment merely because it is just is the infliction of suffering by no means demanded by morality. One might think that in such cases it would always fall foul of the moral rule: Prevent suffering wherever it is morally permissible to prevent it.

(3) McCloskey is of course quite right in insisting that the gravity of an offence does not turn simply on the actual punishment annexed. Not at least in the most morally significant sense of 'gravity'. He is also right in insisting that disagreements among retributivists and others as to the relative gravity of different offences do not show the subjectivity of the concept. But it is surely requisite that a retributivist who aims to deal thoroughly with the question of punishment should try to formulate an objective test of such gravity. This task doubtless is moralizing rather than conceptual analysis, but then I take it that re-

tributivism and utilitarianism are both moral theories, not conceptual analyses. McCloskey comments that there is equally no objective test as to the value of the different goods which figure in the utilitarian theory. Now if it is traditional hedonistic utilitarianism which is in question this is not so. There may indeed be areas of vagueness in the hedonistic criteria proposed but in many cases it can give definite results. If it is ideal utilitarianism the point is correct, although I suspect that our 'intuitions' of value are more congruent than those of the gravity of offences. What this shows really is that ideal utilitarianism and retributivism are skeletons of theories rather than complete theories. They lay down a pattern within which moralizing must take place, but do not determine every detail. So I should only insist with regard to this point that retributivism is not a very determinate moral theory until criteria of 'gravity' are laid down.

Having defended utilitarianism, and especially hedonistic utilitarianism, against various criticisms of it as a theory of punishment, my main positive objection to retributivism is that it breaks the principle: Wherever possible, prevent pointless suffering.

There is, however, one last point about utilitarianism which is of considerable importance. The utilitarian who favours punishment regards it as a necessary evil. If less painful means of keeping law and order are established as being equally efficient, he will drop his support for the institution of punishment and favour these other means instead. That is, of course, provided he has made sure there are no less obvious but greater evils they threaten. Now McCloskey has attacked utilitarianism as a theory likely to lead to too much punishment rather [291] than too little. But retributivists might object to it for the latter reason.

In conformity with the direction of McCloskey's attacks I have gone along with the usual assumptions about the social utility of punishment as a deterrent, etc. I have been concerned to show that the combination of these assumptions with the principle of utility provides an attitude to punishment which is not objectionable in the way McCloskey makes out. But of course the utilitarian who challenges these assumptions may attack the institution of punishment in a way not widely acceptable to date. The question then arises: Does the objection which such an attack is likely to meet arise from a rejection of the principle of utility or simply from the persuasion that the assumptions are after all justified? Only in the former case would it be utilitarianism itself which was rejected.

So as not to evade the issue, I shall simply remark that though many of the assumptions (or explicit beliefs) which underlie the usual utilitarian justifications of punishment may require considerable modification, they do not seem so utterly wrong that the reasonable utilitarian should become an out-and-out opponent of control by punishment. At the most what is required are large limitations on and modifications of penal methods. Of course this is going on (if slowly) all the time as knowledge advances. The utilitarian has a clear notion of the application to be made of such new knowledge. The retributivist who does not justify punishment on the basis of empirical beliefs seems in theory immovable from his entrenched moral position by advances in psychology, sociology, etc. This suggests that as common sense (or the common moral consciousness) modifies its attitudes in the light of new facts retributivism will have less and less claim to represent it.

SELECTED
BIBLIOGRAPHY

The most complete bibliography on utilitarianism available may be found in Nicholas Rescher, *Distributive Justice* (New York: The Bobbs-Merrill Company, Inc., 1966).

CLASSICAL WORKS

AUSTIN, JOHN. *The Province of Jurisprudence Determined.* London: Weidenfeld and Nicolson, 1954.

BENTHAM, JEREMY. *An Introduction to the Principles of Morals and Legislation.* New York: Hafner Publishing Co., 1948.

HUME, DAVID. *An Inquiry Concerning the Principles of Morals.* Edited by Charles W. Hendel. New York: The Liberal Arts Press, 1957.

MILL, JOHN STUART. *Utilitarianism.* Edited by Oskar Piest. Second Edition. New York: Liberal Arts Press, 1957.

MOORE, G. E. *Ethics.* New York: Oxford University Press, 1965. Especially Chs. 1, 2, 5.

SIDGWICK, H. *The Methods of Ethics*. Seventh Edition. London: Macmillan & Company, Ltd., 1963. Especially Book I, Ch. 9; Book II, Ch. 1; Book III, Chs. 11, 13; Book IV, Chs. 2–5.

RECENT WORKS

ATKINSON, R. F. "J. S. Mill's 'Proof' of the Principle of Utility," *Philosophy*, XXXII (1957), 158–167.

BRADLEY, M. C. "Professor Smart's 'Extreme and Restricted Utilitarianism'," *Philosophical Quarterly*, VII (1957), 264–266.

BRANDT, R. B. *Ethical Theory*. Englewood Cliffs, N.J.: Prentice-Hall, Inc., 1959. Chs. 15, 16, 19.

BRAYBROOKE, D. "The Choice Between Utilitarianisms," *American Philosophical Quarterly*, IV (1967), 28–38.

BROILES, R. D. "Is Rule Utilitarianism Too Restricted," *Southern Journal of Philosophy*, II (1964), 180–187.

BROWN, S. M. "Utilitarianism and Moral Obligation," *Philosophical Review*, LXI (1952), 299–311; comments by C. A. Baylis and J. Ladd on pages 320–330.

DUNCAN-JONES, A. "Utilitarianism and Rules," *Philosophical Quarterly*, VII (1957), 364–367.

EWING, A. C. "Suppose Everybody Acted Like Me," *Philosophy*, XXVIII (1953), 16–29.

EZORSKY, G. "Utilitarianism and Rules," *Australasian Journal of Philosophy*, LXIII (1965), 225–229.

FEINBERG, J. "The Forms and Limits of Utilitarianism," *Philosophical Review*, LXXVI (1967), 368–381.

GENDIN, S. "Comments on Smart's *An Outline of a System of Utilitarian Ethics*," *Australasian Journal of Philosophy*, XLV (1967), 207–213.

GIBBARD, A. F. "Rule-Utilitarianism: Merely an Illusory Alternative?" *Australasian Journal of Philosophy*, XLIII (1965), 211–220.

HARROD, R. F. "Utilitarianism Revised," *Mind*, XLV (1936), 137–156.

HODGSON, D. H. *Consequences of Utilitarianism*. Oxford: Clarendon Press, 1967.

HOSPERS, J. *Human Conduct: An Introduction to the Problems of Ethics*. New York: Harcourt, Brace and World, Inc., 1961. Chs. 5, 9.

KAPLAN, M. A. "Restricted Utilitarianism," *Ethics*, LXXI (1960–61), 301–302.

———. "Some Problems of the Extreme Utilitarian Position," *Ethics*, LXX (1959–60), 228–232.

LANDESMAN, C. "A Note on Act Utilitarianism," *Philosophical Review*, LXXIII (1964), 243–247.

LYONS, D. *Forms and Limits of Utilitarianism*. Oxford: Clarendon Press, 1965.

MABBOTT, J. D. "Interpretations of Mill's 'Utilitarianism'," *Philosophical Quarterly*, VI (1956), 115–120.

————. "Moral Rules," *Proceedings of the British Academy*, XXXIX (1953), 97–118.

————. "Punishment," *Mind*, XLVIII (1939), 152–167.

MCCLOSKEY, H. J. "Utilitarian and Retributive Punishment," *Journal of Philosophy*, LXIV (1967), 91–110.

MARGOLIS, J. "Mill's *Utilitarianism* Again," *Australasian Journal of Philosophy*, XLV (1967), 179–184.

————. "Rule-Utilitarianism," *Australasian Journal of Philosophy*, XLIII (1965), 220–225.

MELDEN, A. I. "Two Comments About Utilitarianism," *Philosophical Quarterly*, LX (1952), 508–524.

————. "Utility and Moral Reasoning," *Ethics and Society*. Edited by Richard T. DeGeorge. New York: Doubleday & Company, Inc., 1966.

NARVESON, J. *Morality and Utility*. Baltimore: Johns Hopkins Press, 1967.

————. "Utilitarianism and New Generations," *Mind*, LXXVI (1967), 62–72.

NOWELL-SMITH, P. H. *Ethics*. London: Penguin Books, 1954. Chs. 15–16.

QUINTON, A. M. *Utilitarianism*. New York: St. Martin's Press. Forthcoming.

RAWLS, J. "Justice as Fairness," *Philosophical Review*, LXVII (1958), 164–194.

SINGER, M. G. *Generalization in Ethics*. New York: Alfred A. Knopf, 1961. Ch. 7.

SMART, J. J. C. "Extreme Utilitarianism: A Reply to M. A. Kaplan," *Ethics*, LXXI (1960–61), 133–134.

———. "Free Will, Praise, and Blame," *Mind*, LXX (1961), 291–306.

———. *An Outline of a System of Utilitarian Ethics*. Melbourne: Melbourne University Press, 1961.

STOUT, A. K. "Suppose Everybody Did the Same," *Australasian Journal of Philosophy*, XXXII (1954), 1–29.

TOULMIN, S. E. *An Examination of the Place of Reason in Ethics*. Cambridge: The University Press, 1950. Ch. 11.

WASSERSTROM, R. A. *The Judicial Decision*. Stanford, California: Stanford University Press, 1961. Ch. 6.

WATKINS, J. W. N. "Negative Utilitarianism," *Aristotelian Society, Supplementary Volume*, XXXVII (1963), 95–114.

ANCHOR BOOKS

* Modern Studies in Philosophy Series

12Aa

Philosophy (continued)

* Modern Studies in Philosophy Series

* Modern Studies in Philosophy Series

ANCHOR BOOKS

PSYCHOLOGY

Psychology (*continued*)

14Ba